Silent Awakening

*True Telepathy, Effective Energy Healing and
the Journey to Infinite Awareness*

By Eric Pepin

*Higher Balance Publishing
Portland, Oregon*

This book has been transcribed and compiled from live lectures given by Eric Pepin. Some elements of the live format have been preserved.

Published by Higher Balance Institute
515 NW Saltzman Road #726, Portland, Oregon 97229
www.higherbalance.com

ISBN: 978-1-939410-00-9

Library of Congress Control Number: 2013918891
Silent Awakening / Eric Pepin

Published 2013.

Printed in the United States of America

Other Books by Eric Pepin

The Handbook of the Navigator

Meditation within Eternity:
*The Modern Mystics Guide to Gaining Unlimited
Spiritual Energy, Accessing Higher Consciousness and
Meditation Techniques for Spiritual Growth*

Igniting the Sixth Sense:
*The Lost Human Sensory that Holds the Key to
Spiritual Awakening and Unlocking the Power
of the Universe*

Books by Higher Balance

Bending God: *A Memoir*

To discover more techniques and knowledge from
Eric Pepin, and to experience awakening yourself
beyond what is discussed in this book, visit:
www.higherbalance.com/experience

ADD TO YOUR EXPERIENCE
GET YOUR READERS ONLY BONUS MATERIAL

As a reader you receive special reader-only bonus material you can download for free. You will get new tools and knowledge to enhance all the practices found in the book.

Receive:
- **Video training with Eric Pepin:** Watch as Eric leads you through applying the techniques from Silent Awakening, in practical and powerful ways.
- **Dreamscape Fantasy:** A guided, visual meditation that creates a lucid dream-canvas, exploring a fantasy-filled world. This tool will assist in pulling deeper emotional issues to the surface, with positive experiences, to reinforce healing and empowerment.
- **Guided Surrender Technique:** Listen to Eric Pepin as he guides you through a powerful Surrender session introduced in chapter one.
- **Deep Sleep:** A special album created with binaural technology designed to relieve stress, anxiety and attain a good night's sleep.

Go to
www.silent-awakening.com/readers-only

DEDICATION

My sincere gratitude and thanks to the following Navigators, my personal Dream Team of editors who have dedicated an incredible amount of their time to make this book a reality. Getting my work into print has been my life-long dream. Without their dedication and support to this project, this book would never have been written.

Together, all things are possible.

Editing Team

Loretta Huinker, Team Leader, Editor, Proof Reader
Viny D'Errico, Asst. Editor, Volunteer Trainer, Proof Reader
Ray Ross, Editor, Proof Reader
Justin Schramm, Editor
Diane Pfaff, Editor
Deborah DeWet, Technical Support

With special thanks to the Higher Balance staff members for their contributions:
Frank Kramer, Jesse Borsheim, Peter Ince, and Josh Leavitt

Additional thanks to the following Navigators who helped with the original transcription of the audio modules into print for this book:
Kristine B., Pennie N., Jordan F., Cathy H., Molly McD., Joseph S., Vivien F., Amy P., Loretta H.

TABLE OF CONTENTS

Introduction

THE LEGEND OF the Phoenix is common to most ancient cultures. The Phoenix is a mythical bird that returns to its place of birth to die in a fire, only to rise up from the ashes and live again. The Legend of the Phoenix is about the cycles of death and re-birth and the fluidity of life.

When I imagine this extraordinary event, the most powerful element is the brief, silent moment between the explosive end of this noble creature and its wondrous rise. Infused and radiating all the power and glory of creation, that one, perfect moment where the entire universe is still, silent and present. It bridges the world we know and the boundless eternity of all that will ever be.

Picture yourself looking out towards the horizon from the edge of a cliff overlooking the ocean just before dawn. In the breath before the sun blazes to life, rising from the sea, you reflect, let go and embrace your total nature. It is a death. A birth. An awakening. An awakening born in the stillness, in the silence that crosses the ocean of time and space to an infinite universe within you.

A silent awakening . . .

As you continue your journey through this book, you will learn to let go. To surrender all that holds you back. That weighs you down. That prevents you from flying free. As you let go, you discover that the things you have held onto for so long aren't really you at all.

Letting go can be painful and, at times, may feel like death. Yet with each layer you shed, you rise anew and get closer to the true being inside. To the universe locked within. And like the Phoenix, you will ascend from the ashes, stronger than ever before.

Like water, your mind will begin to move and flow. Nothing can harm it, because like water it will part around each obstacle. Nothing is stronger. Water wears down even the hardest, most rigid rocks. In its perfect state is a constant motion of transformation. Such is the nature of the Phoenix.

Of silence . . .

Between every sound, silence flows, and carries the eternal presence of the universe. This is the veil you will part and, in the end, take a look behind to discover all that has been hidden from you. And all that you have been searching for.

I'll see you on the other side.

Good Journeys,
Eric Pepin

Chapter 1

THE POWER OF SURRENDER

IT IS IMPORTANT to have a clear understanding of the process of surrender because, as a student, it is the most critical skill that you can possess. It will strongly influence the level of reception you receive when you leave this world and how much peace you find in this life. For the truth of the matter is by surrendering, you must truly accept death.

If I could explain this to you in just a few words it would be terrific, but it is a very complex subject. The first thing that should be addressed is the misconceptions you already have of surrendering. When I use the word or the term *surrender*, you see a little white flag. You feel that you have to submit to something and see it as form of weakness. There is a huge amount of negativity you associate with it. Even in your deep subconscious mind, you still think that if you surrender, it is a sign of defeat.

In spiritual terms, to surrender is *absolute*. It is the defining point of your spiritual awakening. It is an act of trust, of faith, and of absolute inner beauty. Surrendering is not easy. It is one of the most difficult things for someone to do. That is because, innately in all human beings, there is a survival instinct. Unconditionally, you must be receptive to absolute trust. You are opening yourself up to the Universe. You are surrendering to the very Source, to God or the Universe that has created everything.

Many people think they have surrendered but they do not have the breakthroughs they have been searching for. That is due to their survival instinct or their resilient will to live. In terms of absolute surrender, death plays a very important role. It means that you must release all of your attachments of holding on to your existence. It is something that happens internally, and you have to just let go. It's time to leave this world now. You're done! You're through!

Your sense of survival is one of the many challenges you face when surrendering. It is your perceived sense of immortality, your desire to live forever. You have a strong connection to your physical body, your being, your is-ness of who you think you are. Even if you say, "I know that I'm more than my physical body," you have little faith in this belief. It's very difficult to acknowledge your spiritual body over your organic body. You may say to yourself, "I am perfectly okay with leaving the physical body. I am ready to do that. I accept it." But that is not the truth. If you internalize and reflect on this, you will realize that you are not ready at all. You are afraid of death just like everybody else. You are afraid of that immortal transition.

There are people who are successful in surrendering. For example, a person who decides they are tired of their illness and is ready to move on. Or an elderly person who has body aches and is riddled with health issues. They have come to terms with leaving this world. There is a sense of calmness about them and they have made peace with themselves. They're not worried anymore about bills, relationships or material possessions. They possess a certain resolve that creates a sense of peace within them. This can only be done when you truly accept the fact that you're going to move on soon. The problem is that you want to be able to achieve *true* -- I do use the word *true* -- surrender. If you can do that, if you can achieve and experience surrendering, you will realize for the first time how trivial life's demands really are.

While watching a program on TV a while ago, there was a discussion about the differences between happy people and unhappy people. It seems there is a significant difference between the two. Those who smile more and have a better outlook on life put a positive slant on things that often go wrong. It is statistically proven that positive people have longer lasting relationships, more prosperity, and generally better health conditions than negative people do. Statistically speaking, it is not even a two, ten or even twenty percent difference; it's much larger figures.

Someone with pessimistic views of life demonstrates a poor sense of security in relationships, financially, and personally. However, someone who can grasp the true concept of surrender, no matter what their personality is like, can take a negative situation and turn it into a positive situation. Their idea of life is, "It'll all work out in the end. Everything is alright." They internalize their beliefs and feel it emotionally. A positive attitude gives you a much better understanding and acceptance of surrender.

When you learn to surrender, life becomes brighter, more beautiful. Everything you experience is like your first kiss or a hug from a loved one. It is the first real sunrise you stopped to watch so you could savor its beauty. It is even better than that. Surrendering liberates you from the collective consciousness that holds you in place, the Doe. You look at your bills and you think, "Well, they are still here. They're going to be here, but I am dealing with them." You find a way to let go of that constant pressure. You let go of people who hold on to you for their own benefit. You let go of the things that are holding you back, preventing you from finding the completion you are searching so desperately to find within your inner self.

The irony is that you reject the idea of surrendering. Again, I say the main reason you do that is because you feel that if you surrender, it will be like giving up your life. That is what really prevents you from experiencing absolute surrender. So through that understanding and observation, you should now begin to reflect on peeling away those barriers. Meditating is very close to that same concept. It gives you incredible tools that help you to surrender. Some people think that they can just surrender without reflecting. Then why haven't they done this in the past? Believe me; you will know when somebody has surrendered. You cannot help but feel their absolute presence when they do. It is profound.

Is surrender a specific act like meditation or is it a state of mind?

Surrendering can start off as a process or a mechanism. There are limitations when performing the act. You can only set up the premise of what you are about to do. My suggestion is to be by yourself in a room. Make sure you are not disturbed. This isn't like preparing to do a meditation. It is a more reverent, humble state of mind, much like a Muslim may prepare to bow and praise Allah. You want to prepare to bow and release yourself to the Universe. Clear your mind, clear your emotions and start repeating, "I forgive all of my past intentions." Then reflect on what those intentions are because they were internalized. Ask yourself, "Am I cruel to other people? Am I cruel to myself? Am I too consumed with money? Have I done enough for others? Could I have done more?"

Bow to the Source. Clear your mind, clear your emotions and start repeating, "I forgive all of my past intentions."

Release those internalized thoughts. Give yourself permission to release those types of things. God is not going to judge you in spite of your religious beliefs that try to convince you otherwise. You do not need to pay your fee to gain entrance into the pearly gates. You do not need to confess to a priest about your transgressions. Forget it. The end result is, *"Are you able to forgive yourself? Can you forgive yourself?"* I don't think anybody can forgive you until you can forgive yourself first. That is the only way you can freely express compassion for the mistakes you have made to yourself and to others. Apart from that, you are just making surface statements to express the pain that you carry around with you. You might be able to show that pain to someone else if you've done wrong to them, but it doesn't mean that you have purged yourself from that negative vibration.

Give yourself permission to surrender, even if it is only temporary permission. Now that may sound odd, but sometimes that is all you need to do to experience what you need to understand so you can release and forgive yourself for your own crimes. You have to be compassionate to yourself as a growing being.

You cannot forgive yourself unless you truly recognize and internalize the errors you have made. You have to acknowledge them. You cannot just say, "I forgive myself." This is the tricky part: you have to truthfully internalize the fact that you would never do that act again. You have to realize this truth both mentally and emotionally.

You have to understand your errors and give yourself permission to be forgiven. Now that may sound self-righteous, but I don't think another person can say to you, "You can forgive yourself now." You have to be the one who gives that forgiveness to yourself. That is what peels away the layers I am referring to and it has to be done unconditionally. You cannot just think you will forgive yourself today or next week, becoming arrogant or self-righteous because now you are free from those issues. That will not get you anywhere. The mind is so complicated. I have often said that you cannot perceive the higher vibrations if you know your own sin, your own errors, your own negativity. Your tonal is irrefutably acknowledged. There is a way to purge that through self-reflection and by internalizing and forgiving yourself. You may not be successful the first few times, but you have to at least try.

There is a part of you that wants to ask God for forgiveness. This is what we have been taught in this dimensional world. This is what the teachers of various religions have taught us. They say that you can only seek forgiveness through God and that you have to do this through religion. They teach you that you can ask God on your own terms to be forgiven, but only God can forgive you. We all want to be forgiven. There is a part of us that lies deep within our consciousness that feels we have never been completely forgiven for our "sins." God gives you the choice to forgive yourself. It ultimately knows you will hold yourself responsible until you have truly come to terms with the issues you are holding inside of yourself. God is not going to say, "Okay, you're forgiven; you can come through the pearly gates now."

You want acknowledgment because, through parental conditioning, you learned to receive forgiveness that way. You are punished for your misdeeds and acknowledged when forgiven by removing the terms of your punishment. "Okay, you can go do that now because you're off curfew." This is social reasoning. This is how we think as human beings. It is integrated into your thoughts, but you never think about just forgiving yourself. You know you did something wrong and you did your penance -- move on!

When you begin the process of surrendering, the first thing you need to do is forgive yourself. And then you have to remember that just because you forgave yourself, it does not mean that the other person has forgiven you. Part of surrendering is to make sure that you have opened your heart wide enough to share that information with someone else, if they're willing to accept it. You want to heal them and repair the mistakes you have made by making it right for them.

You've worked on yourself, so now it is time for you to see if you can make it right for the other person. If you cannot, do not punish yourself forever. You cannot expect someone else to give you that release, nor can you expect to give this release to someone else. You need to forgive those things because they're all like cords. There could be hundreds of cords with each one tied to you. Imagine someone holding the other end of that cord that is tied to you. Don't forget that you also have cords that are tied to other people that you are holding onto. This is holding your identity, your consciousness, who you think you are in this way, in this place.

One of the most powerful elements of the Doe has no name. It has variations of names, but none of them accurately describe what it is. If you don't know exactly what it is, you will never know how to truly surrender.

You should take time to surrender either once a week or once a month; however long it takes. You cannot unrealistically expect to be purged all at once and think that you are now ready for full surrender. If that is how you are approaching surrender, forget it. Give it up right now. It will not work because that is not true surrender. That is ego surrendering. Real surrender starts with the smaller things that eventually lead up to the bigger things. You have to decide where you want to begin. You may want to review it mentally in your mind and forgive it. Then say, "I'm going to let this go now."

Sometimes your ego and your inner mind say, "Well, if I let it go, what's going to prevent them from hurting me again? I am opening myself up and making myself vulnerable. They will take advantage of me." No one is telling you to be naïve. Nobody is saying that you should be stupid or foolish. There is an old adage, "Fool me once, shame on you. Fool me twice, shame on me." Just because you forgave someone does not mean that you forgot what they did to you. You can forgive someone and also be smart enough to know that you need to move on. You are going to surrender that situation away. Maybe it's time for you to let go of that person, if they are consistently hurting you.

You have to forgive yourself so you can let that person go. It is just your guilty feelings that are holding you back and allowing the damage to be done to you. You are not forgiving yourself enough or being considerate enough to let go of this person. It is also your ego that is holding you back. It takes a lot of contemplation to realize this. It takes a lot of deep soul searching. Again, do not expect to do everything in one session. It takes time for true surrender.

When you are ready to release those inner issues, you should kneel down and make it a sacred ceremony. This is ceremonial; you're about to do something that is very challenging and difficult. You are accepting your perceived identity from the brain, that part of you that recognizes your personality in this life. You are beginning the process of pulling out the thorns that have created wounds in your psyche. You have accepted these thorns as part of your wounds that will stay with you for the rest of your life. Instead of carrying the burden any further, dress those wounds one at a time. Think about that. You are patching and repairing all the damage you have previously accepted as a part of who you are. You are remolding your psyche for a new world perception, and your perception of other people.

So, now we are back again having a pessimistic or an optimistic view of life, and the benefits of both. Optimistic people are more apt to allow those thorns to be removed. Because they are willing to do that, they are able to let the light of life, Prana, the Universe come into them. That act requires a more positive outlook on life. You can have that too. You just have to choose to act on it.

Should we try to surrender our most painful issues first in order to progress faster?

There is no particular order for surrender, but don't go for the big issues immediately. Start with little ones. Start with anything that comes to mind. Take fifteen minutes every few days and let whatever pops up come out in your ceremonial process. Create it however you want. This process is between you and yourself. Once an issue arises, you say out loud, "I'm going to release this. I'm going to forgive myself for this. I'm going to surrender this unconditionally. If I get hurt again because of this, I accept the hurt. If I am punished for this, I accept the punishment. If any negative consequences arise from this, I accept them. I surrender to whatever it is that is going to happen, and I accept it willingly."

When you start releasing your issues, your life will get better by leaps and bounds. It is pivotal that you acknowledge yourself as the benefactor of the quality of your life. You can either learn to surrender or not surrender. When I mentioned earlier that there are many levels of surrendering, perhaps you understand now what I meant by that.

As you begin working on yourself, you will release your issues. You may have to release them several times. You are used to them being a part of you, so you will recreate them and will have to release them again. Eventually you will come out on top and progress from there. You are working with layers. Remember, those issues are the perpetrators that are holding the frequency you vibrate outward. Your frequency is how the Universe recognizes you and responds to you. So if you are unhappy with your life and the hand that has been dealt to you, understand that you have played a role in that decision. You have the power to relinquish your unhappiness. It is a choice you consciously make. You can choose to surrender it or you can accept the circumstances and the terms of your life right now.

A basic layout for the surrendering process is that each day, week, month or whenever you feel the moment is right, you will choose a special place. You do not have to vocalize it, but you can. It is really your personal choice. You want the ritual to have consistency. You want to say, "I forgive myself. I release and surrender this issue."

When you start to surrender your issues and do the Foundation Meditation along with the other tools from Higher Balance, your results will be amplified. If you thought you had amazing results before, after the surrender process takes place, it will be a lot more intense. As I've said several times, your thoughts and the vibration you emit is based on how the brain interprets your perspective of the world and your acceptance of what society has led you to believe is your experience. You created a vibration inside of yourself for either reward or punishment. The punishment comes from that learned perspective. That is the bottom line.

When you accept the terms of your life and you don't make a choice to surrender, are you contributing to the hand that is dealt to you?

Everything that I teach is based on the level of your consciousness and experience. Experiences are the vibrational fibers that build your soul and your dimensional body. We speak about reincarnation and spiritual progression; this concept is the foundation of it all. When you leave the physical body, the vibration that your frequency emanates is the deciding factor for the level you move into in the realms of the vibrations of God. It is how you are going to recognize that final level that you are seeking. It also determines the affect and circumstances of your next incarnation.

When you receive the knowledge I'm giving you right now but don't make the effort to attain it, then you accept the level of your current vibration. If you say, "I'm too tired. I'm too lazy. I'm not willing. I've got too many things going on in my life right now," you accept the fact that you're not completely happy with everything in your life. You accept where you are without really saying it. You have to put forth some effort to improve the level of your vibration.

When you meditate, you are trying to build the skills to understand the Universe and your place within it. You want to expand your knowledge base, your influence, and explore. All of these are excellent things to strive for. They are all worthwhile goals to achieve. But if you ask me: "What is surrender? How can I accelerate my experiences? How can I manifest accelerated experiences?" This is how to do it. Drop the baggage you are carrying around with you. Drop it now! Drop it, and continue on with your other experiences. Those experiences are going to blossom profoundly. If you choose not to do that, you will carry around dead weight. But if you deal with that dead weight, you will reprogram your dimensional consciousness to be lighter, brighter and more influential in your spiritual experiences.

Surrender is the most powerful tool you can possess. Your consciousness and your experiences in life, both good and bad, develop the tonal, texture and fibers of your being. Your experiences are fibers that create the embodiment of your dimensional body. Everything you learn from all the other Higher Balance material teaches you how to move that body. You learn to empower it and how to enrich the information you get from these experiences. This, in turn, makes you feel more positive.

All the other Higher Balance material will not teach you how to remove negative fibers from your vibration. Surrender is unique in that it allows you to work with those little fibers. Without surrender, it is also difficult to achieve the results you strive for in those other spiritual programs. Surrender allows you to remove the negative fibers that are interwoven deeply into your spiritual consciousness. It gives you the ability to purge them. After purging all of those fibers, your tonal is so much brighter and lighter. You can experience the tones like a major scale: do, re, mi, fa, so. You experience 'so' without even leaving your physical body.

You can experience a much higher frequency that was previously unimaginable. Also, you can sustain those places longer and enrich yourself with a higher quality of information.

You learn, with Surrender, that even those negative events in your life are experiences to learn from. They are not who you really are, but you have accepted it as fact, as a part of your being. You can release them. You have the power to release them. See yourself from a higher perspective and heal all of those deep psychological wounds. Heal them effortlessly.

Those deep-seated negative vibrations have a lot to do with disease, illness, psychological problems, fatigue, depression, sociological problems and prosperity issues. I don't like compiling them all together, but think about it. Your state of mind is how you come across to other people and how they will react to you. What you internalize emotionally will affect your immune system. That internalization affects the embodiment of this journey in your physical life. Surrender will provide a simple but incredibly powerful method to release those things that hold you back. Simply by forgiving yourself, you transform negativity into a higher vibration.

When something happens to you, it affects your psyche in a very traumatic way. You have personalized it because of everything that your senses have taken in. When you watch something on TV, you do not internalize it the same way but you learn from it and gain wisdom about those particular circumstances. But you haven't internalized it the same as a physical experience. You can take all the experiences from your entire lifetime and, instead of internalizing them and making them a part of you, surrender the affect they have on you. They are not part of you. As a dimensional being, you have the ability to extract them and make them part of your progression and wisdom instead of internalizing them and choosing to have a lower tonal. It is a matter of perspective. It is a matter of simply forgiving a circumstance. You release the hold and those fibers become part of your knowledge instead.

When you die and move into your dimensional self before you incarnate, a lot of the information you hold is digested in the same way. The bigger issues transcend into the next life. You are dealing with all of your issues right now so that by the time you transcend and dump what little is left, the show is over. You are an enlightened being. You progressed to such a level of infinite understanding, it's profound. Even enlightened beings carry those fibers. It is not to say that the fibers will ever be removed totally, but the more you remove them, the greater your experiences will be. How you perceive, experience, and relate with life will be dramatically improved. I promise you it is going to be a very, very pleasant journey.

Would someone be making a critical mistake if they overlook surrender?

You have initiated a quest by searching out someone like me. The purpose of searching is because you want to improve yourself. You want to develop and complete yourself. You search for knowledge that will, somehow, benefit you. Understand what I am saying to you now. Read it over and over and over again. Not all in the same day, maybe not in the same week. But once every few weeks or every few months, reflect on this again and each time you will go deeper. The Doe is going to try to make you forget a lot of this discussion, especially this particular part. I promise you above all other material that you have learned; this one will evaporate from your mind the fastest. There is a reason for that. The concept of surrender is ultimately the most powerful tool to help you awaken.

Can someone surrender or go through the surrender process if they haven't prepared to do it?

That is not a typical situation. You have to be ready to begin the process of surrender. It's not something you can do while driving a car or when you are busy with other things. You might find ways to do that, but it will turn into an emotional release instead of true surrender. An emotional release is when you just need to cry over a bad situation, a breakup, the loss of a loved one or something to that effect. There is a difference between surrendering and having an emotional release. That is more of a biochemical release than an inner-fibered release, like true surrender.

One of the worst things that you can experience is the loss of a loved one. You should not try to surrender that type of loss in the first week or even the first year. You will know when you are ready to release it. You are just not sure how to go about doing it. You cannot move on with your life until you come to terms with your loss. The first step is to sit down and forgive yourself for feeling that you're ready to give it up. That can create feelings of guilt, so forgive yourself for wanting to release it. Recognize that it is okay to move on. Surrender that emotion, that guilt, that pain, that loss. Let it all go. Surrendering that loss does not mean you no longer acknowledge or miss them anymore. It is now a different perspective in your consciousness. It now seems like an event on TV instead of something that you internalize and has a direct and profound effect on you.

You have to remember one simple thing: life goes on. It is selfish to prevent other people from moving on to whatever destination they are meant to go. They have their own progression and their own agenda. When you can accept the fact that they need to move on, you should release them in your consciousness. The feeling is like letting your child go to college or releasing the people that you love and want to hold close. If you really love them, you will set them free. That is the hardest thing to do. The sooner you can do that, the sooner you can grow and allow new opportunities to come into your life. The Universe is just waiting to give them to you.

**How do you know when it is time to
let go of issues like that?**

You will know it is time because you have already thought about letting them go. You know you have to do it. If the time is not right, it would not even occur to you. It would be a non-issue. If you feel a lot of time has passed without even thinking about it, perhaps you already surrendered it. Maybe you need to do a self-check with yourself. A self-check is like a sounding board. You draw up that person's tonal and you say to yourself, "Okay, have I let you go? Am I still holding you here in my thoughts and my will to keep you in my life?"

What kind of love is that? Think about it. It might sound very cynical, but there is a reason I say that. You can love someone so much that you suffocate them. You have to ask yourself, "What kind of love am I feeling? What kind of love am I emanating? Is it a liberating kind of love for the other person? Or is this a selfish love for myself?" It is very hard to let go of selfish love. But if you truly want to grow as a spiritual person, then acknowledge those issues through self-observation and by reflecting it. You already know what you need to work on. Just ask yourself to surrender it. "I want to surrender this hold I have on you. I need to surrender it. I need to set you free. I will always love you, but I am setting you free now."

If you can to do that, you will retain all the benefits of the relationship and dump the negative aspects of it without the usual emotions. **You have the experience and the knowledge that you gained from it, but you released the emotional, vibrational, inter-fibered energy into your being.** What I just said is very important. There is a difference between not letting go and holding on to someone who you will always remember. There will always be a connection. You can release them from the energetic bond that is inside of you. You can free them.

Could this type of surrender be used in a negative context?

This process should never be used in a negative way. For instance, someone you love and still need to continue with in a relationship. If you are looking for an excuse to abuse that relationship by thinking, "I'm going to release them because I want to remove all the people I know." Well, you have to check yourself and listen to your intuition, that instinctual feeling that I've often referred to in other courses. Are you thinking from your ego or are you thinking from that place of sincerity inside of yourself?

You do not have to create more work for yourself. Work on the past decade of your life. Start there. There are probably lots of negative experiences to release. By doing just one Surrender session, the next day you will be amazed in how your life has changed.

Can you please elaborate on using surrender in a negative way?

The power of surrender should not be used to erase people from your life. You only want to surrender the negative vibrations. Don't be thinking, "The more people I can surrender, the less I will relate to this life. The better off I'll be." You are living life to grow as a dimensional being. There is a reason why you're here on the Earth, and it is critically important. You do not want to eradicate everything just because you think your life is bad, that it has caused you pain." Some pains are good pains. Sometimes pain helps you to grow from the experience. You release a lot and gain knowledge when you surrender. Again, use a sounding board to understand what the negative things are that you need to let go of. When you have learned what you can from it, move on. Surrender is about learning right from wrong, not abusing it for everything that you want to throw at it.

Would approaching it that way be surrendering at all?

You are no longer in a surrender state of mind. You are letting your ego stifle this beautiful process that allows you to grow. Approaching it that way is like ignoring the optimistic self that you're trying to develop, and letting the pessimistic self pollute the whole surrender process. You misunderstand the truth behind it. Do you see the need to be in a clear state of mind? This circles back around again to the reason for developing a ritual to help enforce this process so that it cannot be tarnished by the emotional intentions inside of you. Use the Higher Balance material. It's going to help you to achieve this without being influenced by negative influences.

Surrender is a very complicated process. It sounds very simple, but really it is not. Persistence and consistency are the keys. They are paramount to your success, so do not forget that. Be consistent with this progress and you will succeed.

It is possible to surrender and release something and then feel great. But a week or a month later, that same issue starts to take hold again. That is because (1) other people are projecting this issue because of their connection with it, or (2) you are reviewing it in your mind because it's being psychically forced from other places. It's making you reflect on it again and give it structure. You have to be aware of those things and use the other techniques from High Guard, for instance, to give you an advantage. If you are persistent in attempting to release the issue, your energy field or your dimensional body will feel that frequency. The issues will not become permanent. If it does internalize, it falls into another aspect of the teachings and other techniques, such as Foundation. Now you must combine Surrender with mindfulness, meaning that you do not reflect on the negative. You have to be a Kung Fu master and throw the negativity over your head. You utilize mindfulness if you feel these recurring issues trying to grasp onto you again and again. You have to use the tools that you already have learned to advance yourself. But Surrender still is, ultimately, an extremely powerful tool.

Is there any danger in surrendering?

You can abuse it by trying to make yourself feel nothing. That is not what you want to achieve. You do not want to become numb and feel nothing. You just want to remove the deep pain you accumulated over your lifetime. You certainly want to feel life. That is partly why you are here. Life is going to infuse you. It is going to empower and liberate you. Life is a wonderful, wonderful thing. Surrender is about the issues that create a pessimistic view of life, and you can resolve that inside of yourself.

Does surrender have anything to do with why we bow at the end of a meditation?

Bowing is a small part of surrendering. The surrender that we are talking about is much bigger, but you can incorporate bowing in your ritual if you choose. The Higher Balance Meditation is very powerful for what it was designed to accomplish - expand your consciousness. It was designed to increase your sensory or your psychic abilities. Its purpose is to feed your dimensional body clean, pure Prana. It is intended to empower you. If you start incorporating the surrendering process with the meditation, it's like switching into fast gear. Say that you just completed a physical workout in aerobics and now you are all pumped up. And then you immediately sat down and read five chapters of a book without walking around or unwinding first. It's not that it can't be done, but you are putting more of a strain on the process than is necessary.

In the movie *The Karate Kid*, Mayagi begins training Daniel by having him wax his car, sand the floor and do some painting. Each chore uses a specific movement. Daniel doesn't see the connection until Mayagi reveals that Daniel has been learning defensive blocks through muscle memory learned by doing the chores. In much the same way, by practicing different things, we learn techniques that can be used to help us spiritually. This is often referred to as wax on/wax off.

When applying the process of Surrender, it is the wax on/ wax off effect. You utilize the tools that you learned through the Foundation and other Higher Balance material. You quiet the Babbler. You slow down your breathing and place yourself into a calmer state of mind. You communicate with your inner sensory and the emotions that you were trained to feel. Once this is done, you can start selecting the issues you need to release. Then you simply start to surrender and forgive yourself. You give yourself permission to clear them.

However, when you do a meditation, you surrender to the Universe. That is a very profound thing to do. When you surrender, you are working more with isolated issues than just working on yourself. The concept of breathing out at the end of the meditation and releasing yourself can absolutely be combined with a form of surrender. Feel free to let yourself open up. But it is a very broad way of opening up. The big issues will not be released that way. You are still hanging on to those. But you will cleanse those big issues and wear them down over time. Maybe they will turn into pebbles so you can move them eventually. But if you want to speed up your progress and make it more beneficial to you, start purging the larger issues by surrendering them. Then when you surrender to the Universe, it will be more meaningful.

Can anyone surrender or do you need to have some training to do that?

Some people can grasp this intellectually and do a very good job. But the people who have been working on the Foundation Series and other Higher Balance material will have much better results because of their training.

Does surrender enhance your meditation results?

First of all, meditation is based on controlling the Babbler and how long you can keep yourself in the flow. The flow is Prana coming into you. The amount you receive depends on your level of concentration. Prana builds and creates a vibration. As you accumulate this higher vibration, this pure energy of Prana, you move yourself or surf. You actually change your tonal.

However, the issues within your psyche that originated from your brain will weigh you down. They percolate into the mind and try to rewrite and reprogram it. Your issues feed the Babbler, acting like a heavy weight that brings you down. This is what this whole process is about. You are slowly cleansing it. If you purge and use surrender, it will release the source that weighs you down as you reach those higher vibrations. If you drop a lot of the weight while going uphill, it is easier to get to that magnificent view. It is easier to experience it.

Can Surrender help you to develop multidimensional consciousness?

Absolutely, it gets you there ten times faster if you use this in combination with all of the other material. Let me give you an example. Sit in your chair or on the floor and put your feet flat on the ground. Take your hands and put them in your lap as if you are meditating. Now clear yourself, just the way you were trained in the Foundation Meditation. Breathe in and exhale out. Allow yourself to relax. Now, take another deep breath in and think to yourself, "I forgive myself." Exhale out. Again, thinking while breathing in, "I forgive myself." Breathe in once more and say, "I open my heart completely to the Universe. Freely, willingly, openly, and trusting, I surrender to you God, the Universe. Take my heart if you choose." Breathe in, "I surrender."

Breathe in and exhale out. Allow yourself to relax. Say, "I open my heart completely to the Universe. Freely, willingly, and openly. I surrender to you God, the Universe." Breathe in, "I surrender."

Now, breathe in through your mouth, open your eyes, and ask yourself how you feel. If you think that feels good, imagine what true surrender will do for you. It is profound. For men, it will be three times harder than for women because the emotional base in the brain is less sensitive. That's just the way it is. It is the design of your machinery, your body.

It is important to work on deeper releases. If you are very masculine, it might take more work and more time. If you are very feminine, you can probably purge easier. You will be more upbeat and much happier. Women hold pain and negative energy in their lower stomach area. After a surrender session, they feel less tension. It is as if all the pain and negativity was released. A woman can easily internalize thought, emotion, and feeling and allow forgiveness and release.

You are your own judge. You choose to carry your pain. You can choose to free yourself of that pain. God gave you that option. But you can only free yourself if you have learned the lesson from it. Learning from it absolves you. If you have not learned from it and make the same mistake again, it will not go. That is because you are not ready to surrender it. You did not learn from it. You are lying to yourself. You cannot lie to the Universe. You cannot fake it. It's impossible. It's a frequency.

Think about what I just said. You chose to hold the memories, the feelings, and the guilt inside of you. Your guilt causes illness and suffering. Your guilt causes muscle tension and your immune system to drop, so you are more vulnerable to dis-ease. This is fact. This is science. This is something you need to understand.

You do not need someone to remove or give you permission to forgive yourself for this guilt. You do not need a lover to give you permission. You do not need a parent to give you permission. You need to acknowledge the right and wrong that you have done and forgive yourself. Forgive yourself and clear your soul with absolute light and brilliance. You do not need permission from anybody to do that. God gave you that permission a long time ago. You just have to accept it. Maybe the first thing to surrender is your guilt from saying that you can surrender and that you are allowed forgiveness. Surrender the guilt from giving yourself forgiveness.

People can devastate us by manifesting shame and guilt inside of us. You might be ready to forgive others but they may be hanging on to their anger. They manifest, feed and strengthen it inside of you by constantly bringing it up and by comparing the wounds and the damage you have done. In so doing, they imprison you in that place. There is a natural instinct, a repelling mechanism that develops when you want to escape from that person. You will start thinking of ways to get away from them. There is a mechanism that causes this reaction. Your interaction with them creates an illness inside of you. You harbor all this inner pain and you are being told you cannot be forgiven. Then when you are forgiven, it is brought up again. You decide that you will never be forgiven. Your body doesn't understand why it feels that way, but you know you need to escape. You know that, eventually, you need to remove yourself from this other person's life. You are in more anguish and upset at yourself for wanting to get away. Eventually you will. You will run. It is survival. In a sense, you are dying. They are killing you. You are killing yourself, and that same survival instinct is going to kick in. It is just a matter of how long you will fight it.

Throughout this entire process, you subliminally use all of your inner dimensional energy, all of your Prana. Your spiritual fiber is trying to hold you together so that you can move on. All of the psychological cruelty you think you have caused is holding you back.

You have a right to make mistakes in your life. You have that right because that is part of the learning process. You also have the right for forgiveness. But you can only forgive yourself when you acknowledge the mistakes you made. If you cannot acknowledge them, you cannot be forgiven. The Universe has its own mechanism of control. You are forced to acknowledge your mistakes and then move on.

Another person can hold you in place. They use guilt to keep you from freeing yourself. Just acknowledge that and take it for what it is. You have to forgive yourself and surrender it so they no longer have power over you. If you hurt someone and they fear that you will do it again, they need to accept the fact that such is life. You have a right to live. You do not belong exclusively to anyone but yourself. A person must realize that you're with them by choice. They cannot force you to stay. It is your choice to stay or not to stay.

These situations can become very complex, so keep it simple. Surrender it. Let them have their own issues. They have to realize that the reason you are there is because you chose to be there. Once you forgive yourself, you empower yourself. That is what God wants for you. It wants you to grow. Realization is absolute growth.

Does psychic or sixth sense development have anything to do with surrender?

As mentioned before, the sixth sense is critical for your development as a spiritual being. Your five senses have gathered enough information to help you mature intellectually over your lifetime. You understand many of the analogies and concepts so that you can comprehend this missing link. But because your sixth sense abilities are not already highly developed, this is not logical to you and needs to be further explained. So, I am integrating this information in order to bring you up to speed. I am helping you with this while you are learning to develop this other sensory of the sixth sense.

Is there a specific chakra that can intensify or help in surrendering?

Sure, the heart does the same thing. Think about what I have said about surrender and then focus on your heart chakra. Watch how it magnifies the whole process. Now, put that into your ritual. It's that simple.

Can you be in a state of surrender and still interact with the world?

Yes, but it is harder to accomplish because the only thing you want to do is to smile and cry tears of joy all at the same time. It is a wonderful state of mind to be in and I wish I could be in it twenty-four/seven. The reality is that you would not be able to function like you should. It does not hurt to try to be in a state of surrender as often as you can. It is a place to which you have a key so that you can come and go whenever you please. It's a choice that you make. Certainly you can be there, but in this reality, it is extremely challenging.

Everyone thinks that if you are an enlightened person, you are there all of the time. Isn't that where Christ, Buddha, and Krishna were all of the time? However, when Christ turned over all the merchants' tables at the temple, you can be sure that he was not in that place. It is the same thing for all enlightened beings. The point is that you can reside there. You want to do that as much as you can. You achieve that by purging as much of the negativity as you can that is holding you back. When you do that, it releases you so that you can reach those higher states of consciousness. It is a very loving, very beautiful, very cosmic enriching thing. There are no words that can adequately explain it. When I think about it, it draws me into that place. I want to go there and I do not want to come back. It's wonderful, and when you go there, you realize that everything is all right. Everything is going to be okay. Life is just a ride, and you know what? It is a fantastic journey and you love every single minute of it. It is absolutely the best. You realize this only at the end of this lifetime. When you do a life review, that's when you think about everything that has happened in your life. When you account for all of the negative situations in your life, they can easily be erased by finding one good person you have met on your journey. Think about how that person makes you feel right now. Everything else that was bad no longer exists for you. It doesn't matter. The surrender state is like that.

Is surrender the one thing that ties the very highest states and the very lowest states of consciousness together?

Surrender helps you to remove the blockages that have prevented you from moving out of the lower states and reaching the higher states of consciousness. It is not to say that it puts you in a high state of consciousness. It just makes you pliable. It makes your foundation stronger, and it means that you have a broader spectrum to operate within. Surrender makes you feel more at peace, more in balance, and happier in life. When you move into the higher states of consciousness, it allows your wingspan, per se, to open and for you to move more freely. It increases the possibility of reaching the higher frequencies to gather information to bring back down. Surrender is about improving the quality of that flight or that movement into these higher states of consciousness.

To stay in the higher states of consciousness, use your energy mind to force the brain to work with and communicate with it. There is a certain point when you need to come back with the data you received. You cannot remain there for too long because the brain gets overtired. It's like driving your car at 140mph all day long. No matter how good the engine is, you need to give it a cooling off period. That is when you absorb what you learned from all the places you have been. As long as you are in a physical body, there are limits on how far you can push your higher consciousness. You can go there, experience it, and bring back the data. You digest it and journey back and forth. Then you build a structure from here because your brain is more capable of digesting and working with that information. Using surrender helps you with that flow and allows you to take more information with you than was possible before.

What changes in a person when they surrender?

Everything that you did not like about yourself is gone, just like that. You are the garden: You start off as the dirt that later becomes something beautiful. All of the challenges in your life are really about helping you become the person you need to be until you are ready to accept that you can be something more, something beautiful. You are the ugly duckling that becomes the swan. You are the song that raises the spirit. There is hope. There is always hope. It's not a matter of whether or not you can surrender to become this person. It is a matter of acknowledging what you already are.

You are so busy with life, its problems and getting caught up with your issues, that you forget who you really are. You are searching for wholeness. In the midst of the search, you wonder, "Am I good enough? Is there something special about me? Is there something there? I just want to know." There is something about you and I'll tell you what it is: You are made from the fabric of God. You are supreme. You just have to believe it, accept it, and not be ashamed of it. Let it shine, let it resonate with you. If you can accept this truth and embrace it, that you are made from the fabric of God, the finest thing in all of the Universes, you will shine. You will feel it tingle. It just resonates as a beam of light that tingles throughout your whole body.

That is all you need to reflect on. Just think about that, about what you are made of. When you do, you will realize that no matter what happens in your life, you haven't contaminated your perfection. It is just that someone has fooled you into thinking that you have. Life is an illusion, so do not buy into it. Listen to the song, "You Are So Beautiful." It says everything you need to know. Listen to that song. Think about what you are really made of. That's all you have to do. Everything else just falls away from you because it does not matter anymore. Your problems and your perceptions cling because you unknowingly let them cling. Just know what you are. You are made from the fabric of God. God wants you to know that. You are just not listening.

Can you encounter fear when surrendering?

You can encounter the darkest of the dark. You can be in the abyss of abysses. You must simply acknowledge what I am saying. **God leaves no one behind.** Simply put, there is absolute forgiveness. It comes from you. All you have to do is acknowledge what you have done. You will go through your own purging process. You will go through your own inner pain. In the end, the world is made of flesh and it can be harsh and cruel, but it can also be beautiful. It can be kind. Ultimately, life is a journey. It is a journey to experience. If you look at nature, and you look at life, you can say that people can be incredibly cruel and unkind. And I absolutely agree. There is a point when you let that go for your own spiritual growth. You deal with it in human terms. You come to terms with it, and then you need to move on.

Looking at the cruelty of life in nature, such as lions hunting the beautiful deer and unmercifully ripping them apart -- you could justify that by saying, "Well, that's nature. It's different." But it is really your perspective of how you perceive things. You have to intellectually let go of some things. Letting go of something does not mean that it does not matter or it was insignificant. You have knowledge and wisdom for all things that have happened in your life. You don't want to make it so personal that it reflects biochemically in your body.

What is the difference between love and surrender?

Love is surrender and surrender is love, but most people do not think about love. I touched upon one kind of love, a controlling love. There is also love that you have for family, love that you have for a friend, and love for your pets. There is sexual love. There are a variety of kinds of love, and most of them are very biologically oriented.

The greatest love is agape, a love of God. And if you love God, you must love yourself. You are made of the fabric of God. Therefore, if you do not love yourself, essentially you do not love God. People think mostly about lustful or physical love. You certainly can love your children. Your children are made of the fabric of God. Love all people. They, too, are made of the fabric of God.

Every religion shares the same foundation. They all understand this; however, politics gets in the way. You can throw out all of the politics. There is no need for it. In the dimensional levels of the Universe, politics do not apply. Politics only apply to the physical reality and for the most part, it does more harm than good.

Again, there are many different kinds of love. Some loves are not particularly good. Love can be so embroiled, so passionate that it can suffocate you. Perhaps that love is not letting you move on with your life or grow as an individual. That type of love can become very taxing.

If you surrender people that are close to you, could you potentially stop caring about them?

No, you will always care about them. Our families and friends are the people that are closest to us in our lives; however, we often have a lot of pain tied up with them. By separating yourself from them, you probably cause yourself more pain by letting them go. What you need to do is acknowledge the negativity, release it, and surrender it.

Society has taught us a very flawed way of thinking. The mind may think, "If I surrender, it's like letting them get away with all the bad things they have done to me." They know what they did! They may not tell you. They may not acknowledge it. They may act like it never happened. But they know what they did to you. Ask yourself if you have a similar situation in your life no matter who it is, and even if they do not acknowledge it, you already are aware of it. They are suffering because of it and you know it. You do not acknowledge it because you want to see their remorse in a physical way.

If you already forgave them, what else do you want? Free yourself. Don't let them hold you in that place anymore. Take your power back from them. Surrender it. Free yourself from their hold. Look them in the eye and let them feel your forgiveness, your love, and your compassion. They are so engrossed in this dark place that they are acting out in darkness. They have nothing compared to what you have now. Nothing. They will recognize that because they want the same thing. You have tried to inspire them to heal their own pain, their own ugliness and their own darkness. They have their own battles in trying to accept the wrong they did because they cannot forgive themselves until they acknowledge internally what they have done to you. They will eventually face their own demons just like you do when you surrender. You can only let go if you truly understand the error of your ways. You cannot fake it, so just forgive them.

Forgiving them does not mean that you leave yourself vulnerable. Don't be foolish by putting yourself in similar situations. By surrendering, you do not give up the wisdom of that experience, nor do you put yourself in a similar situation. You assert yourself now, but you release the pain and control they have over you. You say, "You no longer have a hold over me anymore. I will no longer wallow in the pain that I carried for all these years, nor will I let it become me. No more."

Take your place as a dimensional being and release it. Surrender it and step forward. Look the person in the eye and forgive them, "Forgiveness does not mean that I agree with your actions or that I am doing your part of you having to forgive yourself. I am not saying that I am giving you permission to release this. I am saying that I forgive you.

Let it go so that I can move on. You need to resolve this issue yourself. I am saying I let it go. You need to come to your own terms with it."

No one else can give forgiveness for you; that's what I have always taught. Only you can forgive yourself, and you can only forgive yourself when you have learned from the error of your ways. Then you say, "I feel the pain that I caused others. I know that I hurt someone. I know I did something terrible and I want to change that. I want to fix that."

You may think that you don't care, that it doesn't matter, but I assure you that it does. You cannot lie to yourself. I believe that you do care and I will bet my life on it. If you want to hang on to it, that's fine. I can look at your tonal and tell it has not changed at all. I know when someone has suffered to the point where they deserve their own forgiveness. And when they do forgive themselves, you can see their frequency change. With someone like me, you can see an octave of frequency changing inside them. That is the only way I can explain it. But if someone asked me, "Do you think I did something bad?" I'm going to say, "Yeah, what you did was horrible. It was atrocious and I would not want to be you." They may say, "Well, I don't care." I'll reply, "I don't care if you care. I've let it go already. I've moved on. But that does not mean I will forget what you did. Do you want my forgiveness? I don't know if I will forgive you. I know that I've surrendered it. But if you asked me if it was a horrible thing that you did, the answer is yes."

Should they repent, suffer, and correct it? That is for you to decide, but you can forgive the situation inside yourself. You can surrender it. No matter how cruel it was, no matter how much damage was done, you can surrender it.

When they surrender it, you look them in the eyes and you see on a soul level by their expression and your intuition that this person took responsibility for what they did and deserve your forgiveness. If you already surrendered it and did your part, you will give them that forgiveness. You will acknowledge that they moved on. They got it. That is what matters.

It is very hard to do that though. Ego wants to hang onto it. Hate wants to hang onto it. Anger wants to hang onto it, but you need to let it all go. You need to let it go or you will be trapped forever in this inner dimensional holding cell. And that cell is locked from the inside. You might think that you cannot open it, but you have the key to open it right in front of you. The lock is facing you on the inside, it's a choice.

How does age play a role in surrendering?

There are many remarkable people, both old and young, no matter what their age. There is no way of knowing, for sure, whether or not there is an advantage with age in surrendering. However, as a general rule of thumb, probably someone in their fifties, sixties, or seventies may have more of an advantage. For women, it is during menopause. During that phase of their life, women gain their strength and self-empowerment. They are more respected by men, if not already. It's kind of an internal thing. It happens a little bit earlier for some women, but this is still regarded as a man's world. Unfortunately, evolution is a slow process.

By the time you are in your seventies, you have already developed wisdom. It is when you reflect back on your life and accept the art of surrender. You develop more compassion and understanding. It comes from the self-realization that you have made a lot of mistakes in your life and have come to terms with it. You realize that you need to acknowledge the flaws you see in others. It is not the fact that you are acknowledging that they have learned from their mistakes. Rather, you acknowledge, with some level of confidence that they are going to get where you are. And because you have that insight, you are more forgiving of their mistakes now.

Surrender is achieved much easier as you grow older because knowledge is the foundation of vibration. It is the refining tool for how your consciousness resonates. It is how you internalize your emotions, your thoughts, your perceptions and your reality. All that changes as you grow older because you are more tolerant of the situations that were difficult to accept earlier in your youth when your reactions were more intense. Wisdom decrees that you stop exhausting yourself. You think, "The last time I exhausted myself like that, I later realized that it really wasn't such big a deal." You cannot substitute perceptions for wisdom.

This is why all of the best presidents were older. This is why Native American chiefs were the oldest people in the tribe. There is wisdom in aging. They have been down the road before and do not generally overreact to situations. They see life and its finer qualities. They may have their own issues. There may be things that they need to work through, but the fact is, they acknowledge that graciously. They will look at their flaws and say, "Yes, I need to grow in that area." Most people do not want to acknowledge or admit that. It is a level of distinction.

Age refines and defines a person. It is like a fine wine. There is a difference in how you perceive things. It is not that you look forward to getting older; rather you look forward to gaining the wisdom. You know age is a tradeoff. With aging, there are advantages and disadvantages. I would say accept them all. Forget about the disadvantages. It's just a constant exchange of growth. That's really what it is in the end.

Can your intention be to surrender everything at the same time or do you have to surrender one thing at a time?

There are times when you just surrender, but you may not understand what it is that you are surrendering. You just have to trust that, in surrendering, it is helping you to release what you have to let go of. You will know when you release something; you'll feel it. It's not necessary to put a label on it. Maybe it is something you do not remember. It's there, you can feel it. Your body will work with your dimensional energy. It doesn't have to have a label. It doesn't have to have an identity. Your dimensional soul does not have a requirement for that. It does not categorize everything like in this dimension.

There might be things that you do not remember from your youth. Things that you have suppressed and are not conscious of right now, but you will feel those things coming out of you. You might not have a name for them. They can just start flowing for no apparent reason. It feels wonderful once they are released. It's a very good experience.

Can things be surrendered from a past life or do you release that when you die?

You can release anything that is in your mind, unconsciously or consciously, within your dimensional realm. If it is affecting you it has to be alive. That means it is in the fiber of your being right now. If it's there from a past life, it is going to surface.

Do you have to go through extreme turmoil to finally let go and truly surrender?

There are as many ways to surrender as there are stars in the sky. Everybody is uniquely different. But it is very normal for most people to feel it intensely.

Are there any big stumbling blocks that could prevent someone from entering a state of surrender; such as their family background, the way they were raised or their religious background?

Sure. Your thought process or what you deem as your perspective on life is based on your knowledge which is based on your experiences. You make many changes throughout your life. You can change your religion, beliefs, and home address. How you perceive things affects whether or not you are able to surrender. It is the complex mind that can prevent you from having a good release.

Society is designed around the Doe, which does not like change. The most successful people with surrender are those who are familiar with the series we offer here at Higher Balance. Someone with a religious background may find it a little more challenging in letting go and releasing their issues. What you learned earlier in your life will or will not permit you to work with your brain and your mind. If you still hold the concept of sin and good and evil, as taught by many religions, you will not have the same results. It is because you believe that you have to be forgiven by a priest or someone of authority. Move past that and take responsibility for yourself.

Understand, without a doubt, that this is an internalized thing. You may not be able to accept that yet, so try to keep an open mind and gain the knowledge that gives you the tools to work with. Those tools yield experiences and those experiences are like reading thousands of books. It broadens your knowledge which, in turn, allows you to reach higher levels of Surrender. It is a self-fulfilling process. I don't like to trash religion, but there is a time when you have to think for yourself.

How does Surrender open the gateways to perform miracles?

It boils down to removing the fibers that keep you stuck in the Doe. If you remove them, you can move up to a higher octave, which begs the question, "Is it possible to stay in the surrender mode twenty-four/seven?"

As you move up to the higher octaves, you resonate with it and receive Prana at a much higher rate than before. You will profoundly affect the world around you. You will raise other people's tonals. When you walk up to someone to say, "Hi!" you will infuse this energy into them. You will affect them spiritually.

Maybe you will learn how to heal others with the help of the material from Higher Balance. You can learn how to open yourself as a conduit to heal others by releasing energy. If you use your abilities in this way, it will just flow from you. There will be less resistance from this dimension. You will change this reality because you are a pure channel of energy that becomes solidified into this dimension. Right now, you are a purer level of energy that naturally flows through you. You have achieved what you have been trying to achieve your whole life.

Would staying in a constant state of love or bliss not be desirable?

That is a double-edged sword because sometimes, if you are too blissful, you stream from much higher energy. You are here to experience this dimension, so participate in this reality. You have to accept the pain in order to find the beauty. It is a tradeoff, but it is not that bad in the end. You can find a happy medium with inner peace. If you want to make a difference in this world, you have to go through the struggle. I, for one, am willing to trudge through the struggle along with everyone else. I can endure the suffering because I know that if I need to step away and heal or rejuvenate myself, I can.

How does the act of surrendering open you up to paranormal and metaphysical experiences?

You remove all of the obstacles that are created by the billions of other programs, therapies, systems and medications. You are using a simple process, although it is a very complex one at the same time. When you remove those blockages in the fluidic sensory of your sixth sense, you free up and increase its capabilities. It is all tied in together. But because it is a sixth sense, it is more of an energy consciousness. It is the highest level of your consciousness that's closest to your physical sensory. By removing those deep-rooted issues, you can free that sensory, enabling it to broaden and expand, opening you to new possibilities.

Are mindfulness and surrender related?

Mindfulness empowers you to achieve the states of surrender. You can be bombarded by negative energies that prevent you from surrendering. They keep you busy by building emotional blocks, which are deeply rooted. They permeate into your spirituality. Mindfulness says, "Oh, no you don't. Out you go." It's the *bouncer* or *doorman* theory. It's the trouble maker that is screaming and yelling, and the bouncer who is saying, "I'm not letting you in. Now we have to clean up the damage you created." Instead of allowing these things to keep doing more damage, you prevent them from continuing. You repair and fix the damage and move on. Mindfulness and surrender are very useful to one another.

Are there noticeable changes in a person's physiology when they enter a state of surrender?

People say there is a different intensity about them or a diverse physiological outlook about them. I think it's because your immune system kicks in. If you have a cold or an illness when you surrender and you have achieved positive levels of consciousness, your immune system will spike. You run the illness right out of your system. If you have a disease, your body copes better and repairs itself rapidly. You will also discover that if you can stay in the state of surrender without asking to be healed, there is a good chance the Universe will heal you. I have seen it happen before, but you cannot ask for it. You just have to work on yourself. If miracles had a frequency of opportunity, that would be the state.

Let's talk about cancer. Many people believe that cancer runs rampant in the body because you give up the fight. Or that it is something that you are not willing to let go. That sounds a little crazy, but going back to what I said earlier about the body being miraculously healed, you can surrender your illness. Accept the terms of it. So, then you might think, "If I accept it, it will run rampant and spread because my body is learning not to deal with it," or "I will not be fighting it anymore." That's not true at all. Every part of your instinct will tell you to fight it with everything you have. It will tell you not to surrender to it. If you surrender to the devastation, you are doing the same thing as when you forgive a person by forgiving the damage they did to you. It somehow relinquishes it. I don't want to say it is definitely going to cure you, but it has cured people before.

What should someone expect from their ego when surrendering?

Expect the same battle as when you are dealing with the Babbler. Ego comes in many shapes and forms. Ego is often associated with pride, arrogance, overconfidence and zealousness. Ego can be a subtle echo, yet have such a profound effect. Ego is like going into surrender feeling that you do not have a problem surrendering. You can do it. Accept the challenge that it might be difficult and that you may not be able to achieve it. Accept it all. Accept the overwhelming obstacles that you face as it is pressing on you, and then surrender it. You will become ethereal. It will still remain as matter, but the weight of it will pass through you.

You cannot allow ego to even be involved. And the only way that you can get rid of ego is to surrender it. At first, maybe you should start off by saying, "I surrender my ego." Say it right now. Sit in the lotus position. Put your hands on your lap, thumbs touching. Take a nice deep breath in. Say aloud, "I surrender my ego" and breathe out. Again, breathe in, saying out loud, "I surrender my ego," and out. One more time, breathe in. Say it aloud.

How do you feel? Something has opened up within you. How much you allow this to happen by releasing your ego will determine the depth of what you are able to release. If you really want to let go of your ego, you will let it go. You are in control of your consciousness, but you do not always choose to exercise the power that you have. It is ego that tells you that you are being arrogant if you think you can control your consciousness, so it defeated you. If you just accepted that thought now, do you understand what I am saying? Think about it.

When you sit down to do your session you say, "I am releasing my ego." Your ego may demand, "What makes you think that I am not here?" Or your babbler may say, "What you believe is your higher consciousness is really your ego telling you that you can get rid of your ego." It really doesn't matter. Continue with phase two of your surrender program and just move on. It's like the whole "blowing out" thing from Foundation. You know you're just blowing out an issue. You are blowing out your ego. Out with the ego, breathe in. What else are we going to take on? I am letting it all go. Out it goes. That's it.

It may sound too simple. You may have to chip away at this, but you will go deeper and deeper into the recesses of your mind. It is as if the problems are layered like sediment. They are deeply rooted and when you skim off the top layer, it is like pulling the top of a weed out of your garden. You may feel relieved and think that you got rid of the problem, but you need to pull it out by its roots. You may not see it anymore but you need to keep working to release it. You will know if you have cleared it or not. Then you will feel deep emotional releases. It will come out in different ways.

Is there ever a time when you should surrender something that you don't think is negative?

If you surrender it and it isn't negative, then it won't flow out. It is already part of your conscious knowledge and does not have any roots. You don't want any roots; that is the bottom line. You can have conscious knowledge to draw upon as experience. You are not letting it dig into you to solidify, holding you to this physical realm to the Doe. You are letting it go. If there is nothing to let go of, then you are just checking to see if there is anything there.

This is such a potent tool to possess. It doesn't matter if you are a victim of abuse, if you have post-traumatic stress disorder or an illness of any sort. I don't care what it is, just visualize it. Feel it. You don't have to feel the full emotion of the problem, but just acknowledge that feeling inside of you. And say, "I release it. I surrender it." Work on it every so often. Move on to the next issue. Don't sit there wondering if you got rid of the problem. It's okay. Sometimes it might take an hour for it to release. You might be sitting down watching TV and suddenly think, "Whew, boy, I don't know why, but I suddenly feel so much lighter."

It is a work in progress. Don't push it; let it take its course. Do your work and move on with your day. It can be applied to everything you do. You just simply feel it as you are doing your ritualistic surrender process. Choose to release it. Breathe in. Release it out. Internalize. Feel the emotion. Release it out. Then deal with whatever emotions surface: the relief, the joy, the pain, the tears, however it comes out. If nothing comes out, just wait. If you don't feel anything the rest of that day or the rest of that week, go back and do it again. It will surface when it's ready. It's like a loose tooth for a child. It has to wiggle and take its time, but it is going to come out eventually. Don't be ripping it out before it's ready. The fact that you're dealing with it is telling you it's ready to go. It's loose.

Are there events in life, like dreams or meditative states that can trigger surrender?

There are people who are probably more spiritually evolved from previous lives. In their dream worlds, they are able to act as their own therapists to help with their release because dreams themselves are mechanisms to help you release those issues in life. The reason we dream, in the first place, is to cope with life on Earth.

There also are beings that have a vested interest in you and they will work with you in your dream state to help you release things. If you find that you've accepted something or you say you've accepted it, it really means you've surrendered it. In many cases, I work with individuals on a dream level because there are fewer issues, consciously, to battle. I can work with a vast amount of people in their dream reality versus the conscious state. Many people are aware of the work that I do in a dream state. But if ever you feel uncomfortable about that, it's your ego putting fear into the overwhelming possibilities. I would never do anything negative to someone. It is just inner fear, the inner-mind working. It's a matter of being overwhelmed with ideas of what I could or couldn't do.

How does someone begin to surrender?

You decide whether or not you are ready to surrender. Breathing is the key element. Breathe in and think about the area on your body where you will be surrendering. If you feel tightness in your chest, and you exhale out, that is an indication that you are ready to start the process. If you don't feel a subtle feeling inside of you, then you are probably not ready yet. Once you are ready, you must have quiet. You must have privacy. You must have alone time because you may cry or you may laugh. You may be thinking, "This is the happiest moment of my life because I am finally able to let this go." But you are going to need private time.

Start off by standing, facing north. Do a few breathing exercises, breathing in, blowing out the basic issues for the day. "I'm not going to worry about laundry. I'm not worrying about my bills right now. I'm not going to worry about those things." Just blow them out like you are doing a traditional meditation. Maybe do a meditation first. When you are finished with the meditation, stand up to change the feel of what you're doing. I would recommend choosing a slightly different spot than you normally would choose for meditations because that's a very special energy you're developing there. You do not want all of this released baggage in that vicinity. So select a different area, but if that is the only area you have to work in, do it there.

Then, as you stand up, do your breathing. You want to feel that you are ready to start releasing. You might want to sit in a chair, feet flat on the floor, not crossed, hand within hand as you would in meditation. Then go within, and work with the first big issue that turns up.

You know what you need to surrender already. You know what your issues are. It does not really matter whether they are health, emotional, or family issues. Just choose one. If you feel more than one issue, then say, "I surrender all of it." It'll start to flow out. You will feel it. Just use your breathing. Breathe in and when you surrender, just let it out. Say to yourself in the most intimate way, "I surrender. I forgive myself. I forgive myself," over and over again. "I forgive myself. It's okay." Just keep using those words. "I forgive myself." Or say your name, "Eric, I forgive you. It's okay."

You are really talking to your physical self, which affects your spiritual self. It's okay to talk in the second person because you are internalizing your spiritual self with your physical self. It's a duality, but it's not that much of an issue, in this particular case. Just keep working with it, saying that to yourself. Then maybe go to your heart chakra and fill that space with positive energy. Smile, and then breathe in through the heart chakra. And then let it back out again. When you feel a little tired or you've gone through your emotional run, it is time to stop. Bow to the Universe. Breathe out; breathe back in, just as you would for your meditation. Then get on with your day.

Is there anything you'd recommend outside of the Higher Balance system for someone who has buried away some of their deeper issues?

See a therapist. Seeing a therapist is not weakness. It's not a bad thing. A good therapist does not judge you. Sometimes you just need to vent. Sometimes you just need to talk to someone who will hear what you have to say and give you an unbiased opinion or help you to resolve inaccurate perceptions. This understanding can facilitate the removal of a lot of stuff from you. If you cannot afford a therapist, sometimes just a good friend can help. But you need to say to them, "I just want you to listen to what I am saying and acknowledge it. If you feel like you have something to add, briefly give it to me because I am releasing this with you. Are you okay with that?"

Do whatever it takes. If you don't have anybody to do this with, release your issue into a mirror. Talk to yourself in the second person. Give advice that you might give to someone else. It may sound crazy, but there is a point of logic in this. You've got to help yourself any way that you can. The bottom line is that, inch by inch, you gain a mile. If you are ready to release something and you catch your hand in the door, I am willing to bet it will be a while before your hand stops demanding your attention.

On a very basic level, if you just ate and usually fall asleep afterwards, then you are not helping yourself. If you are doing things that affect your physical body, then it will affect the outcome of your session. If you eat a healthy diet, more power to you. Be conscientious. Your body is your temple, so whatever you put into it is going to affect you biochemically. Your brain will affect your mind because it is a stronger center point. You are here utilizing this body to hold you in this dimension. It is a very powerful mechanism, and your conscious mind is rooted into it until it has run its course. You are really reverse engineering to reach the mind, who you truly are.

Whatever condition your body is in will have an effect on you, whether you drink too much caffeine, soda or sugar or too many fatty foods. Do the best that you can. I do not consider myself the best advocate on physical health, but even I know my limits. I know that I have to exercise some willpower and say, "Okay, I cannot do that." I certainly have more advantages than most people, but I still reserve my own physical health.

Take care of your physical body through physical fitness, such as walking a mile or so a day. Here is a key thought to remember: **walking is one of the best exercises that you can possibly do.** If you walk a mile a day, every day, in rain, sleet, snow or shine and you have a lot of issues on your mind, by the second week you will find that most of your issues start to unwind.

It's almost as if the answers start popping into your head. Do you know why? Because you are physically moving the body and historically speaking, human beings were very nomadic people. As individuals, those were calmer times. Just by walking, with nothing in particular to think about, your thoughts unwind. Your inner consciousness can communicate with you without anyone else interrupting you, and without any other responsibilities. In this modern age, the computer, the TV and other forms of technology divert you from self-reflecting. You neglect or ignore it, and you are numbing yourself instead. When you take a walk, you exclude other people from easily accessing you. Walking is the best therapist and it is free, so just walk and you will reap the benefits.

Can Dreamscape sessions be integrated with surrender?

A dreamscape is a therapeutic tool for revealing and handling issues that are troubling your mind. It provides a means to explore various possible higher states of consciousness, like those experienced in lucid dreaming. It will guide you into a vivid dream-like reality, opening doors that are normally only available to you in a dream state. If you are working on *Surrender*, you will find that more stuff comes up in your *Dreamscape*. The *Dreamscape* certainly complements it, but *Surrender* identifies specific issues that are probably things that you need to let go of. Therefore, you are bringing them up with a very powerful tool that was specifically designed for releasing them. The *Dreamscape* is not going to draw on major issues unless you are really ready to handle them. *Dreamscape* will effectively help to release some issues, but not as thoroughly as with *Surrender*. It is difficult to compare the benefits of the two; however, *Surrender* is a huge instrument for *removing issues* very rapidly. *Dreamscape* can bring up some big issues and help you to resolve them. I don't think there is a fair comparison between the two as it's like comparing apples and oranges.

Does surrendering open you up to a direct experience or connection with the Universe?

As stated before, clear yourself from everything that acts as a resistance for attaining the higher levels of vibration. When you clear the debris or the logs, you clear the path for this absolute experience. Once you have that experience, it does not matter anymore. You are exactly where you need to be.

Can you develop multidimensional consciousness without surrendering?

It is harder to accomplish, but yes, absolutely. You will end up dealing with the same issues though. It's just that you will probably deal with them a bit differently. It's a longer process. It is still a lot more progressive than any other methods out there.

Do you consciously return from a state of surrender?

There is a settling back in to yourself period, but the difference is that you simply feel new and improved. You feel clearer. Your mind is clearer. Your sense of well-being is amplified and you are happier. The only way it can be explained it is that you now have a more positive attitude. You let go of a huge weight that you carried around with you. You released it. Now, you remember the happier times that you had forgotten about. You think, "Wow, now I'm in the same place I was in before those things affected me," and you feel relieved. This, in turn, changes your whole perspective on life. The optimism/pessimism switch begins to take root.

Can surrender be fueled by desire?

Of course it can, and do not be ashamed of that. You have a desire to be a better person; why is that so terrible? You have the intention to sit down and do this. That is perfectly okay.

How does being honest with yourself come into play with surrender?

You cannot surrender unless you are absolutely honest with yourself. If you hold back, you don't get the same results that you are looking for. You will know that you are not being honest. You will feel it. You internalize it. You know it.

When you ultimately surrender are you surrendering observation as well?

It is a combination of the two. Observation is how you communicate the damage that was done, whether a visual or a mental observation. You acknowledge how it became a part of you. It is how the experience was recorded and, therefore, it is part of the process that is removed.

When you're in a life or death situation, how or when do you know if you should just surrender rather than take some kind of direct action?

You go through all of the natural physical responses. How extreme those physical responses are depends on your training and how you perceive the situation. If somebody has a gun in the room, you will obviously perceive this as a threatening situation. Your physical body may lock up. You may not believe that could happen, but it will. You may seek a method of escape or you may start hyperventilating. There is a point that your mind takes over, but your body will still go haywire.

Naturally, you want to survive and the survival mechanism is what you should be utilizing. Surrender, in this particular case, is not the process that you want to use. If you are in a situation where there is nothing you can do and you want to live, you do not have to ask yourself that question. You already know the answer. It is your intention. Just surrender and say, "Okay. I'm surrendering this situation because it is above and beyond my control. I am letting the Universe come into me knowing that what I really want is to live. I want to see my family. I want to say my good-byes if I am going to pass. But I accept the situation, no matter how it is dealt to me." You internalize all that.

One time someone pointed a gun right at me, pulled the trigger and it didn't fire. I'm not going to say the same thing will happen to you, but I am willing to bet on my particular situation. It was a good-working gun. The trigger was pulled, but the mechanism didn't work. I think the Universe will hear your request without asking, if you accept the situation for what it is.

When you talk about being conscious as well as having flow, is that a different way of describing the state of surrender?

No, but it is very similar. When you are not surrendering, you are stiff. You are rigid. You may not even realize it. If you stop right now and think about your body and your mind, you realize that you are very much in the now except more structured. Your consciousness is very thick. When you surrender, you must become like a reed in the wind. When the wind is blowing if it is an old stale, thin branch, it will snap off. It cannot resist the power of the blowing wind. When you are imitating that, you are limber and swing randomly left, right, up, down, back, right and left. It is like you cannot even feel it.

If you observe the trees and the leaves, there is a certain dance of synchronicity that happens. It's harmonized, meditative, and very relaxing. Flow comes from surrender. The most powerful force in the Universe comes from surrender. You are not physically designed to handle the full potency of the Universe moving through you at any given moment. When you are fluidic and surrender your sense of controlling how you want to be, then the Universe can move through you without harming you. It is profoundly powerful. It is profoundly perfect in its movements. You want to be in a state of surrender. You know that as you work with it, you will develop that sense. Then when you are unconsciously thinking about it, you will just react.

The Universe is neither male nor female. It is a balance of the two. More specifically, it is a combination of both masculine and feminine energy that creates a third polarity. And that polarity is a balanced masculine and feminine energy which is a relaxed state of being. There is a power that flows from it: the feminine being flexibility and the masculine being potential or the amount of creation that comes from it. In essence, you are in a state of surrender and you have a certain confidence of trust that emanates from it. That is the masculine and feminine polarity within. You can emotionally allow it to move through you.

The ideal for many Eastern spiritual methodologies is to achieve a state of non-dual awareness permanently. Can non-dualism or seeking the state within permanently prevent someone from truly surrendering?

That is like detachment from reality. I disagree with that philosophy. You are here to experience this dimension. You are here to be plugged in. Do not deny that; accept it and then you can find the correct balance between the two.

Many seekers believe that by pursuing spiritual growth, they desire it. They think that enlightenment is something that you cannot pursue and it is only achieved by letting go or surrendering all desire.

You acknowledge your intention by the simple act of giving up everything. You can desire to achieve enlightenment; there is nothing wrong with that. You can want this absolute level of higher consciousness, if you will. Just because it is what you are looking for does not mean that it is going to affect how you achieve it.

You have to give up your ego or your desire to want it, but you still have to acknowledge what you are trying to give up in order to get it. Accept it, and when you accept and internalize it, do not make a big deal about it. Just know that it is something that you're trying to achieve.

You do not need to abandon your desire of wanting enlightenment but do not think about wanting it at the same time. If you surrender the ego, the ego includes what you are trying to achieve. You are simply surrendering. Yes, it is true what they are saying. But what is the point of acknowledging it just to make an issue of it? By making it an issue, you create an even bigger duality just by thinking about it.

Is this surrendering the same as Buddhist detachment?

In Buddhism, detachment means to let go of your need for material things. There is some truth to this, but do not take it to the extreme like the Buddhists do because it detaches you from your life experiences. You need to have those experiences because you should experience life in its fullest. It's really about your perspective in life rather than the need to detach from it.

I want to experience. I want to know that I was alive while I was on Earth. I just do not want to cling to all the negative experiences that are part of my journey, letting them anchor me into a non-functioning being. I want to be alive. I want to feel the grass under my feet. I want to laugh with my friends. I want to watch a sunrise. I want to dance with my partner. I want to experience life to the fullest. Along the path, there are always a few jerks and a few lousy experiences that you have to deal with, but I don't want that to stop me from appreciating life, the creation of God. If you want me to experience detachment, to what level is your expectation and from what perspective? I do not want to be detached from life.

It is not about wanting or not wanting a car or having or not having a car. Want it. Have whatever car you desire to have, but don't let it engross you. Don't let it control you or dominate you. You can say, "I have an old beat-up car and you have a sports car. It just shows that I am more detached from necessity than you are." Well, you can have a horse-drawn carriage if you really want to. You can walk everywhere if you want to. You can give up your shoes if you really want to. You can give up all your clothing and your robes if you want to. It is a matter of personal choice.

What it really comes down to is this: Who are you in your life? Are you kind? Are you compassionate? Are you forgiving? Do you enjoy the things that life has offered you? Do you enjoy the gifts created by God? Do you smell the flowers? Do you feel the grass under your feet? Do you help a kindred person on your journey? Do you feel that you did enough to thank God for giving you the opportunity to experience this life? If the answer is no, then you have a lot of work to get started on and there's no time like the present.

I think people get too caught up in all of the details of how they should live their lives. Recipe books are what I call them. The Quran, the Kabbalah, the Old Testament, the New

Testament, and the Bhagavad Gita are all recipe books on how you are supposed to live. You cannot live your life through a recipe book. You already know right from wrong, internally. Wherever you live and whatever part you play in this world, whatever society you live and progress within, you had to adapt to that experience. There is not one single book that will work for every single situation. I don't care if they say, "Yes, it can." They are forcing it. They are interpreting it and bending the rules to fit their own agendas. You already know the answers internally. You already know. All you have to do is release all the baggage inside of you. Surrender it and you will feel a difference in your life. That's it. It is that simple.

THE SURRENDER TECHNIQUE

The first thing that I would like to say about the surrender technique is that once you have learned it, you should do this on your own without the written instructions. But for now, think of me as a voice or guide, not as a person or teacher. I'm like a subconscious echo.

You want to be in a nice, safe, quiet place where you will not be disturbed, sitting on the floor or in a chair. Simply sit for a minute, be still and take in a few deep breaths . . . and release. Breathe in . . . and release. Breathe in . . . and release.

Repeat after me, and then think of something that you want to come forward. It will come forward on its own.

"I invoke the pain of my childhood."

"I invoke the pain of my childhood."

"I invoke the pain of my childhood."

Now see yourself as a child and as the adult say to yourself,

"Forever you are loved."

"Forever you are deeply protected and wanted."

"You are the most beautiful thing in this world."

Now say,

"I surrender the pain."

"I surrender the pain."

With a smile on your face, "I surrender the pain."

Deep breath in . . . exhale.

We're going to work with whatever comes up. See what emotions or memories come up. You can apply them as you feel they are appropriate.

"I invoke the pain in my life."

"I invoke the pain in my life."

"I invoke the pain in my life."

"I set you free."

"I choose to set you free."

"I am setting you free."

"You no longer hold the chains in my heart, my soul, or my spirit."

"I am free."

"I AM FREE."

Breathe in . . . and exhale. Repeat after me:

"I am the power."

"I have the choice."

"I choose the liberation of my life and my soul to be now."

"I will conquer every challenge in my life."

"I will climb every mountain and I will even stop to see the view along the way."

"I am healed and I am healing every day."

Take a deep breath in . . . and exhale.

Now, slowly, choose a painful moment in your life, whether it is a person, a place or a shameful moment. I want you to briefly visualize the scenario that has caused you this pain. Now I want you to artificially change the experience. I want you to take control of the experience. I don't want you to harm the other person or harm others, but control it in such a way that it becomes a positive outcome. Visualizing this, I want you to say now,

"It is done and it is complete.

"It is done and it is complete."

Each day, I want you to choose one to three situations like this and spend at least five minutes working on them. Take every negative experience you've had in your life, and even though you remember the truth of what actually happened, I want you to rewrite it for your brain or mind. See the scenario and then change it into a positive outcome. When you are finished, take a deep breath and say this:

"I surrender the pain in my life to the Universe."

"What was once bad and painful, is now changed to good and light and healing. So be it."

I'll give you an example of how this knowledge and tool of rewriting information has helped me in my life. I went through a rough period of time in my life with an abusive step-father. In one particular situation, I was doing my homework at the kitchen table when he came into the room. He often drank instant coffee, if I remember correctly. He would put the kettle of water on the gas stove, turn it on and wait for the whistle to blow. Then come in, make his cup of coffee, and then go to his workroom. I didn't think anything of it. He came in, he was doing something in the kitchen, he left and I continued working on my homework.

He came back into the room and said, "What the hell are you doing? Why did you shut off the hot water? Who the hell do you think you are?" And I said, "Huh? What? What are you talking about? What's the matter?" He said, "I know you shut off the kettle of water! You think I don't know you shut it off?" And he stormed off. I really didn't know what to make of the situation. I was slightly fearful of him to begin with for the abuse that he put me through.

I remember hearing something thumping behind me and before I could react, I remember seeing a bright flash of yellow and red. It was very bright. I must have lost track of time. Anyway, I opened my eyes in what seemed to be a few moments later to this intense pain -- like somebody stomping on my head and I looked up. I was on the floor and looking up at my stepfather. My stepfather had a board about the size of a 2x4, but I don't remember exactly. He was yelling at me while shaking the board saying that if I ever touched his hot water again or thought that I could play games with him that I had better think twice about it. Then he marched off.

That was a very painful, abusive memory, one of many dealings with my 'wonderful' stepfather at that time. The surrender method really has helped me to be at peace with myself, with my stepfather, and the cruelties he put me through back then.

In this particular case, I sit in the lotus position and review my memories of this situation. Then I simply clear my mind and go back to that moment when he came in and yelled at me. You want to keep as much of the situation as you can to make it as real as possible for the brain to process. As my stepfather comes in and I hear his footsteps, instead of taking the wallop on my head, I see myself and visualize myself in detail. It's very important to put as much emotion into it as you can. Keep it as real for the organic brain as possible. I spin around in my chair, grab the board that is coming down on me, hold it, jerk it free from him, stand up and I say to him, "You better leave me alone or else! Now get out of here!" I throw the board on the ground and he becomes terrified and in his intimidation he runs off. I feel the confidence that comes with it and the reward of being able to defend myself and take a stance.

Now, that may seem a little silly to some people, but somewhere in your brain, it will re-write that memory. Instead of a painful memory, it now puts it into a positive, assertive, perspective instead. This is the beginning of building a level of confidence that comes with it.

Now you might say to yourself, "Well, I know what really happened." That doesn't matter. The brain doesn't necessarily work as a complete unit. It has its own little compartment for storing facts, information, and experiences. If you continue to do this, whether you believe it or not, you will balance yourself out more emotionally and not react to the circumstances that were once fearful. I can allow the fear to take hold of me whenever I hear somebody behind me, but instead I just jump around with a fearful expression.

Because I feel that I have rewritten and reprogrammed many of the negative experiences in my life, I have limited the amount of psychological damage they could do to me. It is not a cure-all, but in the end I certainly feel that it is an excellent form of therapy. And you can also use this for any mistakes that you made yourself. Maybe you will not receive the forgiveness from someone because they've already passed on or moved on. Or they are not willing to give it to you. There is a part of you that needs that forgiveness. By re-inventing that experience, you now see them as a loving mother or father who never has loved you properly or perhaps just making better decisions and having a better outcome.

You can re-write the script. You may feel a sense of guilt that you are giving yourself something that you may not fully deserve, but the real question is: Have you come to terms with it? If you have and that person is not willing to forgive you so you can move on, then I say it's okay to give it to yourself. I say it's okay.

You make of it what you will but be the best person that you can. The only way that you truly deserve the forgiveness and will receive it is, in your heart of hearts, you are truly sincere and appreciate this gift that you are giving yourself. Above all, love yourself. Love yourself as if you are another person. Love yourself. Go back through your life and turn every bad moment into a positive moment.

I like the saying "Forgiven but not forgotten." My stepfather and me, we don't speak anymore. I have moved on with my life. He has moved on with his. I know that he is a very, very, deeply disturbed and ugly human being for his actions. He is filled with anger and rage and that is just who he is. If I see him, I say "Hello, how are you doing?" You better believe when he looks into my eyes, there is a sense of fear in him. Because there is an absolute sense of confidence in mine and that's something he never took from me. I have conquered him. I am the warrior. I am the person alive, and he is the dead, dying person for his ugliness. And I can't help him. I haven't forgotten what he's done, but I certainly have forgiven him so that I don't keep dwelling on the past. I've moved on and I'm grateful that I have.

Chapter 2

FURTHER DISCUSSIONS ON SURRENDER

WHEN YOU HEAR the word surrender, you automatically think that it means to give up, throw in the towel and admit defeat. So, when I talk about surrender, it is a very complex subject to explain to you. The best way to simplify surrender is this way: the mind is amazingly intricate, and because you are a biological creature by nature, your feelings, ideas, and concepts are habitually ingrained. You do things because that is the way you always did it and never give it a second thought. But when you commit to something, you tend to see it through. The belief system that has been engrained in you is, "I don't give up," or "I will do it anyway." In difficult circumstances, it is easy to make the wrong decisions when lacking the correct information. If you do have the right information, you tend to do things much better.

What is a positive example of Surrender?

Here is a good example of surrender that is very simple to comprehend. Before I started Higher Balance, I had a number of students that I personally taught on a one-on-one basis. At that time, my policy was, "If somebody is persistent and dedicated enough, I will teach them." That was my style and that is what I focused on. But there came a period of time when I wanted to take all of the lessons I was teaching to a higher level, which later became The Higher Balance Institute. At that time, I was not sure of which direction to take the lessons or how to fully go about it. So, I became consumed with teaching people individually. This, of course, took away from the time I needed to develop Higher Balance. It became obvious to me that I had to sacrifice my commitment of teaching people one-on-one, and I knew that I had to start turning away the few people in order to help the many.

I will always remember this statement that I once heard -- I think it's from the movie *Star Trek* when Spock said, "When I sacrifice myself, the needs of the many outweigh the needs of the few." I realized that if I surrendered my commitment to teach people one-on-one, I could reach out to a lot more people. Therefore, I stopped teaching individually and in small groups so that I could develop a format that would reach more people. It would still deliver the quality and intensity of the information that was so important to me. It was a surrendering process. It was an instinct, a habit I had developed that was very hard to break away from.

How does guilt play a role in Surrender?

I will give you an example of how that works. In many situations in life when you commit to friends, family, and a job and you also want to develop spiritually, you are taken advantage of by those other people. Not that they have bad intentions, but sometimes it is hard for us to say, "I'm going to let someone else help you." or "You need to get help from another professional instead of me." You feel guilty when you do that. Separate your mind from your duties and realize that, "This is a sensible thing for me to do," and, "Why should I be guilt-ridden by freeing myself of this responsibility?" It's the guilt that is the real problem. The real question is, "Should you even feel guilty?" Your higher consciousness always knows the truth. If you are going to surrender something, then you probably already know that you should not feel guilty about doing it.

Can Surrender be used for eradicating addictions?

Surrender can be used for many, many different things. Another example of surrender is releasing your cravings of alcohol. It can also be used to clear ego issues; such as someone with a strong ego who desperately wants to reach the higher states of consciousness, but feels that their ego gets in the way.

Surrender can be used for almost anything that is within the realms of inner truth. What I mean by "inner truth" is using surrender for the wrong reasons. Like if you commit a crime and want to remove the guilt -- that is a problem. In that case, your inner-guide communicates with your biological self and says, "We need to resolve this."

I often look at the biological self or the brain as if it were a computer. When data is put into it, it simply responds and automates. Your mind or higher consciousness silently talks to you and says, "This is an issue. This is a problem and you need to resolve it." The fact that your mind even brings it up and that it occurs to you is the first sign that you need to deal with it. You need to remove this perception that is inside of you because guilt and manipulation can have a profound effect on your spiritual growth. You have within you something that drives you to evolve and seek out the experiences of life to the fullest intent. That intuitive mechanism within you to direct the will of the Force is called the Navigator. Your Navigator is saying, "We need to solve these problems so you can move on."

What, in your view, is the one most important factor for permanently dissolving blockages or negative emotions?

Of course, the topic of this conversation is surrender, so make sure that you truly surrender your issues. A lot of people go through the process of surrendering, but they do it more like they are cleaning windows. They go through the steps and do what they feel they should do or what they were told to do, but they do not reflect within the depths of their consciousness to pull out the issue that needs to be surrendered.

Here is a good example for this: I have an aquarium in my office. Every time I take a look at it, it is overgrown with plants. Today, I pulled a bunch of plants out, and you know, you can pull out a few plants and it looks great. Everything looks fine for a while, but the plants grow back. So, if I really want to get rid of the overgrown plants, I need to be consistent in finding the root of the problem. The solution is to make sure that I clear it all out and leave nothing behind.

Many people treat the situation quickly, like Windex on a glass. They clean it and move on. They're not very fussy about the edges or the corners or finger prints that may be left on the glass. You have to be thorough. You have to be deeply earnest in your pursuit of releasing the problem so that you can surrender it. It has to be done from the depths of your soul. You must bring it out, release it, and surrender it to the Universe. This takes a lot of self-reflection. You cannot just sit down and go through the motions, like it's a recipe book. You have to deeply reflect on it.

I seem to be blocked from connecting with my Higher Self. My meditations are nothing but blackness. Can the surrender skills and techniques help me to reach a level beyond relaxation?

Absolutely! I will do a little walk through process to help you with this. You can add this to your meditation. It is critical information: **It is all in the details.** When you reflect on entering the void - the blackness - and you say, "Nothing is happening," your expectation and the act of looking for something will prevent something from happening.

Now, I know that that may sound a little strange, but the Universe doesn't necessarily show you what you want to see when you want to see it. In other words, if you are looking for something in particular, then you are probably looking for something that you can already conceive or understand. So, you might say, "Okay, I expect to see something beautiful. Maybe yellows and pinks and blues or I expect to see a flower." You do this without even being aware of your expectation. Surrendering relieves you of that expectation. Surrendering allows something very profound to come through. And, of course, that is very hard to do.

Surrender the need to go beyond the black void. Be happy with the void. Be content. Absolutely love the void. And when you come to terms with the void and you are at peace with it, just rest there and be placid. Just be there. Don't have any intent. Don't have any expectation even if it takes a week or a month. I promise you, profound things will eventually happen.

Many years ago, I first entered that void of absolute nothingness and wondered the same thing, "Nothing is happening. I'm just going to this place and nothing is there. I'm just hanging out and that's it." When I came to terms with this, I realized there is a peaceful feeling with no demands in the absolute nothingness. I just enjoyed being there. I even forgot about enjoying it because that's a whole other thought process. It was just existence of non-existence.

Then I realized that I was moving – literally. It was like being in a starship moving through a galaxy and you see all the stars zipping past you like on *Star Trek*. You enter this area where there are no stars and it looks like an inky black hole. Not that it's a hole or it is ink. It just doesn't have any stars to mark distance or space. You enter it, and as you go further into it, and deeper, and deeper, it doesn't seem like there is anything there. Eventually, what was behind you can't be seen anymore. So it looks completely black. And as you're moving, you assume you are not moving at all because you cannot see anything to orient your progress.

There is nothing to gauge it by, so it feels like you are not moving at all. But you are moving faster than the speed of light until, eventually, you realize there is something on the other side. It looks like sparkles of haze or fog. Trying to interpret it is the first mistake that you make. That's what keeps it away, and that's a million dollar statement! **Don't try to interpret it. Just let it be. Let it exist.** Let the Universe manifest what it wants to show you. It becomes a profound experience. That's when you get to see what is on the other side. Have faith in the Universe that this is all a good experience and I assure you, it is.

Just come to terms with the black and realize that it is not black at all. You are actually moving. Most people think that the black is a void where nothing is happening. They are just there. There's nothing going on. This is a test. This is a barrier. This is a wall that prevents those who should not be there from moving beyond it. It's a way to fool them and make them turn back.

Just go with it and move. The more at peace and relaxed you become, the faster you will move across it. If you consciously start to think about it, it will weigh you down. Thought is heavy and it slows you. Let yourself cruise. Let yourself move through that space. And remember, when you find an inner peace inside of you and you go on with your daily routine, believe it or not, you are still moving. You are still moving in that other dimension. Even though you are going about all the things you do in your daily life, you are still moving as long as you can hold that feeling, which is right in the inner chest area. It is this very relaxed, indifferent, non-emotional feeling, but it feels very good. It feels like you are very calm. You just move and you will know when you get to the other side. You will be very grateful and very pleased with what you find.

**It seems that when I see the word surrender,
I have difficulty surrendering to the idea of
surrendering itself. How do you deal with that?**

First, decide what you interpret as surrendering. What does surrender mean to you? I struggled with this same exact concept. I am definitely a fighter. I don't think I have ever thrown in the towel on anything that I considered worth fighting for. When I say surrender, it's about the things that you are hanging onto unconsciously. It's about the things that are weighing you down and that prevent you from progressing further.

Making money, spiritually working on yourself and doing all of these things . . . they are all positive attributes. Who would want to surrender those things? Let's say that you went through a separation and your ex moved on with their life. They got married but you are still thinking about them, so you cannot move on with your life. You cannot meet other people because, emotionally, you cannot manifest the energy inside of yourself to put into other people. So, you say, "I really need to surrender this because I cannot give it up. But, logically, I see that I need to." This is an issue to surrender.

Now you can say, "Well, I will get them back." But logic says there is something better for you, and your ex has a right to the happiness they found. Therefore, this is something that you should surrender so that you can accept better things to come into your life.

Another type of surrendering is something you are obsessed with that just doesn't seem to be working out. You keep hammering at it to no avail. Now, you might say, "Well, maybe this one time it is not going to work out for me." Really, it is just a matter of asking yourself, "Am I listening to my inner guidance or am I letting my brain get in the way so that I can force it to work, whether it's right or not. I'm going to fit the square peg into a round hole and I know it can be done."

My question is, "Do you think there is a better way to go about that?"

Some people might need to surrender the pain of losing someone they love. And they, again, are stuck. Most of the time, surrender is used for emotional issues. Emotion is the closest thing to a universal language, meaning God or the Universe or whatever you wish to call it.

When you are a soul or a spirit, you do not have vocal cords. You are not going to talk like a human does. There is a different way to communicate. It is very complex, but it is essentially based upon emotions. Emotionally, we internalize words and they get into our mind or our higher consciousness and clog things up. Our Navigator says, "You need to deal with this. You need to resolve this problem so that you can progress." This is the process of letting go and coming to terms with the issue rather than hanging on to the people who have already left. The whole world is passing you by and you are stagnating.

So, those are the kinds of things that should be strategically surrendered. It is about finding what you feel you need to surrender through your Navigator. Your higher truth is something that is stifling you, preventing you from progressing. Write a list of the things that you feel should be surrendered. Simply sit back, relax, clear your mind and ask yourself internally -- don't even verbalize, rather feel, "What are my issues?"

Do not expect to hear a voice in your head that says, "Well, you have to deal with your child, etc." Watch for images or emotions that come up. The emotions usually are tied to an image or a particular situation. You will know exactly what the emotion is. It has an abundance of information and you will know what that is. And then write it down as something that you may want to look into further. Often, the things that you need to surrender are the things that you are not even aware of.

I emphasize that you should just sit back, clear your mind, create your space, and go inside of yourself. Let things surface. Internalize the question, 'What are the blockages that

I need to release?' There is a sense of awareness in all of us that communicates to us unconsciously. It almost prevents us or misdirects us, and you need to understand that it is a kind of intention or resistance that tries to keep you within the Doe. It is kind of an elusive consciousness that communicates to you and makes you forget about surrendering. You have to trust your Navigator, not so much your brain, to interpret what you are feeling.

Do not try to figure out what that is. Jot it down and then write down what you think it is connected to. Just let it flow. Put it out and then go back to it later and analyze it, but don't analyze it as it is coming to you. That is the million dollar secret: **don't get emotionally caught up.** Treat yourself as a second person. Be the mind, which is perfect. You would be amazed what can happen when you set up rules for yourself. Just acknowledge it by saying, "Okay, I'm not going to get emotional about this. I'm going to treat this as if I'm assisting someone else, but it's me."

Your soul consciousness is perfection. It is the brain and all the experiences from life; like emotions and all of the organic processes that get us all jacked up. So, you need to trust the Navigator to ask your organic brain the question. The organic brain, as long as you are not being emotional, will respond without thinking about it. And then you just jot it down.

There is a module from Higher Balance Institute called *Reverse Engineering the Self* that explains how you can identify the "I's." That will identify other consciousnesses in your mind that are not necessarily you. They are part of your brain mechanism. When you isolate all of them, you have a lot more ability to decode all of this.

How does the ego get in the way of surrendering? What are some instances or techniques to try to break through that?

I think some people erroneously think of the ego as something that is bad. I certainly have an ego, and a lot of people are shocked when I say that. I do not think that I could have achieved the level of consciousness or the abilities that I have without the ego. I see the ego not as *myself* but as a tool to push myself. I see the ego in the sense of confidence and a source of *willpower*. I believe that if you set your mind to something or you tell people, "This is what I am going to do," your ego or your pride makes you follow through.

You can also have a negative ego. A negative ego is the kind of ego that blinds you. When you have too much pride or too much arrogance, you blind yourself to how your actions can affect others or even yourself. So it is very important to acknowledge the difference between your positive ego and negative ego. As a point of interest, all of the spiritual masters from Christ, Buddha, and Krishna were considered extremely arrogant by outsiders or by other spiritual people. It really comes down to the fact that your actions and communications express the message you are sending to others. People are genuinely shocked when I say, "Spiritually you can find enlightenment, but you will also have an ego." Use the ego as part of your organic self to push you to attain the higher states of consciousness.

White cells should acknowledge that there is something very different about them. It is engrained in us that we are not supposed to feel that way. We are taught that is arrogant and that is where the problem begins. We become our own worst enemy by accepting the concept that we are not supposed to acknowledge ourselves as being different. We have to acknowledge that we are different. If you want to call it special, then call it special. I did not call it special. You have to *feel your uniqueness*. You have to acknowledge your uniqueness. You have to empower yourself with the idea that you are important. There is a reason why you feel it. We always hear, "You think you are better than everyone else." I've heard that my whole life and it really was not about that for me. It was a need to serve some kind of greater cause. I understood that. If other people do not feel that, then it is not my problem. I am not concerned with whether or not they understand that or not. I am concerned whether or not I feel it. I need to figure out what I should be doing with this feeling. I want to fulfill my purpose. I feel very proud, very privileged, honored, and mostly humbled by the fact that I feel a sense of being connected to something -- the Universe -- God – something greater than myself.

White cells are like salmon trying to find their way back to their point of origin as they face all sorts of dams, rotor blades, bears, wild animals and many other obstacles. This is just another obstacle, but a very psychological one and nobody wants to call it out. You have to be very careful what you define as your ego, and what you are trying to release.

How do I focus on surrendering one small issue without being distracted by other minor issues?

I would not surrender any of the outer issues. Instead, look into your psyche. It comes down to how you are designed. It is the design of your organic brain. It is like you are trying to direct everything down a one lane highway but you have four lanes merging into one lane. You need to construct a better mechanism for processing things. It is definitely an emotional issue that you are taking on. In other words, all the problems that you have going on are not necessarily *the major* problem. You want to take them all on at the same time. And the part of you that feels the need to take them all on at once is what you need to isolate and surrender. The desire to do that is overwhelming you and creating the overload. If you remove that, you will replace it with something more advanced. You will be able to deal with those issues a lot better. It will allow you to reach higher states of consciousness in everyday life and in business.

Since I was a baby, I've struggled from sexual abuse and I have been disabled for the past six years. So, how can I tell if that is part of what has held me back for so long?

Since you are bringing it up right now, that is a good indication that there still is a problem. It is generally because something is telling you, "These memories are my problems and my issues." That is what surfaces in your consciousness.

Personally, I think the way that I have lived consciously all my life is because so many people around me treated me differently. I always felt different. I let them dictate to me, not the bad or the horrible person they thought I was, but it has been a big challenge for me. Even with my own family. There is a need in us as white cells to appease people. We do not want to hurt anybody. We want to make them happy. When they ask us to give up our identity and not to acknowledge it in anyway, we give up ourselves. We are our own worst enemy, in that case. It is not that we do it on purpose; it's just our nature to appease others.

I'm going to walk you through the Surrender technique, so prepare yourself by ensuring that you are not going to be disturbed by this. Find a nice place to sit back, like a comfortable chair or a couch. You can lie down if you like or recline in a chair. I do not recommend sitting in any chairs that do not have arms in case you happen to slouch over unintentionally.

You might want to grab a notebook or something to write on and a pen. I want you to jot down at least four things that you think are the issues that you would like to release. So, go ahead and do that now. You are going to go through a session and I am going to help you decide what you are going to work on. It is very important to selectively choose something significant to surrender. Don't choose a group of things or plan to surrender your ego. You have to be more specific than that. You have to decide on a specific issue and chip away at that one particular thing.

You should not surrender more than one thing a week. You can keep working on surrendering that one issue if you do not feel like you have fully released the issue. Spend a week working on it if you have to, and that will make a difference, especially if you are using the Higher Balance material.

So, now that you have chosen a few things, select one concern out of the four. Now, sit back in your chair and relax. Do not cross your legs or your hands. Place them by your side or somewhere comfortable or on your lap. Do not have them crisscrossing each other or folded on top of each other, and the same goes for your legs.

Feel your forehead, your ears, and your inner ears. Relax and just let them go. Feel your throat and your shoulder blades sinking. Relax your arms and your hands. Feel your chest relaxing and sinking. Relax your stomach, your lower back, and your hips. Your mind is floating and easing. The brain is easing. The body is easing. Relaxing through your thighs and your knees, your calves; feeling relaxed and comfortable. Feel your whole body as if it were made of lead.

Now, allow the issue you chose to surface -- something that you are going to surrender. Know what it is that you are calling on. What is the problem? Speak it again in your mind. What is the problem? Feel it. Associate the feeling with the problem. Now, see it from an outside perspective as if you were feeling it from outside of yourself. You are feeling for yourself but it is not of you. Now, feel the vibration. Feel the feeling of what it is that you are choosing to surrender. Feel the familiarity of it.

Now envision a clear box inside of yourself, a transparent box that is holding that feeling, and it's residing inside of your chest area where your heart is. Visualize it being lifted up by your hands, but don't move your hands yet. It's as if you are taking the box inside of your chest and bringing your hands to the sides of your rib cage and then lifting it like it was a big box or cake. Inside of the box is the problem. This is the emotion that you choose to surrender. Say it with me, "I surrender this. I surrender this. From the depths of my being, from the depths of my soul, it is time to set this free. I choose to free this. I choose to surrender this. I choose to liberate myself."

Now, lift the box upward from your sides. Lift it up slowly, higher and higher. Now, release your hands and like a helium balloon, see the box floating away. Floating away. Floating away. Keep seeing it floating away. Feel it going away. Releasing it; releasing it from the depths of your being. Releasing it; seeing it getting smaller and smaller and smaller in the distance. It's becoming a little dot and it disappears. Send it now out to the Universe.

Again, say with me, "I free myself of this. I no longer carry this. No longer is this a blockage. I release it. I am at peace and one with the Universe. I invite God within me. I invite God within my being, and I ask that God, the Universe, purge me of all my blockages: remove from me all of the negative energies and blockages that may be within me; let them surface and release them. Surface and release them. Surface and release them.

Feeling relaxed and comfortable, take a nice deep breath in through your nose and exhale out. Deep breath in. I want you to release any last bits of that energy as you exhale this time.

Thank you again for your time. Thank you for choosing to spend it with me.

Chapter 3

UNBOUND

IN THIS CHAPTER, I am going to put more of the pieces of the puzzle together for you. All of the teachings are done in layers that build on itself, which makes it easier for you to understand. So, let us begin with a relaxation technique. Take in a nice deep breath. Now take in another. This last time, I want you to think about the Prana that is coming into your body, filling that empty space within. See the energy coming in. You can only affect the Prana that comes into you when you think about it. It converts to the same frequency as your tonal. If you do not think about what you are breathing in, then you are just breathing in air. When you think about the Prana that is in the air, you take Prana in.

Look around and see the energy in your room. Believe in that energy and tonalize with it. See that energy and breathe it in now, and then exhale. Notice the difference in how you feel just by thinking about it for only a couple of seconds. One more time, see the Prana energy. Open your arms to the Force that you have forgotten. Open your arms to the God-Force; to the power that you have neglected, forgotten about and starved yourself from. It will come to you if you think about it. So, embrace it. Now that you are feeling relaxed, I am going to open this up to any questions that you might have on your mind.

Why is it so difficult to be spiritual
during the winter months?

Throughout history, there have always been highs and lows in the affect the Force has on this planet. At certain times, the Force is very strong and then it becomes weak. Being weak does not mean it is not present; it just means it is weak. There are times when the Force will reach out and speak to you. But during other times, it's just not going to be there at all so you have to turn to it. Winter is a very low point for the Force. It has to do with the position of the planet in its orbit. It depends where the other planets are also, not because of astrology but because solar frequencies are the method the Force uses to talk to us.

We know the sun throws off solar radiation that bombards the planet in multiple frequencies. This is how we receive communication from the Force. Not that it is the sum total of our communication, but it is a portion of that. Because of the position of the planet in its orbit, we do not receive as much of that signal. As spiritual people, we look for that signal to motivate or steer us. When it is weaker, the tonal of the planet, the machine, and the tonal of the red cells dominate. That is what you feel right now. If you were feeling spiritual before, you are now starting to feel depressed because you are being sucked back into the tonal that you tried to escape from for so long. You feel so unmotivated, you cannot even save yourself. You are not drawing on the Force. You just allow yourself to float adrift in the ocean of the collective consciousness.

You have totally forgotten your practices. You get washed if you do not practice the ways of the Force every day and do not think about it. When you do not integrate the Force into your life and you start to feel depleted, you do not feel the change right away. It washes you so you do not even feel it happening. It just removes who you are, layer by layer, until you are demystified. Until what you know just seems to fade away from you.

Why do spiritual people forget to
keep up with their practices?

My teachings are not just information. They are a living knowledge. They are alive. Think of this knowledge as a species, an organism. My words are an organism that permeates you like an energy virus, but a positive virus that becomes a part of your soul. It lives inside of you. When you do not think about your soul, when you do not ponder and reflect on it, you forget about who you are. You become a biological machine and you lose yourself. Sharing this with you is food for this living thing inside of you. You are feeding it with energy and with consciousness. You are feeding it mentally, and that is why it is alive. Perhaps, you are starting to feel it now. This is what you are craving. It is what you want. When you forget who you are, when you stay away too long, you are washed. You are erased. It will happen to the best of you; therefore, until you are enlightened, stay close to the teacher.

If you drift away, you will lose yourself. Then one day the Force will be strong. You will get up out of bed and ask yourself, "Where have I been?" You will see how all of your money, all of your possessions, and everything in your life is meaningless. Your purpose in life is gone because you have lost who you are. Rest assured, if anyone happens to drift away, that is their choice. They know what you know now. If you do not feed and take care of your spirituality, the collective consciousness of the planet is so very powerful that it will wash away your memory. It will wash away who you really are. It will wash away your soul and you will become a working organism for this planet. All you will think about is eating, sleeping, how to gratify your flesh, and what your next adventure will be. Only those things become important to you. You will forget who you really are.

By becoming more aware, will I be more apt to resist the planets suppressive tonal?

By awakening in this life, you become a visitor. This is a working organism planet. It is a machine. As you awaken, you become a guest. You begin to become aware of all the people working around you. At some point, were you more aware of your path than you are now? Do you remember what it is like watching other people? You forgot who you are. You are becoming one of them now and that is the problem. You are becoming just another worker for the planet. That is what you have struggled against. That is where you once were. You finally managed to get away from the mechanism and became aware. You have forgotten the word *aware*.

When is the last time you thought of the word *aware*? It is such a powerful word. You have to remember to feed your awareness. You have to feed your soul. You are miserable because you forgot your spirituality. When you think spiritually and feed your spirituality, you are not unhappy. But you are miserable, unhappy, and negative when you are not aware.

Is being aware similar to being enlightened?

Enlightenment has multiple levels, not just one. It is something that you have already entered into. You can enter it very quickly, but it depends on each individual. You were there once, so find your way back to it. You are miserable, not because of the lack of money, your relationships or because your life is not moving forward. You could be a millionaire and still be miserable. It does not matter if you are in debt or have a lot of money. You would still be miserable because you do not have awareness. Instinctually, you were aware once before, and nothing compares to that. You can think about all the material things in your life that you assume will satisfy you. But none of those will fulfill you. That is the illusion of red cell thinking.

You have to remember awareness again. If you have awareness, you can go to Alaska in the middle of the winter and it will be wonderful. If you have awareness, you can work in your job and you will not be unhappy. Remember who you are and your past lessons. Remember the Force is everywhere around you. But remember the most important thing: The Force cannot become one with you unless you choose to understand It enough for It to merge with you. *If you do not think about the Force, the Force cannot touch you.*

You are made of material from the Earth. You are an organism. It is your tonal, your spirit that separates you and allows this body to commune with a higher source rather than a lower source. When you do not think about and practice what you know, you become part of the frequency of the Earth. You know what the difference is. A spiritual person can see spiritual phenomena and a non-spiritual person cannot. This is because they exist at two different frequencies. You reflect more when you are aware. You have interesting dreams and strange or unusual experiences.

When you reach the higher states of consciousness, do not think it is just a coincidence. If you feel that way, your state of consciousness can lose its importance when that happens too often. The Force dropped its frequency of our planet and you dropped with it because you were not paying attention to it. You lost your signal like a satellite. You are running around in circles not knowing what to do with yourself, and the world just sucked you right back in before you even realized it. Your whole life became about bills and your relationships. All of that is trivial! It is trivial. Believe in the Force. Trust yourself to the Force and all things in your life will have meaning again. If you were meant to be poor, accept it. Do not depend on material wealth while you are here on Earth. Instead, prepare for the riches of Heaven. In other words, prepare yourself for what's beyond this world by doing the work now.

So one should not desire material things?

I am not saying there is anything wrong with having money or material possessions. In this life, you will always have bills to pay. There will always be people who try to bring you down, but all of this is just trivial stuff. If I lost my house tomorrow, it would really suck, but it's a trivial thing in the greater scope of things. I could just write it off. If I lost the school, I could write it off. But you know something? I am a very, very rich man and I know that. I know how a millionaire or billionaire feels and I know that they wish they could have what I have. They would give me everything they have to get it if they thought they could attain enlightenment that easy. I truly believe that.

You will be much happier if you remember the teachings. Go back to your toolbox. Go back to your practices. Practice what you know. When you are constantly thinking and stewing on the problems in your life, you give away your power. You give in to your miseries and the unimportant things.

How can I stop myself from overly focusing on the petty things in life?

Feel the sun on your face. Smell the air when you take a walk. Feel the Force in your life, and thank God you are here to collect all of those experiences. Then you will realize how trivial and unimportant everything else is. It will all work out. Your bills will get paid and your life will get better. The machine pushes you through. It is going to push you no matter what happens. It is like a wave on the ocean. You will be pushed ashore sooner or later.

So, do not be so hard on yourselves. Read the **Desiderata**. Be kind to yourself. Only when you can relax will you let the Force into you. If you grab the bull by the horns, so to speak, you will not win. You will only get tired. Yet this is what you are doing. Somewhere you forgot who and what you are. You forgot your teachings. Instead of being like a reed in the wind, you are getting stiff. You are pushing against it. Remember your teachings because life will be a lot more rewarding. Do not think for a moment that I am above all of this because I get caught up in being a human being, too.

Will being aware lead to awakening?

Awakening is not something that just hits you on the head. Awakening comes from logic, reasoning, deduction, and training. When you meditate, think about your spirituality. Think about your awareness and the Force. Then subtly think about what you need to accomplish in your life. If you need a better job, trust it to the Force. ***Praying to God is talking to God -- meditating is listening to God***. The Force knows what you need. If you simply apply to your needs, it will fulfill them. I truly believe that. It's like baking a cake and adding the salt. Now salt is not bitter, it adds flavor, but it depends on how much or how little you use. You are baking the cake of your spirituality. You have to add the desire as a pinch and it will be perfect and resolve itself.

Have you ever been aware of what happens when you are depressed, but after meditating, everything seems to iron itself out? I had a student come to me once who was almost in tears. I told him time and again to meditate. Finally he did. Almost overnight he got a job and the situation with his house was resolved. Every problem in his life ironed itself out. These dilemmas in life occur because you become part of the machine; you become part of the product. Walk *In-Between*. Remember your teachings. Remember who you are. Awaken. Stay awakened. Feed yourself. Remember that you are a spiritual being. You are no longer part of the machine.

Once you are aware of this knowledge, you can never go back. You can never forget it. The knowledge is always with you, and that is the reason why you are so miserable. It is the part of you that feels so unfulfilled. You can never fit back into that square peg anymore. You are not square anymore; you are round. That is what you have to realize. It is not anyone else's choice but your own. You will always be miserable doing anything else. The only way that you can be happy is to find a way for your life and your spirituality to walk the same path in duality together. You must harmonize the two. If you do too much focusing on your work and not on your spirituality, you will not be happy. If you do too much spirituality, you will not be happy with your physical life. You have to balance them both.

Even though you have heard a lot of this before, you know that I am right. You can feel that I am right. You can feel that it is changing you right now. Isn't there a part of you that acknowledges how good this feels? If there is another part of you that is still fighting it, it is because you are still caught in your humanness. The more that I can share with you, providing these thoughts to you, the more you can understand. Then you can become part of this hologram rather than it becoming material for you. This allows you to move freely as a conscious being. You have to understand more of the Force than you already do. The more you can understand the Force, the more your brain will accept the greater reality of all of this. Let me turn the tables on you. Give me an example of evolution.

What comes to mind is infections and penicillin.

In what way?

Bacteria, after being treated with penicillin can become immune to the effects of penicillin because the bacteria have learned to deal with that problem.

How did it learn?

It reproduces quickly. Eventually the bacteria will mutate slightly so that it is not susceptible to the antibiotic.

How does the bacteria know about mutating?

Its goal is to live, no matter what.

Are the bacteria intelligent enough to know how to mutate in order to fight off the antibiotic?

No.

There is a Divine Force that thinks for it so it can specifically do what it needs to do to overcome the threat of the penicillin. Evolution is that Force. It is an act in motion. It is when things happen beyond coincidence. I always think of new ways to prove that the Force exists. In religion, they say to just have faith. I always look for ways to help you to better understand. The day that you really understand is the day you too can walk through walls, that you can do incredible miracles. But you have to make absolute sense of all of this so you can say, *"I'm no longer bound by the rules of this dimension."* You will always be bound to this dimension as long as you mentally cannot break free from how it works or how you understand it. If it's not truth to you, you cannot break past it. It has to make perfect sense to you. Until that becomes absolute truth to you, you will not understand it. You will not reach that next level.

The other day, the Force was hammering me with an explanation of why you are losing yourself and why the Force is weaker right now. Winter is a very weak period for the Force. It is always weak at that time of year on this part of the planet. If you think back, you have always been in this state of mind around this time of year. Sometimes you are worse, sometimes better. It depends on the axis of the planet, of course, but right now you have to empower yourself to get through this. This can go on for several months during the winter. That is why you need to motivate yourself to do classes right now. Now is the time to do that. The Force is everywhere. It is thinking for the planet and this is proof that you can tune into it. Evolution is conscious thought.

Think about this. This is so amazing. What intelligence tells a butterfly to make its wings look like the eye of an owl? We know, scientifically, that certain butterflies mimic an owl's eye. An owl is predatory to birds, so the birds stay away from owls. The birds are now afraid of the butterflies because the butterflies have wings that appear to look like owls. According to science, this happens for a reason. They do not say how the specific genetics of a butterfly, an insect that has

biochemical thoughts on the lowest of levels, can allow for the thought process that is needed to rationalize this. How does the butterfly know? Something manipulated it. Do you think a butterfly looks at an owl and says, "Hey, now that would be a cool thing to have on my wings? I think I'll just manipulate my cellular structure to perfectly imitate that." Think how astounding this is! On the level of intelligence that an insect has, it probably cannot even relate to an owl. It is probably not even capable of seeing an owl, let alone knowing what the owl's purpose is. Yet the butterfly mimics it. There is a Force that intelligently understands that in order to balance some things in life; it must manipulate things in certain ways.

The Force is everywhere. When you look at a bug that imitates something, how does it know to mimic it? What logically told it to shake like a leaf every step it takes? Common sense supports this theory. How does it know when to take a step and rock back and forth? They call it evolution. Well I ask you, what part of evolution makes this conclusion? What part of evolution rationalizes what needs to takes place for this to happen? Evolution is a process of thinking. The planet is a living organism. It thinks and the Universe affects it. Something tangibly affects everything around us, but we cannot see the thought process because we move at a different vibration. That is all it is. Something tangibly makes things think. It is astounding.

We don't see it in our lifetime because evolution takes hundreds or thousands of years to manifest. We know by the size of the planet that its thought must be slower. Everything is slower in proportion to its size. The bigger it is, the slower it is. However, there is conscious movement of manipulations even at molecular levels.

I was watching a butterfly on TV and it looked like an ant was carrying the butterfly. The tentacles of the butterfly were waving around and its whole body was writhing. This is how nature gets other insects to peck at the wrong side so that the butterfly has a chance to get away. Did this butterfly rationalize that if it flipped its body over and wiggled all around, it could fool the birds that were trying to peck at it? Think about the intelligence of that thought process. That is amazing. Does the insect manipulate itself or does nature do it? They say, "Well, that's just nature." *What part of nature tells it to do that?*

How does it rationalize all of this? What aspect of rationalization makes the butterfly know what colors and what configuration is needed for its wings to appear like the eyes of an owl? How did the other butterfly know to move its antennae to mimic being carried away by another insect? Something intelligent paid a moment's attention to it and manipulated its cellular structure to resolve the issue. Cells don't know how to do that. The insect didn't know how to do that. Everybody takes the word evolution and assumes it is just a process of trial and error. What taught nature how to do this? How did the butterfly know that it needed to change because it was getting pecked on? Out of a million combinations of possibilities, why did it decide to make a perfect rendition of itself upside down? How did it intelligently know what it looked like? Does it say, "I am"? Does it recognize itself? Does a butterfly acknowledge itself as an intelligent species? How did it know to make that decision? Out of a billion decisions, it made that particular decision. The only logical answer is it did not make the decision on its own.

Nothing on this planet makes a decision on its own, even you, and that is the point. If nature is affected by some unseen Force that logically makes decisions for it, do you think that you are excluded from this same Force that affects every living creature on this planet right down to molecular structure? It is the Force or God.

I find that astounding. You know my mind is always off in the cosmos. I've always understood this, but I never thought about explaining it this way. Do you understand the power of the Force? How can you dispute this? How can you say it doesn't exist? Everything on this planet has been manipulated by the Force. That is evolution. Evolution is the consciousness of the Force. It actively thinks here. It thinks on every single level, and affects every cell in your body right at this very moment. All you have to do is choose to think of it and it will become one with you. That is the one thing that we humans have. That is awareness.

So humans are subject to the Force's will?

Human beings are subject to the same puppeteer of the planet's force. The same thing that is changing the butterfly is the same Force telling humans their purpose and how to function. When you are aware, you acknowledge the puppeteer pulling the strings. You look at the puppeteer and help it pull the strings. That is the secret. The more that you can look at and study nature, the more you can understand it. All of the secrets are there. Ask yourself how and why it all works. It only comes down to one thing: there is an intelligent Force manipulating everything in the Universe. *Chaos Theory* has basically said that everything is being manipulated by some kind of intelligent Force, right down to the smallest molecular structure.

If you can ponder and think on this, it will change who you are. By understanding this, you can look at things and understand them. You will then become more as God than a byproduct of God's actions. Tell me what I mean by that.

I will help to pull the strings.

That is awareness. That is enlightenment. It is to move from the opposite end of the spectrum of just *being affected* to the other side of *making an effect*. The more that you understand, the more you bridge the chasm and you can see the actions. Not only can you see, but also you will begin to understand what it takes to make these actions happen. Maybe looking at a butterfly means nothing to you right now, but that simple logic will unlock something inside of you. If you think about it long enough, it will make sense to you. It's an insight to something you are not supposed to understand. You are supposed to be a product of the Earth, just like the butterfly. But all you have to do is understand it to become part of it. That is all. You do not have to be it. You just have to understand what is going on.

Anything that you can understand, you become. You are no longer unaware that you are being moved by the current. You move with it now by choice. It is very hard to understand. You become more spiritual by the simple fact that you are able to acknowledge what is going on. It is like your electrical energy tonalizes to mimic the process. You are now aware of how this works, and by that fact alone you have a different perspective. By understanding that the Force manipulates all of these things in nature, you become one with it. It empowers you. You already know all of the secrets of the entire Universe. All the secrets and all the knowledge that I have is somewhere inside of you. It is the same concept as DNA, yet different. You just need to understand how to bring it out of yourself. That is really what I am trying to emphasize here.

You have lived many times and are an old soul. Genetically speaking, the matter that you are made of affects other matter. I want you to remember that you are made out of matter. Matter is energy. Everything that has to do with matter is recorded as a collective continuity and the interaction accumulates as thought. In other words, there is a collective consciousness in every single molecule in the Universe.

All you have to do is figure out how to tap into it and it will all come together. That is how I do what I do. It is part of the Akashic records. We are all part of one thing. If you can accept that this is how it works, then you can separate yourself or become a central point of the process, but you need *realization*. That's what the word realization actually means – *to become fully aware of it as fact*. This is why you must sit down at a brook and observe the water. Do not try to figure it out; just study it. Observe how it flows, its transparency and its wetness. Observe the whitewashing of it and be astounded that it holds itself together instead of dispersing into molecules. Marvel how it is transparent, yet solid. Solid, yet it is soft and penetrable. Feel what it is like for it to flow down among the rocks.

If you understand the Force and you think about how It affects all things, you will begin to understand things in a different way; more than you have ever before in your entire life. Sit and look at a tree. Just stare at the bark of the tree and do not even think about what it is. Just admire its structure, its continuity. If you do this, you will begin to have realizations that you were not aware of before.

Become part of the Force. See everything as the Force sees it. Feel how things are obedient to the Force. Feel how the Force is changing to improve things, but also remember that the Force is moving slowly as a consciousness. If you can slow your mind down as you study things, you will understand how the Force thinks. It is essentially just an understanding of different perspectives.

Slow your thinking down to a different speed and then you will become one with It. The more that you can understand It, the more It will become you. To become you means to become aware. You can step outside of It and move to any frequency in any dimension. It is like riding a wave once you set your mind to it so that you can flow with it. It is like throwing sails up on a boat. You can ride it. Just get up and look around and see things in in a different way, but you have to match that frequency. Get your mind to go into that altered state of appreciation. It means that it becomes you. The frequency that you are constantly at is the frequency of the planet. It is red cell.

Right now you are advancing beyond the red cell level because you think more spiritually. You can slip into an altered consciousness if you allow yourself to ride it. Sit and stare at something, and then when you are in, just go with it. It's like staring at one of those pictures with the images hidden in the background. You stare at it on the surface and as you are staring at it, suddenly you see within the depth of the picture. The images start coming to the forefront. You got in and you can see the structure of the environment, but now you are afraid to move your eyes around too much because you might slip out of that awareness. After a moment, you realize that once you are in there, you can look around with no problem and get back to where you were before. Once you feel comfortable with it, you are not afraid to step out of it.

It is the same concept whether you stare at water or a tree; you will know when you slip into that state of mind. Then you can move around and you will know that you have to be careful of your thoughts. You have to just be in this translucent state of mind. You will see and feel things that you never saw or felt before in your life. The moment you reflect on the act itself, the second you think about what you are doing, you will snap out of it. You will see this full dimension. You are walking in this dimension, but there are other things going on beyond your perception.

What is a good way to build your skill in this type of exercise?

You need to meditate, clear your mind, and start thinking about your spirituality again. I suggest that you do rituals. It is the hardest time of year to do that, it always has been. If you think it's tough now to think of your spirituality, it is even more difficult to do that on the east coast where I once lived. It is winter there with no leaves on the trees and everything is gray. And because of that, at this time of year it has very low energy. Here in California, there are scenic views to capture your attention. Remember something: spiritually is in hibernation. It is logical when you reflect on how the Force affects the planet. The Force affects the planet the most when there are living things that reciprocate or capture the energy. Then the Force can manifest and it makes life flourish.

Winter is the time for hibernation. All plants recess their energy and pull in during this time of year. They go into a sleep state. That is what is happening and why people lose their spirituality because everything in nature is now pulling in. Even here in California, the trees are pulling in their energy.

Even though they are maintaining some greenness, they are still pulling in. As the Force loses its hold and backs off a little bit, you feel this dissipation of your energy. At this time of year, you have to work at least three times harder. So read books, practice and reflect on the things that you learned so far to get you through this hibernation phase. The stronger you keep yourself now; your energy will triple when the spring comes. You will move forward instead of being burnt out and having to recuperate again. You want to carry over strongly. Educate yourself, feed yourself, and feed the spirit inside of you.

The energy now is moving away from us, and that is why there is a lull, a feeling of stillness. That is why you have to focus harder right now. Winter is the collective of the whole planet because the northern hemisphere is tilted from the sun. The sun pulls away from the northern hemisphere, the signal weakens and the opposite hemisphere is tilting towards it. We are tapping into a source of energy that is not just the west coast. It is the collective consciousness of the planet as a whole and its relationship to the Force. Rather than meeting with other people and creating a higher frequency of collective thought, the people in the northern hemisphere are now staying in their homes and out of the cold. This means that all of this energy is dropping into a hibernation state for probably the next six months. Focus on your spirituality in other ways.

What should be the focus for this time of the year?

During this time of year a lot of vortexes open up, such as the Bermuda Triangle. Do you know when the strongest time of year is for the Bermuda Triangle? It's December, January and February. All the dimensional phenomena start to happen at this time of year. Instead of being connected consciously and spiritually, more dimensional and UFO things happen. There is more UFO activity now than in the summer. It has its yin and its yang. You have to compensate; thought can provoke new thought. Take in the information you have learned right now and you will expand what you already have by applying the knowledge. It will prepare you for even bigger things later. You can read something right now and understand it much better than most people because of your lessons.

Let six months of the year go towards mental and spiritual training. The other six months should be material training. Build a pyramid to meditate in, or design equipment that will affect us all. Spring through early fall are the spiritually oriented times of year. So, this time of year, get into the material aspect of building dimensional gateways and doorways. Investigate hauntings and anything to do with the physical aspect.

People spend more time in their homes in the winter. By doing so, it's apt to create dimensional vortexes and hauntings. So you have to stimulate yourself by working on that kind of knowledge in winter, instead of seeking enlightenment where you sit down, meditate and have great experiences. It is very hard to do that in the winter because the energy has shifted. In the winter months, focus on your intellectual side. Go out and investigate things. That is how you will pacify yourself but propel yourself to move forward. Reinvent yourself. Recognize that the first thing to great success is to realize your weaknesses. When you are familiar with your weaknesses, you will compensate for them. That is how you survive.

You are feeling a lack of the spiritual state of mind. Compensate for that by finding other things to interest you until the energy returns. Experiment with some different types of things, such as looking into a mirror to see if you can see spirits and entities. In a "black room," do a séance type of thing, where you call on different spirits and look into a mirror to see other entities reflecting back at you. You can have some pretty amazing experiences with that kind of thing. So take an active role in seeking out something new and innovative.

I find haunted places by talking to people. One lady came to me with a story of a haunting that led to a much bigger haunting in an apartment complex that that had not been rented for years. That is how it all begins. If you keep researching it, then you will find out a lot more information.

Do you think that being in this low period we will get fewer results investigating things?

I think that once you are motivated, it will generate enough energy to sustain you. It will not be a problem at all. Remember, the Force will always double whatever energy you put out. If you put out zero effort, the Force will put out zero effort. If you put out two percent, It will return the favor, but you will gain four percent. If you give ten, It will give you back ten, but it will equal twenty percent. That is all you have to do.

When a different season arrives, such as spring, the Force will push itself on you. All you have to do is open yourself to receive it. But at this time of year, you get what you put out. If you can create a maintenance schedule of meditating for fifteen minutes a day, the Force will reciprocate. If you withdraw from it, you will not only feel depressed about life, but also the pain of being spiritually starved and deprived. That will bother you the most and it will make you miserable.

Remember that there are a lot of spiritual people that go insane. They end up in mental institutions because, at one time, they were highly spiritual people. Yet, they pulled back from IT and it is as if IT takes from who you are. When you better understand awareness, you will have more experiences in meditation so you can attain a higher state of being. You will create a multidimensional consciousness despite the fact that you peaked and then dropped to a lower level when you withdrew from your spirituality. If your spiritualness pulls away from you, you get depressed physically.

For most people, the highest level of depression starts in November. If you look at clinical studies, this will make sense to you. The highest amount of suicides happens in November through May because those people are very in-tuned spiritually and they have pulled away. Even non-spiritual people get depressed. They are the ones who normally get depressed, which you are feeling in the collective consciousness. Your depression is amplified because your spiritual starvation is falling in line with your regular depression, which creates an effect. That is what you are feeling.

It is like a form of therapy. If you can recognize the problem and acknowledge it, you can resolve the issue inside of yourself. Your instincts will pull you together, but you probably will not understand why you are feeling a certain way. So you just keep pulling yourself deeper and deeper into depression. If you look at the last two months before winter, you will see a spiritual high. Then, as the season progresses, you drop dramatically. But you can rebound with a little effort put forth. Inspire yourself to start on the new cycle. If you acknowledge what is going on and you say to the Force, "I want you to be strong with me. You know I am not going to abandon this," and you draw in energy, you will still be very powerful. Just give the Force more attention. It's not tapping on you saying, "I'm here." You have to tap on it and say, "Hey, c'mon." That is the secret right now. Every year it's like this.

It's like existing in a desert environment spiritually. It's horrible.

That is why you have to focus on other things like spirits, ghosts, and entities. Turn to more project oriented things rather than meditating and drawing on your subconscious and tuning yourself. Direct yourself towards other things to carry yourself through it, and find ways to reinvent yourself. If you do not do this, you will suffer. Make yourself meditate. During the summer, you feel like doing spiritual things. The Force takes you and says, "Come along." When it's winter, you have to use your tools. It's about survival. It's about cleaning your room. It's about creating the environment and the energy. Sit down and meditate. That is how you empower yourself. That is how you get through this. You can actually have great experiences, but you just have to put out more effort.

One insight I gained from all of this is that evolution and the Force are one. You told us to slow down so we are at the same speed as the Earth's consciousness. But really you have to slow down because, in comparison, you are like a bug that only lives for a day.

Right.

For it to fully understand why we do what we do, it would have to slow down. When you think that the Force is the size of the Universe, I understand why you have to prepare ahead of time to start sending energy towards a meeting that you are having next week because it is doing so many things in just such a wide space.

Or you could say that it moves extremely fast even though there are trillions of living organisms. It moves so quickly that it almost seems to move slowly. Calculating each thing to progress in that way is just astonishing.

For me to realize and be able to explain this to you in that way got me excited. By explaining this to you and you observing and understanding certain things, it can put you into a state of mind that would slip you into the *In-Between.*

Everything is about improving. Every single action is about improving to the perfection of the Force. The Force is dealing with the microscopic levels of this planet. The planet is a tiny molecule in retrospect to the billions of stars and planets that are microorganisms on their own level. The Universe is like a beach. Each grain of sand is a solar system filled with dozens of planets. On this beach, you can dig as deep as you want or go as many miles as you choose to. All that you will see is only one tenth of one little corner of space. If you can imagine that and try to visualize and encompass it in your mind, the Force will draw stronger in you. It is drawn to you because of that act.

I wish I could plug my brain into the TV for you like a DVD so you can see what I see in my head. I think you would be amazed. The moment I think about the galaxy or the Universe, I see it. It's like a hologram in my brain. I move at the speed of light, swirl around different things and just move on. I can zoom into the atmosphere of a planet and go through the whole planet at the speed of light. Even now, I am thinking about the Earth and I just took in the whole planet. I can't even explain it. It's just amazing. That is because I am in tune with the Force. Don't just try to get in tune with the Force. Since everything is a collective consciousness, you should be trying to get in tune with the energy of the Earth, the consciousness of the Earth. Everything is consciousness. It is an accumulation of collective work. Every single planet has its own version of the Akashic records. All of those accumulate to become one Akashic record of the solar system. Each solar systems has their collective consciousness that contributes to their galaxy, and that is an Akashic of consciousness. It becomes one total conglomeration of energy that includes what we call the Force. However, for you to try to take that in right now is foolish. You are not going to get it. You are going to get frustrated and you will give up. Focus on this planet's Akashic, energy, inner dimensions, vibrations and tonals. Then ride that wave to the higher levels.

Chapter 4

THE STRUGGLE TO AWAKEN

WE ARE ALL a part of something and when you are a part of something, you can easily understand it. You just have to believe that you can. Now, imagine the complexity of the matrix or collective consciousness. If you can wrap your mind around it, imagine the possibilities. The planet is a thinking organism, and that thinking is a prime example of what you believe is the matrix. It is just a little different because that reality is all energy.

The Earth is vastly complicated, even on that level. Yet it is but a grain of sand on a thousand mile oceanfront. Every other grain of sand is just as complex as the first one. Now, mentally move past the sand and think of the complexities that put the oceanfront together. Can you begin to conceive this? It is the galaxy, the Universe, multi-universes, the totality of it all. This is way beyond anything you have the ability to comprehend.

You have to deal with here and now. That is what I am saying. If you want to pursue this path of awakening, that's fine. If you do not that is also fine. You can choose to be a red cell or you can choose to be a white cell. It is very simple. However, the only way that you are going to be a white cell is by an act of will. If you want to be a red cell, then do nothing at all. Just go through life and do whatever life tells you to do. It is the easiest path to take.

As difficult as it is to follow the path of awakening, there is a point when you are done with the hard work but it is a tremendous undertaking to get there. It could take you your whole life or even many lifetimes. But it could also take just a week. There is a point when you reach a level where the path becomes you. It's like an arm or a leg; it's just you.

There are students who put forth so much energy trying to force their awakening that they forget about the box. There is a box. If you envision it in your mind, you see a box floating. See it now. Close your eyes. Inside the box are all the secrets that you need to attain enlightenment. It has all the secrets of the cosmos and the Universe and everything you have ever wanted to know. You know it is all in there; an enlightened master is telling you it is in there. There is just one problem: the harder you try to open the box, the tighter it becomes. The only way to open the box is with absolutely nothing. Then like a flower feeling the rays of the sun, the box will automatically open.

So you can't force the Universe to give to you?

Correct, everyone wants to force it. You don't realize it, but sometimes even by learning you are forcing it. People try to find the answers in so many different ways. There is one thing for certain that I can tell you, "In this world, nothing is exactly the right answer." I'll teach you what I know, but it is through all of this knowledge and how you put it together that you will realize *it is nothing from this world*. But it will be the right answer.

Other students reach a point where they hit *maximum velocity*. This is what happens with the majority of students over time. They work very hard. They are dedicated, committed and their heart is in the right place. But they reach a point when they ask the question, "Isn't this enough? Aren't I ready yet to move to a different level? Haven't I achieved something that is worth acknowledging?" That is what I call the *breaking point*. They have just about reached maximum velocity and they want to be accredited. They want to be acknowledged for something that they have spent a year, 10 years or maybe 20 years working on. Their ego takes over and they are missing the whole point. The point is to **expect nothing, gain everything**. By the simple fact of expecting to be at a certain level, they gain nothing. In fact, they set themselves back, and that is a problem.

It's so hard not to want and expect to reach higher levels.

Of course it's hard. If it were easy, then everybody would be doing it.

If you don't force the box, you cannot even try to open it.

I gave it to you in an analogy so that you can better understand what I am talking about. What was the analogy?

The box.

Let me show you something. I've never shared this with anybody and no one has bothered to ask or to even think about it. Everything that I collect has a meaning to it. This little box actually has something inscribed on it. Do not open it; you are not allowed to see what is in there. There is something very special and mysterious inside. Everything I have means something. I buy these things because they are significant; they are tools for teaching. Sometimes, I don't remember to use the tool. Sometimes, the opportunity just doesn't present itself. The opportunity is here now and I am sharing it with you. What do you acknowledge about this box?

It has flowers on it.

Yes, there are flowers. What makes a flower flourish?

The sun.

That is not the right answer even though I do admire the sun. There is a secret in the sun, but it is not what you think. You do not think correctly. You think like a human being. You think only with what you can see three dimensionally. You can only think with what you are able to comprehend, and that's the problem. It is the whole problem. The box is like a flower. It is a bud. Have you ever taken your fingers and tried to pry open a flower to see its full blossom?

It wouldn't work. You would just destroy it.

You would never get to see the full beauty of the flower if you did that. Can the wind open the flower? Can the rain, the dark, the cold or the heat open the flower? Absolutely not! Using an analogy again, the flower opens when everything is perfect and the sun is shining upon it. It opens perfectly *when it is ready to open because there is an unseen harmony and it listens to the Force.*

How can I unlock the knowledge inside of me without forcing the process?

I'll tell you part of a fable. There is a leather bound book that had beautiful little flowers painted on it. Inside the book were all the secrets of the Universe. It contained everything from the beginning of time, from all universes, and from all galaxies. All the knowledge of the Universe was in this one book. When you opened the book, you saw that the first page was a mirror. The next page was a mirror. Every single page was a mirror. What do you think that meant?

The secrets of the Universe are inside of you.

Yes, that is true. That is one way of looking at it. But how can we look at that in a forward-thinking way? This fable is from thousands of years ago when thought was more simple-minded.

I am a universe.

How?

I have living systems and I am a giant organism with smaller organisms within.

Yes, now we are getting somewhere. Let's keep working on it and give it some more thought.

By reflecting inward, you can see what is outside.

Well, that's on a spiritual level. Let's take this to a different level. Let's go to the place that most people do not really think about. We know that, scientifically, you are made of molecules that billions of years ago were actually suns that went supernova. Supernovas happen when a star becomes so old and ancient that after millions or billions of years of existing, it explodes. The explosion is like millions and millions of nuclear bombs going off all at once. When stars go supernova, they blow all of its matter throughout the galaxy. In fact, most of it is still moving. That is why part of the Universe is still expanding. You are made from molecules that have existed for billions of years from the beginning of time. You are made of substance that has existed since the beginning of creation. Think about that.

In one form or another?

Inside and all over your body in this physical form, you have molecules that are billions of years old. You cannot destroy energy. You can only re-create it. In some way you see yourself, but what you see isn't completely what you are. What would happen if you could see yourself and everything that you are? Some spiritualists teach their students to travel backward mentally when they meditate. The idea is to go backwards until you get to the pivotal point of creation before it all began to create the Universe. What happens when you get to the very beginning of matter, to the beginning of creation? What would happen if you went through? What is on the other side? Maybe all of the answers you ever wanted to know. Maybe all of the answers that you believe you can find right now, you could have found a long time ago.

In some ways, this is the same kind of thinking as the old masters, but in other ways it is not. It is about *self-reflection* and looking within yourself for the answers. It is about all the simple stuff on the surface that you should acknowledge about yourself for your own spiritual growth. Without acknowledging those things, you cannot really acknowledge the deeper knowledge that is inside of you. The process is incomplete. It is like leaving on a journey to cross a desert without water or shoes thinking in your head that you can just go across. You must build the foundation so that you can conceive and comprehend on your journey. It's very important to always have your teacher work with you.

You think in a structured method. Everything is structured in your mind, and rightfully so. You live in a very structured world, everything is three-dimensional. Everything has a beginning, an end, and a purpose. Sometimes you have to move beyond that. The reason that you cannot move beyond it is you do not have enough trust. That is what keeps you here. It is what keeps you solid in this realm and in this dimension. You cannot think that you will be able to totally surrender, hold your breath, and then somehow you are going to make it to the other side. It does not work that way. You must have everything right in your mind. Everything that you are doing has to be right. It is about "wax on, wax off" to the point where you can do it without thinking about it. It becomes a natural process for your consciousness. That's when you're there. Learn to think without thinking and experience without having to physically throw yourself into something. Trust yourself to experience perfection. When you experience perfection, you will become like the flower bud. You will simply bloom.

You are trying to reach a place in your mind of not controlling something, but getting to that point through control. It is the only way you know how to get there. When I tell you to sit down, put your legs this way, sit straight, touch this spot, and think about nothing else except that spot, I am teaching you to do everything in a systematic way. I am trying to teach you not to think at all. Doesn't it sound a little bit odd? I am teaching you not to think at all, but I am doing it by teaching you a structured way of getting there.

**By using a very structured way of thinking,
you are teaching us not to think?**

Correct. I do not want you to learn not to think or just to have silence in your mind. I do not want you just be quiet. I am pushing you through to the other side. You need to think in a way that you have not thought before. You will still be in control, but it is a different kind of control than you can understand in this dimension. Once you are there, and you bring it back through you, you will understand.

What is the purpose of this type of thinking?

It is for you to control your brain, and shut down your body so that you can just listen inside to tonalize. You have to be able to comprehend and have a theoretical understanding of all that it entails. This takes years to learn. There will be times when you are tired of it and maybe you will want to move on. People go through life in phases. Unfortunately, the human condition on this path is no different. Unless you are exceptional, you will only make it just so far. So, you have to hope that you are exceptional. Time will tell.

Ultimately, I am teaching you to think differently and to become more flexible in your consciousness. By doing this, you will awaken. It is a very simple program. Don't have anything going through your head and you will comprehend. This way of thinking shows you how to exist in a way that is non-existent, but is very present. How do you know God is there? How do you know if the Force is here? It is like the rays of sunlight. Sunlight is always here but you cannot smell, hear, or taste it. You technically cannot feel it. The after-effect is what you are feeling. To keep it simple, you cannot look directly at sunlight, but it is here. You just trust that it is. You simply know that it is.

It is the same way when you are trying to understand this level of thinking. You have to start thinking differently. By using these examples, everything I am showing you helps bridge you over to comprehend this. You have to take those examples into consideration. It is natural that you may forget them. That is just the way it is.

What is an example of how you can utilize this way of thinking?

For many years, I predicted the future as a means of making a living. I was highly accurate. If someone asked me, "Is the future predetermined?" I would say, "No, it is not." How is it possible to predict the future then if it is not predetermined? Most human beings are limited in their thinking, as you are at this moment. But I am going explain it and you will understand what I mean.

Pretend we are in a room that is very small. There's a colony of ants on one side and there is a colony of ants on the other. As you study both of these colonies of ants, they are not aware of one another because the room is too big, too vast for them. But on one side, you have an ant that you monitor and you recognize its habit. It likes to go out to explore. It is always going out further than every other ant and then going back. There is another ant that is on the other side of the room that also likes to explore. You see that this specific ant is always going out and exploring new places, and then showing the colony the location of this new batch of food. But there is one thing that is a bit different about this other ant. He always attacks and bites the head off of any ant that he comes across that is not from his own colony. Now, all of a sudden, we have predictability here. We have one ant that's constantly going out exploring from one side, and we have another ant that's constantly going out exploring from the other side. It is inevitable that sooner or later, they are going to meet. And then, what will happen?

They are going to fight.

Who is going to attack?

The ant that always bites their heads off.

That's right. What's going to happen to the ant that doesn't attack the others when he goes out exploring and runs into the ant that does attack?

It will have its head bitten off.

Would you say that is a high level of predictability or would you say that is the future predetermined? A computer holds a lot of data. When you ask a question, it computes the answer for you because it's been predetermined. Did it know you specifically were going to ask that question? No, the programmer anticipated the fact that somebody might ask it. The computer does not think. It has everything predetermined so that when somebody punches in a certain amount of information, it answers that specific question. But it was prepared by somebody who determined that someone would eventually ask that question. Was it predetermined to have the answer because it knew that you specifically were going to ask it that particular question at a specific time? No. It knew that particular question was going to be asked sooner or later, so it had the answer ready.

What do you know for sure? We know that you are going to grow old. Your teeth are going to decay. You are going to get wrinkles. And you are going to eventually die. Is there a level of predictability there, or is it predetermined? The Universe is much more complex, by far. We know from chaos theory that everything is predictable. If you take a super ball and bounce it in a square room, do you know where it is going to land? No, but a computer can calculate a billion different possibilities for the outcome of that situation. It can determine something from this particular point, with this amount of velocity, at this specific point of release, at this specific angle, that you need to take three steps to your right, one forward, put your hand there and wait. How does it know?

There is a high level of predictability.

Did it perceive the future?

No, it just estimated the outcome.

Is the future predetermined?

No.

These two concepts are parallel. Just because you cannot perceive something does not mean something much bigger, like the Force, does not perceive it. In this same perspective, we could be the ants.

It sees the baby being born that you will marry someday because it can highly predict what the two parent combinations are going to do, and how and where the child will be raised. It sees the airplane being built that's going to kill your father because of the career path that he has taken. It can see all that because its consciousness is so vast. It's a cumulative intelligence.

Everything is predictable because there are only so many variations. It's just how much mental capacity you have to be able to see the whole picture. Maybe you saw all those ants over there but there were so many of them, you could not quite figure out the pattern and habits of them all. Maybe there were 20 ants and you figured out all of their patterns. You also figured out the other 20. You knew which ant was likely to do what, and you had a complete understanding of what would happen with a particular ant and when.

What if you had an infinite amount of intelligence? Don't you think you could have an infinite amount of predictability for what is going to happen through time and destiny? When I predict the future, I tap into the matrix. I cannot say that I am 100% accurate, but my accuracy is around 95%. Let's say that God knows 98% of what is going to happen. Is it more interested in *what if*? It knows everything else. What it is that is **not** going to happen. The meaning, or the purpose of life throughout this entire Universe, is for God to experience the unknown. *It is waiting to see what's going to happen.*

Researchers can see patterns in the running water of a brook, if studied long enough and put on a TV screen where they can add a huge amount of colors to it. But we cannot see this same affect with the human eye. To us it looks more like static, but they can see patterns and eventually predict the rhythm of running water.

That proves that everything in the Universe is a formula.

It is intelligence. It proves that God exists and that there is an intelligent system to all of this. What science may not understand is that it's all about that two percent. When God experiences everything, the process will be finished. God comes from an energy being solidifying into mass, entering through this Universe, collecting copious amounts of mass, formulation, and experience. Eventually, the experience becomes educated and becomes energy. We do the same thing as humans when we become energies and beings of light. We become this light process of energy. The energy we collect from our experiences becomes energy that returns to the Source energy, God, with new data of its experience in its journey.

When you try to explain this in simple terms to most people who study math and physics, they do not get it because their mind is only equipped to understand things in a left-brained scientific way. As intelligent as they are, they do not really listen to what you are saying. They cannot believe that anyone without a formal education could conceive such an idea. So already in their mind, they decided that you are not smart enough to know about this. You do not have the technology, so you are written off.

Is predicting the future possible because of someone's ability to recognize people's patterns?

It equates to people who can enter the matrix and get bits and pieces of information that applies to you. Your life seems very complex but you will live only about eighty-six years, which is the average human life span. Eighty-six years old compared to the age of the planet, the solar system, the galaxy, and the Universe. It is like watching those ants for a week. Their life seems very complex to them, but they just lived their whole life in that one week. It is the same for humans. Our lives are not so complicated, it just feels that way. It is only one way to look at things. It may make the world seem very dull now, but at the same time look for the two percent in everything because it makes life more interesting.

When you tap into the matrix, and the more psychic you become, it gives you more of a shared knowledge. This is an infinite amount of knowledge, if you think about it. Now you can take that data and incorporate it into this world.

What is the difference between being dimensional and hyper-dimensional?

Dimensional is a place. It is a whole different place to explore, like this reality is. This is the third dimension but there are other dimensions. Hyper-dimension is when you collectively have self-awareness of yourself on every level of those dimensions at the same time. That is a collective consciousness and it is a complete consciousness. Most people cannot do it. You have lived many other lives, and in all of those other lives only a small portion of them comes through. You are a singular being at this moment, yet you are a composite of possibly over five hundred people that are complete total experiences. Dimensionally, you can say that if you slip into one of those other places, you can become another person from another life. You would forget who you are now, yet still be aware of it because those experiences are recorded perfectly through the sensory of your body. The experiences exist.

To exist hyper-dimensionally is to take a thread and pull it through all of the other dimensions and the entire thread-line makes you one. Just like the cells of your body collectively make you whole; hyper-dimensionally who you really are is separate from whom you are right now. Try to reach your hyper-dimensional consciousness. Study and become enlightened by threading all of your consciousness together and becoming one being right here, right now at this moment. Then you can explain and teach perceptions on the level of quantum-physics, and convey it into this dimension so that the average person can understand.

Hyper-dimension is the totality of you?

More or less, yes.

You want to get to the point where you can reach
the part of yourself that has infinitely more
knowledge than the consciousness you now have.

Right, you already have that consciousness, but it goes
even beyond reaching a part of you. It is becoming the
complete self. People go through life not feeling complete
because, biogenetically, they see themselves as an organic
being. You are seeking to find a partner and you feel that
finding a partner will complete your life. However, you will
never feel complete in that way. You just have a partner and
have come to terms with it. It is really an interpersonal self
where you try to bring your feminine and your masculine
counterparts together, because as biological creatures, our
origins are from the ocean. We were whole once and then we
split into two sub-species so that we could protect our young
and gather food.

Energy-wise, when you leave your body you are both
feminine and masculine. And on the same token, you also
have several different identities that you accumulated as
consciousness. It is just that the organic body cannot handle
any more than one of those at a time. You are trying to
build an energy body that can work beyond all of this, but
at the same time utilize the physical brain. It is like having
static energy moving around outside your head that is your
consciousnesses. But it is all working together to filter through
this little machine so that you can work in this physical
dimension. When you can do that, it is true completeness. It
is enlightenment.

You still are a micro-version of God. God exists in all of
those other dimensions; they are all still one embodiment.
This dimension is about flesh and blood, meaning mass for
God. But it is still interwoven with energy and Prana, the
Force. There are multiple dimensional levels. Maybe God is
not even completely aware of all of itself. As we are micro-
versions of the same thing, things do repeat themselves

consistently. If you slice open a seashell, you will find that the spiral will mimic itself similar to galaxies. This is a form of Chaos Theory. It is the same thing just bigger and smaller, nevertheless, a beginning and an end. So is there the same process over and over: dimensions, energy consciousness, and hyper-dimension. Everything in micro levels is macro levels for the Universe.

When it comes to God, there is no masculine and feminine.

There is, but it is one; yet they can be separated into two. What did I say was the secret to the Universe that science will find some day beyond quantum physics?

The system of three.

I need a cup to hold the water before I drink the water. I have to grasp the concept of a cup before I can hold the water. I have a concept of ice. I have a concept of cold, but I cannot quite experience those things until I take a drink. Fluidity, masculine and feminine energy is just a tool to help you have the mindfulness to understand something like this. To hold what you need to hold, you need the fluidity that it takes to create this. This cup I am holding is the perfect example because it's a thermal cup and it holds the cold in without the cold escaping. It can contain a form of energy, which is cold, longer than the typical cup. Fluidity would think of something like this, but man would not.

If you ever watch the movie ***The Mahabharata***, there is a part when they describe how the sons of the prince created an entire castle or an empire that was like glass. They said glass because they did not know what to call it. It was energy. It had structure; yet it did not. When you reached out to touch the water that you thought was there, the water would not be there. You would walk where you thought there was a doorway and you would hit a wall because there would be a wall there. Somebody else would walk through it and laugh at you and say, "What's the matter with you? You can't see the wall?" Fluidity.

Fluidity, a tremendous task in itself gives you the structure to comprehend what you need to do to move on. What else is fluidic about this cup? The water is transparent, yet solid. There is ice that's absolutely solid, yet it is transparent. If it was totally clear, you could not see it all but it would still exist. However, all of this is an illusion because none of it is really there.

We have four stages of transparency: the outer cup, the inner cup, another cup containing this and the part containing the energy and its intensity. Not only that, we still have transparency in liquid form. We have the same transparency on three other different levels. It's very multi-dimensional thinking. When you can perceive it all and piece it all together, it creates one total experience. Drinking it allows me to experience it again.

You do not have to understand how this works, that's the trick. If you were fluidic, you would not try to understand it. You would want to know it, but you would not have to understand it. It is like the cup. This entire cup is one thing.

But it's still three?

Correct -- ice, water and cup with one result. It's three because it is cold when it's touching me. When it's touching me, it is liquid and when it's touching me, I have to hold it in order to be it. When I drink it, it becomes me. When you can understand these perceptions and you accept them as truth, then you can move through space, time, and other dimensions.

Am I drinking the water to quench my thirst? Or am I thirsty because my body wants to get minerals to give to the electrons to create thought? Does all of this exist because I want it to exist? Does all of this exist because it is making me exist? Do all of us exist because I am already moving out of all this and this is all an illusion? When I accept that, I can move beyond it all.

Instead of dying and remembering who and what you really are, do it while you are living, breathing and aware. Bring all those consciousnesses together in this physical moment, and then use that supreme intelligence to do something here and now. If you die, it does not serve any purpose for this dimension. The Universe brought you here so that you could have this conversation. It knew it would affect you somehow, in some way. Maybe sometime in the future, you will figure it all out. It most likely already knows what is going to happen from this conversation.

Try to become aware to awaken here and now. You will do that through theoretical conversation, which we are doing right now. Your mind will grasp things and expand now. Attain as much energy as you possibly can because conscious thought is energy. The more energy that is infused within you, the more your consciousness will expand. You use all of the tools that you can so that you can create enough consciousness to bridge into the matrix, which means then you can affect this dimension.

If you are connected to everything, it is like electricity and water. The water appears not to be connected to anything but the electricity is invisibly connected to it all. This means the electricity is one solid globular of water. In the same way, when you hold a spoon in your hand, what is the difference between bending your finger and bending your spoon? It is all your perception. When you believe and you understand that, there is no difference. The spoon will bend. I'm not drinking water; the water is drinking me. Fluidity.

Stop trying to make yourself achieve bigger things. Appreciate who and what you have become. Love who you are and be comfortable with whom you are and the rest will follow. Pursue your spirituality, pursue your life, your teacher, and the rest will unfold. Just be happy about how far you have come. As long as you are unhappy, frustrated and think that you have to do more or do better, you limit yourself. You are structuring yourself.

Do not wrestle the bull, you will lose. Be at peace with yourself. Love how far you have come. Be content with that and you will become your own inner sunshine. Your box will expand and open on its own. When you can be happy and content with the leaps and bounds you have already made, then you will have found the flowers inside. You have found the sunlight. You have found the box. You are ready to move on because you found fluidity. As the karate master said to the karate kid, "Your best karate is still in you." That is all that you have to remember. There will come a point when you find relaxation in yourself and peace in yourself. Let go of the demand to push forward and not be content with where you are at. As I say this, I fear that you will become seduced by too much peace and not pursue. There must be a perfect blend of both. You must have a high level of pursuit, but in a manner of absolute fluidity and absolute peace in yourself that creates the ultimate warrior.

You mentioned that the matrix was looser earlier in history and it's tighter now. With the way we evolve and the way that technology is evolving, does Gaia give white cells more room before it pushes the door on us?

Are you wondering why I would say it is tighter now than it was before?

Not exactly. Technologies are advancing but not in the way we think. As white cells, Gaia

**wants to keep us down, so does it give us more
flexibility now than it did in the past?**

I would say it is harder now than it was in the past. In the past, it was hard but for other reasons. In this particular case, because the collective consciousness has more human beings than ever before, we create a stronger collective consciousness. Not just that, but the data from one civilization to another is becoming so ingrained, so interwoven, it's like one piece is interwoven into the other piece making a tighter stitch. Earlier in history, there were fewer people and less communication from one culture to the next. So, the Gaia consciousness was much looser, like a child's mind. The reason why it was harder back then is because of the consciousness. It was easier to go into a deeper state of mind because there was less conscious fog, like too much thought in the matrix. You could go in but the matrix was not as well knit, so there was less room to expand through it. It was harder to permeate into those other frequencies. You had to be extremely skilled just to find those upper bandwidths within the Gaia mind. So there are pros and cons for both eras.

**Why is Gaia or the Doe constantly pushing down on
white cells? Wouldn't Gaia want those experiences
so that Gaia could grow and evolve herself?**

Gaia does want those things but if it has too much of them, then Gaia will not want to be here. So Gaia will not connect with this dimension and it will turn on itself.

**That's kind of like you or I sometimes
wanting to leave our body.**

Right, exactly. Gaia needs to want to be here, so its primary drive is to be in this dimension. In a sense, it has the opposite polarity of what we have as white cells.

Is Gaia more towards automation than awareness?

Yes, it is unfolding in this dimension and God needs it to want to be here to keep it unfolding. But it has to unfold as it is still progresses so that it does have that element of progression. Gaia is constantly changing and constantly evolving. Nevertheless, God doesn't want it to evolve outside yet in a higher dimension. It must stay here long enough to collect data, then convert it into energy, which is trillions of years into the future, and then return all of the data back into energy. It would be too fast too soon if it happens now.

Do other planets have white cells and enlightened beings on them?

All worlds have beings, like white cells, on them. White cells are scattered throughout the Universe, without a doubt. If the Gaia mind is moving in an evolutionary process, we are seeded here to help guide it and move it towards the future of becoming just energy. If we were not here, Gaia would almost turn on itself, consume and solidify into what I call the Darkside.

I will use another analogy. Look at this similar to a bowling ball with every inch marking a trillion years. You take the bowling ball and you roll it, but in this particular case, you do not want the bowling ball to go straight down the middle. You want it to move from one end and slowly move to the other end without going into the gutter too soon. It is as if there are three pins that you still need to get. You've already got the majority of them, but you want to get those last three. So you take the bowling ball, throw it, and it rolls down the lane. It needs to slowly, not too quickly, start leaning over to the right to get the last three. That is what's happening.

You are like a little speck on the bowling ball that is trying to maneuver time as distance as it is rolling. You maneuver it ever so slowly to the right. If the ball is not positioned just right, it would simply go straight and drop right off. You need to see the history of the bowling ball moving through time. That is what white cells are trying to do. You try to cultivate it in the direction that you want it to go. All worlds throughout the Universe are the same; it is just a bigger bowling ball.

In other words, God chose us to guide Gaia.

Exactly, human beings are actually the fingertips of God. Are your fingertips you or are they just a collection of cells working for you? Your fingertips are cells working for you, reaching out. As humans, we are, in essence, all fingertips of God throughout the Universe. So, humans are like cells. Cells are independent but they are willing and totally dedicated to do your will. Everything else is just living cells existing, but white cells are the ones helping them move in the right direction.

White cells are here in this world and all worlds throughout the Universe. Some worlds do not care for white cells because the Darkside is more powerful. It is harder for them to integrate depending on the elements of that dimension, the life forms on that planet, and how society is developed. It has to do with each alien species and their biological and biochemical capabilities.

So what will happen eventually with those worlds?

Some of them are lost. Some are gained, while some of them rapidly accelerate. It depends on where they are, what the advantages are, how life develops, and if we are able to integrate our consciousness to help affect or seed that particular dimension or world.

Do you think the Earth can be compared to lighter worlds or darker worlds? Would the Earth be in the middle?

I would say that the Earth is a little bit above the middle. At times, it's been a challenge.

Is that because of all the red cells or because there are not enough white cells?

Well, you don't want too many white cells in the mix, but you don't want to have too many red cells either if there aren't enough white cells. On Earth, there are always white cells. It is a matter of the white cells being conscious or awakening to create the desired effect. In other times throughout in history, there were only a few white cells and Earth has constantly struggled to get enough of them awakened.

At this particular time in history, there are quite a number of them who have already awakened. It's almost equal to earlier times because the density of consciousness is so strong, so the Earth needs more white cells to affect it. Because of that, it's a matter of quality over quantity right now.

I keep thinking about the evolution of the people's psyche, the white cells. Did the changes after 2012 affect evolution of consciousness?

Well, 2012 was not the finishing point nor was it a checkered flag. In my opinion, 2012 was the grand marker of whether or not we would slip into fifth gear or whether we would stay in third or fourth gear. It's like a car.

I was thinking more like a check point than a checkered flag. You're running a race and you have to go through this check point.

The marker was whether or not we would end up downshifting or upshifting. The goal of humanity was to upshift and it was felt in your consciousness. Not everyone was able to fully acknowledge it, but as white cells, we were able to experience it. We recognized that this is what we had to cope with so we would adjust, no matter what.

As we continue to shift into fifth gear, because it's an on-going process, will it be a whole lot easier to come out from underground?

Let's say you were driving in fourth gear. What happens when you're on the highway and you go into fifth gear? How does it feel?

Exhilarating.

It feels smoother, doesn't it? It feels like something has been released because there is less energy, more flow, and it takes a minimal amount of energy to glide like you're moving through space. It's just a lighter level. So what happens if you make a mistake and you put it into third gear?

It grinds up.

Yes, it's like you can feel the weight, right? You can feel the density and there's tension. As you continue to elevate your frequency, that is what you feel internally. You feel a tension or you feel elevated when you're navigating your sensors.

What gear would you say we were in before 2012?

We were in fourth for a while. It's taken a long time for civilization to get to the fourth gear.

Was it about a twenty percent increase in tonal, if you look at it that way?

Yes, it was significant. Twenty percent is huge. It's very interesting because you can look at this in many different ways. Let's forget about what's going on in the solar system. Let's just deal with the human collective consciousness and that aspect of it.

How many times, in history, have all the people on the planet been collectively thinking of the same thing? Maybe 9/11 was something that affected the global consciousness significantly enough so that everybody was thinking about the same thing at the same time. Very few things happen that way. Maybe the Olympics, to a certain degree, but how many things have an undertone with a certain expectation about how it affects the world?

How about Y2K?

Yes, but Y2K wasn't a global experience. It was more of a technological concern in the advanced part of the world because older computers weren't designed to work in the years 2000 and later. So the computer software had to be modified to work on the older computers.

When we look back at 2012, the vast majority of people in the world felt an expectation that we were closing in. They were building an expectation that something could happen. Many people expected devastation or the end of the world. Other people said that nothing would happen. The one thing that, collectively, could be said is that we all knew that something was going to happen. That state alone can affect the human brain. If you have stress in your life all the time, it releases a certain chemical and your body accommodates it. If you constantly feel joy, your brain will adjust its consciousness based on what you're feeling or thinking. So people were anxious about what could possibly happen. That anxiety was determined to go in a negative or positive direction, which depended on the state of current events at that particular time.

Since the world was thinking about this, it created a doorway of opportunity. If there was no door, then no one could get in. So it depended on whether or not people were consciously aware of that possibility. If people were aware of it, then others could move through that doorway with them. If people didn't think about it, there would be no door to be concerned about and there would be no way to affect world consciousness. You have to present the idea in order to start thinking about it, pondering it, and to contemplate changing the mindset of the people. The result was a more positive affect.

Was that part of the reason for the Higher Balance Institute?

A center has the advantage of affecting more people on a conscious level. In a classroom situation, you can provide better training for the students. Things can be created to help permeate their consciousness. And you can build and demonstrate certain things, as well as provide a curriculum.

Higher Balance Institute is now able to cover a different topic every week with just a small group of students. We try to do that through the modules and we do a fairly good job of it. Is there anything better than having hands-on experiences? There's no substitute for that. A center is a place where we can have specialized classes on specific subjects. We can provide a small building to create a haunted environment and a place to create portals for training purposes. The students will have hands-on experience in that type of environment. We can create a room to enhance mental projection and set it up so that there are particular frequencies in the room. We can recreate it anywhere, but the idea is to be able to concentrate on that type of training in an advantageous environment.

Do you think we're operating on that concept too little too late?

Absolutely not. I don't think it's ever too little or too late. I'll be very honest with you. I'm fairly satisfied with where we are, but if I settle for that then we all lose. So I will never settle. The knowledge that I teach is of the highest caliber. Five years ago, I was only able to reach maybe a hundred people, whereas now I'm able to reach thousands, if not more. I am very satisfied with that because we are still in the minority. We're very small, but I am very excited about quality versus quantity. That is what I'm after.

Since you're the founder of the Higher Balance Institute, what is the direction that you see for this organization? What are you trying to accomplish?

People tend to define an organization as something in particular and people like to tag things with a definition. How are we going to define Higher Balance?

So, the question is, "Are we a following? Are we a religion?" I think of religion as a cult. I think a cult is a religion. I think a philosophy is a religion. A religion is a philosophy. I think they are all interconnected. It comes down to *what we do and how we are reacting with the world.*

Are we becoming an isolated group of people or can we relate to the outside world and share what we have with a sense of mentoring the rest of the world? To me, that is the defining part of what we are. *What will we contribute to society?* What will we offer to others? My hope is that we simply continue to teach, that we continue to look for white cells and help to heal the world on a vibrational level, frequency, and consciousness. I think we will continue in a very positive direction, working on things like the ecosystem of the world so that we can make a contribution on some level. That's how I look at it.

I think we're more of a philosophy. I don't see myself as being a person for people to idealize. You can do as I can do. You can do greater. I try to teach you that. I teach you free will, free independence. It's always about the Force. I don't tell you to make homage to me at all, but I am the hub of the information at this point. I think it's just a matter of perception. If people want to perceive this in a negative way, then they will see Higher Balance as a negative organization. If they want to see it as a positive thing, they'll see it as a positive organization. The latter is my hope.

If Higher Balance is ever to become a larger organization, how will it exist in this world? Most

of the things we do might be looked on with skepticism, like Telepathy or Astral Projection. It's like craziness to them because they don't understand.

Well, I don't think it is nonsense. Christianity has a seven headed dragon coming out of the ocean and they're waiting for the second coming. There are countless generations of people thinking that they're going to see it in this lifetime. They have lived, paid thousands or even millions of dollars to the church thinking that they're going to see the second coming, but it comes and it goes. They're going to be waiting a long time. It's just not going to happen.

There are religious groups that tell you to lock yourself up from society, go to a monastery or a cave. Extract yourself from the world, find God and live in solace. I don't believe in that. We interact with life and enjoy life to the fullest. That makes us healthier than all of the philosophies and religions. That is why you are here. Don't forget your spirituality. Be one with the Universe, the Force; but be one with this beautiful world that we are in and experience it fully.

We accept a red cell world but we are also explorers. There's a thirst in us that says there's more to this world than what people see. Why should we accept it on a limited basis? To us, there is a bigger purpose. Some people live their entire life in one town. Some people live their life traveling the world. Instead of traveling the world, we want to travel the Universe, but we're still part of this world. It's just how much your mind can perceive.

So, if people want to look at us as being unrealistic, that's fine. We hold a job, a home, and family. We have love, but we're also complete in our souls. There's a deeper satisfaction in our relationships and our perception of life. In the end, what matters most is whether or not we find inner peace, and on the last day of our life, we feel comfort in knowing that we moved to something much greater and didn't squander our time here on the Earth.

So, it's a matter of perception and value. I would say to someone who judges that value, "You spent too much time eating food and sitting around the house, doing insignificant things instead of living your own life." The person who's usually the most judgmental is the one who is always reading "how to" books. Instead of reading those books, why don't you write the book and live your own adventure? You're not living life. You're living life through somebody else's dreams. I'm on an adventure! That's the difference with my life.

As a white cell, you are pursuing your own journey. You will have your own inner reflections and someday will say, "I met Eric Pepin once. I sat down with him. I got to speak with him and this is what I got out of it. There are the other things that I did in my life. These are the reasons why I did them, and when I look at them all, I'm richer for having those experiences I sought out."

That's the bottom line. So on a realistic level, my game plan is to awaken as many white cells as I can to teach them, form them, educate them, and develop their sensory, their skills, and ideally quality over quantity. I want to continue to help those people to direct and contribute to the upshifting into the fifth gear of consciousness, and to make a contribution with their skills and their ability. My ideal goal is to continue maintaining and moving into fifth gear, but specifically to look at people on an individual basis. I'd like to help them reach and attain a higher level of consciousness to become more fulfilled on an individual basis, and to help them attain enlightenment. That is my continued objective, to work on each person to define a blissful state of relationship with the Universe, with God. I want to extend this evolution, fulfill it, move it and progress it.

What's the end result? Is evolution more white cells, higher psychic abilities, powers, or whatever you want to call it? It has taken eons, not just lifetimes to get to this point. What's beyond? Is there an end?

Well, there is and there isn't. It depends on your personal goals. I consider this the end of a chapter. We are all collectively part of God's consciousness. In *The Handbook of the Navigator*, I've taught that God is trying to explore within itself. There are mysteries that God does not even know. This is the reason to create life. Why create life if one knows everything already? It is to define and to learn new things. What else is there left to do? I believe they will find this when we start interacting with other species. It's not just human beings that have a drive to explore, to learn. Without the desire to learn and explore, there is no purpose for us to move forward.

I think there's a constant battle concerning moving progressively with evolution and devolution. Devolution is death. To me, it's stagnant water. It becomes poison. I think there is a certain perspective within red cells that nothing needs to change; keep everything the same. Let's just be, and that means no progression. What is the purpose of everything then if you just know what you know and don't want to continue to grow or change? What is the meaning of life then?

Coming from a religious background and seeing what religion has taught historically, it's not the truth as Christ set out to preach it. The church has gone in the opposite direction against the Christian teachings. Even the Bible says that we will become sons of God.

Well, we won't become sons of God unless we get off our asses and progress ourselves. I have certain frustrations with religion because I think it is a very dangerous thing for civilization. At times, it actually prevents progression. They start to follow a pattern of life and they're told that this is how you do things. This is the way it is, and there's no room for growth. Any growth is very minimal.

When I look at different cultures, like the Amish, I think they're beautiful. We admire them to a certain degree. But could you imagine if each person in all of civilization is told that they should not use modern tools, they should not invent, and they should not move forward with progression? If that kind of thinking stagnated them two hundred years ago, then they would be clacking stones and saying we can't have a horse and carriage. We can't build wooden chairs to sit in. We can't have a dining room table because we're not allowed to use these tools. So, at some point, they did progress to a certain point and then said, "We need to stop this." Eons ago, in the Lower Paleolithic period during the Stone Age, if a lightning bolt hit a tree and made fire, the people would run for their lives until they understood what it was and could adapt and learn how to utilize it. Fear of change is human nature.

Religion often prevents people from growing. It tells them that this is the way you have to do things and it is controlling. You must fear God and you must keep only this religion. You have to do the same things over and over routinely. Don't question your life, and accept that's what God wants for you. It's a business because there are people who benefit from it. Those are the ones who are traveling the world and enjoying the riches from it. When people get smart, they don't share their money so easily. They like to spend their money on their own travels.

Since everything evolves, when you're no longer here, how will we preserve the purity of the teachings while still evolving? For the next generation that follows Higher Balance, there's always a watering down process. Yet there has to be an evolution because there are new generations surfacing.

I think these teachings are already evolved, at least years beyond our current society. I think students will see the deeper truths in what I am saying and have more revelations. There are a lot of things that probably go over your heads, even to this day. As technology advances, you will to say, "My God, this is what Eric was talking about! Or this is what Eric meant in using the terminologies that he was using," and the students will have a much broader understanding of what I am talking about -- the evolution of consciousness.

I've talked about modern technology. I've talked about how it will be used to move into consciousness, how psychic abilities will actually be manifested through technology, and how to train the brain to extend beyond using our current technology, such as telepathy and things like that. The human brain will be used to amplify through the pineal gland, just like they are using cell phones right now. In one thousand years, they will have taken that and continued to evolve with it. There will always be a level of truth, but there will also be greater levels of consciousness to understand.

So, to maintain the quality of the information, we have an advantage that was not available two thousand or more years ago. There are the recordings, the videos, the internet, access to all of the data, and now the books. That's what will hold the quality of this information compared even to somebody like Gurdjieff, which wasn't that long ago actually. There's a minimal level of his conversations and direct teachings still available today. He did not have a camera sitting in front of him 24/7. I've already compiled much more data than Gurdjieff and others like him. It's not that he didn't teach it, but the amount of data that was able to be recorded was far less.

One can look at the Higher Balance video tapes now and have a better idea of what I said. There will be another kind of watering down and it will be the greatest sin of all. You know what that sin is going to be? It's going to be manipulation of the video and audio CD's to make it look real, the same thing as they're doing now by creating fake UFO's and similar things. People have the technology now to have me look the same as I look now, but with a completely different message coming from me.

Can't they do it now?

Yes, but it's still very detectible. It will be ego, pride, manipulation and control. It will be certain individuals who will want to control other people and they will manipulate it and say, "This is the material that never got out. This is the secret stuff that never got out, and this is what he really meant. We're the ones who will know that." Then they are going to say that Eric predicted in the future that some other person is going to be teaching and they'll have me saying, "Oh yeah, it's this and this is what he looked like and this is his name, and he's the one you should follow then," and that's what it will be.

Will it be coming from people who have the time and money to do that?

Well, it won't even take money. Even now, most people can do it on their home computers. In ten years, the technology will be phenomenal, and it will happen soon. So what it comes down to is copywriting. And the copywriting will have to be watched over carefully. It is basically going to show your qualifications and your connection with me. Then you will be the authority for looking at a video and saying, "That's not something that Eric would have said. It's not something he would have taught," and they'll respect you because your qualifications can be confirmed through Higher Balance or whatever authority is present at that time.

People can go online and say, "There's this person or there is that person. You can see that they did learn from Eric. They've met him. They knew him. They learned from these other teachers." That's what will authenticate the work and that will only last so long. In the future, there'll be many instructors long before we have all passed. People like you will end up teaching.

So, as we move into fifth gear, will that loosen the matrix? Will it evolve enough so that we can move a little bit more freely than we do now in fourth gear?

Well, on the simplest level, when we move into fifth gear, we will probably have another three to five hundred years of the same mentality that you see right now. Science will always progress to a certain level, but it will be watched over closely. There will be squabbles over stem cells. Most people think that stem cell research should have continued because in another five years, the amount of research that would have been done could mean that everybody would live to about one hundred and twenty years old with a higher quality of life. Arthritis would be gone. There would no longer be diabetes or some of the degenerative diseases. You would feel like you were fifty years old at the age of eighty or one hundred.

Because of ignorance and all of the fears that were created, that will not happen now. It will take time to build-up the research again. Research needs time to build. So, if you think about all the hypocrisies of the past hundred years, never mind the last thousand years, space travel would be a common thing. How people think affects all of us right now. There will be more fear in *old world thinking* or world religion rather than progressive thinking and embracing science and spirituality. You will feel that there is more liberation with a respect for life.

I didn't get anything out of a lot of the information that I got from you, especially in my earlier days. I think that I was only getting part of the data. I didn't understand the other part, so I was frustrated.

Right, but then you also referred to yourself as a red cell that became a white cell and I would agree with that. The real question is, "Why did you keep going with it? Why not stop if you weren't really getting that much out of it?"

I could go in different directions with that, but I'm going to go to my childhood where I had psychic abilities.

So you knew there was a level of truth in the teachings, and you could feel it in there. You knew you weren't getting it, but you knew it was there.

I was getting the material, but I couldn't even meditate for five years because of the house that I lived in. But I continued to receive the material anyways.

What made you get it?

A level of truth.

There you go. So it was still talking to you. It was still doing the job. Today, even if you've already read it three or four times, you could read *The Handbook of the Navigator* again and still reap information from it. After listening to other modules, you will get something out of it that you did not get all the other times and you'll think, "I don't remember him saying that. I don't remember reading that." It's because you were prevented from seeing it.

I listened to the module and said that I didn't get anything from it. Then I'd play it again. I thought I knew what was being said, but I wasn't sure. So I played it again.

Sometimes I had to play it maybe five or six times before
I got the idea, let alone knew what was being said.

But you kept doing it. Something in your soul said, "Keep
listening to this." If you sit out in the rain, you're going to get
wet. If you keep listening to the material, something is going
to start clicking in that cemented brain and you're going to
see the light. You'll awaken. You just have to expose yourself
to it.

In one of the modules, you talked about
structuralization versus fluidity. You said that we
shouldn't take a role because it's too much like the
Darkside. Yet in another module you said that we
should specialize in something, get good at it and
then move on to the next thing. This seems like a
contradiction. Can you explain what you mean?

If you ask me in the context of the material, I'm pretty
consistent. It's just whatever comes out. I need you to provide
me with a more in-depth description of what was being
discussed. That way, I can shed some light on what you are
really asking.

You were talking about a series of thoughts that leads
to a stage of enlightenment. Then you went into
structuralization versus fluidity. You said that we should
be fluidic. But in the beginning, you teach people in
a structured manner. You want students to become
more fluidic. Yet, you are surprised that they do not
select a particular role, become proficient at it and
move on. Then you become proficient in everything.

Do you think that's contradictory? You said that I told you to learn something to a certain degree and then move on to the next target to learn to a certain degree, but you're also saying that I told you not to take on a role. If you just take it on temporarily, wouldn't that mean not taking on a role indefinitely?

It makes sense when you put it that way.

I'm trying to guess what you are talking about. I think my emphasis was not to focus solely on developing just one skill or ability. For example, I don't like it when someone defines himself as a healer. That is what they do for their whole life. They heal people or do telepathy or astral projection or they move their mind to explore. I don't think it is a good thing to accept just one role.

It is excellent to dabble in something and experiment with it. Learn and develop that skill, but don't crystallize yourself in a specific place or say that you only heal; I don't think that is good for your spiritual growth. If you are to serve humanity, that is fine, but you have to ask yourself, "Is my role to serve humanity or is my role to grow as a spiritual being in this dimension? Am I to utilize my time on the Earth to develop as much as I can before I move back into just consciousness?" So, I don't see this as being a contradiction at all. I just think it's a matter of perspective.

Should we strive to pull ourselves completely out of the matrix? Should we strive to disconnect ourselves? You said that we should have a human experience, be in the nitty-gritty, feel the emotions, struggle and have pain because experiencing that is part of why we are here. Won't someone who is able to pull themselves from the matrix be able to manipulate or change reality from that state?

You don't want to completely remove yourself from the matrix. If you do that, what is the point of even being here? Eventually, you will pull yourself completely from the matrix anyway. It's guaranteed that we are all going to die sooner or later. It will take a lot of work to get you there. Many people are just here, growing through their experiences. For you to be here in this life, in this moment, it's really a choice you make. *You came into the matrix to work within this program, this consciousness.* When I discuss the idea of moving outside of it, it doesn't mean to ever leave it completely. You are operating from this particular physical body. So even if you move yourself outside of the matrix, which would be to move yourself out of this program, you're still anchored here. So you are never one hundred percent off the map. It means that you have learned to operate temporarily outside of it, but you are still very much connected to it. If you completely disconnected, that would be a complete disservice to being here.

The idea is to move outside the matrix to have self-realization. When you can move yourself outside of your body, your mind expands outside of your five senses. For the most part, you are literally moving outside of the general matrix.

There are many levels of matrixes. *If you were completely outside of the matrix, there would be absolute nothingness.* In the end, you are in the mind of God. That is the grand matrix. If you go outside of that, there is really nothing else. Therefore, there is an ever connecting level of consciousness. It depends on how deep you go.

Let's say that right now, this reality is your main matrix. When you dream, that is another matrix within it. That is a whole separate reality where you can smell, taste, hear, relate, have sex, love, and hate. It's very, very real. Yet there are different factors, for its law of physics, for your reality. Maybe you are able to fly, or you lick something to taste it, but you don't really taste it; rather you feel it. It feels like fuzz rather than sweetness. So the matrix rules are a bit different in that other reality.

When you take your mind out of the matrix, this main reality that you are operating in, it sometimes gives you a better perspective for seeing what you are a part of. When you're able to step outside of it and take a look, you get greater tools to operate inside of it. When you function inside of something, you just function. You exist. You don't realize that you have any power to change something because you can't comprehend that there is something, a mechanism, behind it all. That's like saying that you are part of the watch hand, but you never get outside of the watch to see that the whole purpose of the watch is to tell time. Once you go outside of it, and you understand that the whole purpose is to keep a measure of time, you can go back into the gears with an understanding of the process. You can understand why there might be a smaller wheel versus a larger wheel and why there is a coil winding up. You can also discern the purpose of that coil.

Of course, if you wanted to tamper with those things, you could actually manipulate time if you understood the purpose of everything around you. You could say, "Well, I'm going to slow the clock down by loosening up the winding coil." At one time, you never even knew that the winding coil was a winding coil. It was just simply something that was spanning around you in a circular motion. It could have been anything until you were able to step outside it and perceive.

So when you step outside of this matrix and are able to perceive it, or even comprehend a small part of it, you can achieve a state of consciousness where you have a knowing. That knowing is a level of enlightenment. It's a deeper understanding that separates you from everybody else who is simply functioning. Everybody else becomes the wheels, the clock hands, and the fabric that makes up the track, which is actually the coil that keeps time. You are able to perceive it differently, which means that your interaction becomes completely different. You are no longer part of the mechanism. If you can understand the mechanism, you are in a duality where you are part of it but you are not a part of it. You can choose to function separately because you are no longer being moved to do something in the process. Your purpose is to be that wheel. You now realize that you are the wheel and you can stop doing what you are doing simply **because you have self-realization**.

Should you insulate yourself with energy and knowledge instead of isolating yourself completely from the world?

Yes, but again to the benefit of everyone else, if you see yourself completely outside, then it's just like when your body has a virus or a bacterial infection; like a pimple. It begins to push it out. So will this dimension. So will Gaia. It no longer sees you as a part of it. Therefore, you can go into a schizophrenic state or mental depression. It can create chaos in your life because you no longer can understand your purpose and that becomes madness.

Many white cells are prone to doing this in their awakening or enlightenment cycle. They start to see reality as being something very separate. It usually starts off with relationships on a sociological level. They start to look at other people and find it very hard to coexist with them, to intellectually find a level of agreement. They start seeing the mechanism. They see all the people as a herd of motions all doing their job as a group. They see the matrix in segments as masses of thought or masses of people doing operations. Then they start to see the mechanism of their daily operations. It's like a clock. They go to the bathroom at a certain time. They have an argument a certain way.

Everything begins to become very predictable, like the movements of a watch. Once you become intelligent enough, once you can step out of that and see all the mechanisms moving, you can make yourself insane because you then wonder, "What is the sense of this reality? Where is there something that isn't measured, weighed, and predictable?"

You start to think that if everything is predictable, what is the meaning of life? What is the meaning of existence? There are all these mechanisms and eventually if you can be observant enough, there are also creations within these mechanisms. There are moments of pure creation: something that wasn't predictable, something that couldn't be timed, or something that wasn't patterned.

Those are the moments that God looks for. Those are the moments that the Universe looks for. So there are revelations, but since you are going through the enlightenment cycles, you may miss that. You have to focus on that in order to want to be here. So there is a kind of madness and sense of separation, if you are not careful. Everything becomes very predictable.

When I was a red cell, it seemed to me that my life was a result of the activities I randomly did before. Now that I have become a white cell, it seems like I'm more predetermined. My life is already set before me.

Well, you have the ability to see further ahead. That creates that feeling. Before you became a white cell, your head was tilted down so you didn't really see where everything was coming from; everything seemed very random. Now that you have the foresight and the ability to see distance, it does seem like you have that predictability. You are starting to see all of the patterns and that can be very depressing. It can be very minimalizing because you think there has to be something more; and there is. The idea is to find those things, operate within them, and affect them.

How do you bring your spirituality closer but not put it on a pedestal? What are some ways, techniques or perspectives to do that? Sometimes I have a problem

putting myself out there. I play the blame game and say, "It's your fault that I'm not meditating twice a day."

How can you blame them?

I know. I can't blame them.

No, you really can't. Everybody is uniquely different. In your particular case, I can see that there is a very strong spiritual pull so there's a battle inside of you to remain there. You get angry about being pulled out all of the time. You are probably contemplating whether or not to try to escape, to find a place to escape from life. You have to be very careful because you need to find acceptance in this reality, and I think it comes down to the terms that you perceive. Right now, you see it as an enemy. You see it just exactly the way you said. You are angry because everything is pulling you out of where you want to be. You believe that if you could just be where you want to be long enough, you would have your final moment of an enlightenment cycle. You don't realize that you are already in an enlightenment cycle. You are already there, and I think you can feel that.

There are times when it becomes very frustrating for me to be here and I just want to escape. I feel sometimes that the world is suffocating me. I feel that the Darkside utilizes stuff to pull me out of my spiritual state of consciousness. So it comes up with greater ways to force it on me because I'm so resilient. I've built up such a resistance to having it pull me into the Doe; but we're all at different levels. It is the terms of which you accept life. You have to love life. You have to look at it differently, and I'll explain how.

This dimension is profound. It is extraordinary. Until you can realize how extraordinary and unique it is and what it can offer you, it will be vexing to you. You have to realize it for what it is. In this dimension, we can smell, taste, hear, and optically see. You can't do these things in an energy body. You have other sensory.

You've existed probably hundreds of millions of light years away in some form of existence. It's just that time is very different. You think, "Well, why wouldn't I be wiser?" It's because your perception of time is very different. In a sense, you are young but you are old. It depends on how you want to perceive time. You can't smell in the other dimension. You can't hear sound in the context that you hear it now. You can't even see structure the way you see it now, in an energy format. You can't taste. You wouldn't be able to hug or touch. There are other profound senses which are equivalent to these five senses as an energy being though.

You take for granted the five senses here in your life. You want to go back, but if you went back you will just wonder, "What was I thinking?" You will realize that you made a great error in your haste to relieve yourself of your life on Earth.

Sometimes people come to visit people like me. When that happens, you have the opportunity to speak with me and ask questions about the things that you have always wanted to know. When you leave, you are going to want to kick yourself because your thoughts are going to be, "I was sitting in front of Eric Pepin. He's an enlightened being. During that time, I saw him as a man and maybe for just a few moments, but I just wish I had done something more. I wish I had taken a great opportunity to do something more with it."

There will always be "something more." So you will feel even more regret when you leave this world because you hadn't spent more time feeling the sand beneath your feet, observing the trees and the branches, or smelling the flowers. Maybe you'll regret not spending enough time touching the face of your mother, or sitting and listening as she was speaking to you, talking about her normal daily activities, about life, and how much you miss it! Only when she is gone will you truly know what you are missing. That is what I often think of to remind myself how much I love this world. I need to savor it every minute whenever I long to be somewhere else.

I often think about the students that I've had in my life, how much I love them, and how much joy and appreciation they bring to me. I feel the passion that I have to teach other people in this dimension, to tell them about the other dimensions, and to awaken them so that they do not wish to escape from this reality. I don't want you to escape. I want you to be whole. I want you to feel more complete and more comfortable doing what you need to be doing. You will return to where you long for soon enough. It is those things that make me want to slow down and exist here. When I let my mind go too far in the dimensional spaces, I long to be there, but I have to remind myself to leave and come back here. No matter what happens in life, it is going to end. You are going to go back home when everything is finished. Why not resolve to savor the things in this dimension? Savor your life, savor the people, and savor your experiences -- no matter if they are dark or not.

Have you ever had an experience in your life that was uncomfortable; perhaps a camping trip? You were uncomfortable and it was damp and cold. You spent the whole night laughing with your friends and you had a really good time. And now you miss it and you wish that you could go back to that moment? But at the same time, you were miserable when it happened. You will be unhappy many times in your life, but you will desperately want it again when you have departed. Hence, the reason we always come back again.

Are we reincarnating back here?

Not necessarily here, but in this dimension. While you are trying to experience more of the spiritual dimensions, don't be in such a rush to push this physical dimension away. It's alright to want to experience spiritually and to do those things, but don't make it an irritation. Don't make it into something that it is not.

Sometimes when you win, you really lose; and sometimes when you lose, you really win. Pull the little irritations that you have in life closer to you, instead of seeing them so negatively. When you pull them closer to you, you'll move through them and you'll find exactly what it is that you need to work through. Now, in some strange, other-dimensional way, it makes sense. Let me explain this differently.

At any given time, I know that I can take an ordinary environment and I can move this place. I can shift it. Even now at this very moment, I can shift the energy, the environment, and subtly move it into a higher dimensional frequency and we will all begin to move into it. Feel the shift slowly. I can make it very intense if I want, but it's not something that we want to do right now.

Take the moment and accept it for what it is; and then move through it. When you go into a haunted house, you could have the attitude of a realtor or a contractor. You could look at the old boards and the structure and think of what you can do with it. And if you have that attitude that is all you will ever see even if there are a million ghosts hopping, jumping, or flying throughout the whole place. None of it will exist for you.

If you go there as a spiritualist, you may not see the structure of the wood, the paint, the colors, or anything that's not of interest to your consciousness. Your interest will be to feel the frequency, the dimension. It's like a dimming bulb: you turn that frequency or luminosity up, and those things become more relevant to you.

If you see life as a frustration, you must understand that behind every mechanism that affects you, there is a reason it was put there. There is a reason why it has been laid in front of you. You can see it as a thing that affects you or you can see it as a thing with something inside of it that you must escape from. It's all a game. There is something to be gained from each person in your life, even a red cell, through either confrontations or experiences. Once you accept what you need to gain, and you accept it for what it is, you will no longer see it as a challenge. Then, all of a sudden, they will move out of your life. They will dissipate.

It's the same thing with your work. If you find that your work is relocating you, simply ask, "Where do you want me to go? I'm happy to go." Then once you do that, maybe you will find that you're sitting on the stone right alongside Don Juan because he happens to live down the road from the place where you just moved. Or the mechanic that you are working with says, "You know, if it wasn't for my spiritual, Yaqui Indian teachings, I wouldn't be able to handle this job." You will wonder, "What did he just say?"

You have to simply accept the situation for what it is. Do not fight the bull by its horns. Let it exhaust itself. Let it run through the cape. Be gentle. Be calm. Let it move with you. You are going to get frustrated. You will forget what you are saying now. It all sounds simple enough until you get into it. You will probably end up deciding how much you hate your life. Try to love it for one week and watch what happens. Watch the wonders that come from it.

If you want this place to become more spiritual, you have the ability to do that. Your intent is constantly on the ball. You're constantly looking for enlightenment. You're constantly looking for your way home. You're constantly looking to complete yourself. You're constantly looking for spirituality. You're constantly looking for the answers.

Look for the answers. You don't have to go to a mountain in Tibet to do that. The answers are sitting right in your home. The answers are sitting in the people surrounding you. Just see them for what they are. As you deal with them, let your intention be to find whatever pearl you are supposed to find. You won't be able to see that pearl because you only can see the work of a contractor that you need to do: the lines of the wood, the color of the paint, the structure, and the bones of the house. Look for the soul in them. Look for the soul wherever it is in the job. Look for it. There's an answer.

I've done everything from telemarketing to car sales, just like anybody else. The interesting thing about my life is that I've never seen my life as an act of doing. Of course, I thought, "I've got to go to this ridiculous red cell job and deal with Margaret and her doughnuts and whatever paperwork she wants to do," but I always felt like I was James Bond. I always felt like I was incognito. Even though everyone knew that there was something unique about me, that there was something there, I didn't let on. I just responded back to them like a normal person; incognito!

I always found that greater mysteries would find me because I always felt that there was a greater mystery to be found. It's all about "looking for the windows in the house," and then just waiting for them to show themselves. I can tolerate working through life by accepting that there will be something there and I just have to wait for it to be there. It always comes.

If I look at all of the things throughout my life, and all of the students I've found, most of them were from my work place. Or I found them by going to a very mundane place. I would bump into them; they would sense me, and I would sense them. Then something would happen. I might have to be there for three, four, or even five months before it happened. The Universe doesn't set its clock by you. You set yourself to the Universe. The sooner that you do, the faster things will happen. *The more you resist it, the longer it will take. So, the slower you go, the faster you will go.* Remember that!

Chapter 5

THE ART OF HEALING: WHITE FIRE

WHEN YOU THINK of healing someone, you naturally think of the biblical teachings and when Jesus walked the Earth. However, in recent times, there are evangelists that set up large tents and make a public announcement for everyone to "come to the prayer service and dedicate their life to Jesus so that they will be saved." Their intention is for a healer to "fix what is ailing you." To me, it is just a dog and pony show where the healer makes an announcement, calls out a name, and someone gets wheeled up to the center stage. The healer then lays their hands on the person and suddenly that person is miraculously healed!

I do not believe that healing process is the power of God nor do I believe that healers are sent down to Earth by God for this particular mission. It is a ridiculous concept, in my opinion. God does not randomly select someone to be the "healer of the night." It does not work that way. Everyone has the ability to heal themselves.

How are those 'healers' able to heal people in those Evangelistic meetings?

There is an energy field surrounding our body that is called the aura. You can actually see the aura with the help of Kirlian photography or Electrophotography. I want you to think of the body as if it was a computer that automatically runs and works fine most of the time. Then one day, the computer locks up. Something is not working right and it cannot be fixed. You cannot get the keys to work no matter what you do. You cannot get it to function properly. Everybody knows that the first thing to do is shut the computer off; let it sit for a second, and then turn it back on. This resets all of the programs so they can function normally. This will usually correct the problem.

However, as more programs are added during the lifespan of this computer, the processes of running the programs changes. One program that worked fine at first somehow develops a problem, which starts to root its way into the normal cycle of the computer. By shutting the computer off, it removes anything that should not be a part of the process. When you turn the computer back on, the only thing left is the original settings that make the computer run perfectly, so there is no problem with it.

Well, the human body is very much like that. Your DNA, brain, organs, and the chemistry of your body are set at a certain calibration that is similar to a blueprint. The human brain follows this blueprint when determining how much liquid to send to the liver to secrete, digest, and process. Illness occurs when the blueprint is misread or ignored. So the organs raise or lower the level of input/output on their own. Then the brain sends a wrong signal to the body. It may start by producing too much of the wrong chemical and sending it to the kidneys. The kidneys cannot process it and moves it along because the secretion is now too acidic. This miscommunication creates "dis-ease" and starts deteriorating the body.

The people who go to these "tent healers" are like a locked up computer. They line up and a healer exclaims loudly, "you're healed" as he smacks them on the head. But what he's really doing is releasing energy that was created from his excitement, and this energy affects his energy field. The individual who receives the healing is also building up their energy field through their excitement. They feel the intensity and believe that when this person touches them, they will feel the power of God.

Have you ever gotten a tingle for no apparent reason? When you think of something pleasurable or when you become excited, your hair stands up, and you get tingles for a second? That is energy running through your energy field. In their excitement, the person's energy builds to a blissful state and when they are touched, it releases endorphins in the brain that overstimulates the brain for a second. Then they blackout; the release overwhelms them like a circuit breaker hit with too much electricity. The energy shorts the brain. In that moment, they are "reset," just like rebooting a computer. The brain is cleared and recalibrated with a whole new process. It returns to the original blueprint and gives them a better life.

After they fall over, they wake up, open their eyes, and they feel healed. They probably are healed because the body corrected all the problems that hindered its performance, just like a computer does. It had nothing to do with God stepping in and performing a miracle for that person. The person reset their brain using the electricity in their own body. It's the same electricity that travels through your arm to your brain and back down again when you reach out and touch something. That's what is actually happening. It corrects the body chemistry, all the rhythms, and all the biorhythms back to their normal function.

What about a person who was deaf, but now can hear?

Most likely the hearing loss was due to physical damage. After they are healed, it is apparent the ear is still deformed. So how is the hearing restored? Your natural senses are set at 10 on a scale of 1 to 100. Haven't you ever smelled something very intense and were surprised at how strong it smelled? Your sight is set at a scale of 10 out of 100. Your hearing is set at a very low level, still considered at the low end of the normal range. If your ears get shot while operating at a 10 and the level of hearing drops to a 1, you still have 91 levels to go. You are able to raise it that much higher. In fact, you can take a person who only has a 10 percent hearing ability, raise the brain's ability to process sounds to 1,000 times higher than normal range. All of a sudden, you have better hearing than everyone else. Sound waves still hit the eardrum. The ear still physically reacts to sound. It has just lost its ability to process it. The brain enhances what little machinery is left to intensify and process sound in a more refined way that makes the sound come in clear again. Their hearing appears to be healed but the damage is still there. It just raised the capacity to 20 percent rather than 10 percent. Now, the person is really hearing what all of us are hearing at 10 percent even though they are now set at 20 percent; but they are processing at that level.

The same thing goes for people who lose their sight. It isn't necessarily losing your vision; rather it is the interpretation of light affecting your eye. Sight is about how well the nerves process the light. If a person is blind, they can amplify the few cones that do work by allowing the brain to take that small amount of cones and intensify its abilities to process light. All of a sudden, they can see again.

> I had a situation where one leg was longer than
> the other and I saw my leg grow! It happened
> right before my eyes. The healer pulled it
> and it grew and it's been fine ever since.

I can explain what happened. Doctors are now breaking the bone and then resetting it to lengthen people's legs. They surgically implant a device that spreads it apart a hairline at a time so there are only millimeters of space in-between the two pieces of bone. Then the bone grows to fill the space.

And just as the growth is almost completed, they stretch the pieces apart a little bit more. So, the body is building bone in-between the space. Doctors do this until the body has built the bone to the proper length.

I need to take this explanation to a microscopic level, but in order to make sense of this, it is important to acknowledge that humans really do not understand electricity. We can harness it, and we know how to utilize it. We also know how to get it to do the things that we want it to do, but we don't really understand what it is.

When the healer pulled your leg and it elongated, the microscopic molecules were spinning rapidly around each other even though it looked like solid mass. The molecules did the same thing that the doctors do, only at a very fast speed without cracking the bone, at speeds far beyond what we are able to comprehend.

I felt it.

You allowed the program from the healer to affect the cells of your body to release the energy. Multiply the bones growth by 1,000 times faster than normal. This is because electricity and energy can intensify the spiraling of the electrons in the cells of your body.

I felt that it was very hot. I remember an intense amount of heat in my lower back and I remember it was like my whole back cracked. And I saw it just like that. That was it; my leg was fixed.

That process basically redesigned your bone. The energy you both released went directly to the blueprint. By referencing it, the energy knew exactly what the bone length should be. It is the same energy that's in your body; it's just that it's not vibrating as fast as it can. If you speed it up, it's like turning up the dial to build it at a faster rate. It is not God; it is you allowing the will of your energy to work with a combination of somebody else's energy. Then, fusing the energy together, it accessed the blueprint to allow the energy do its work. You all have these same capabilities. Your brain contains a giant blueprint of how everything should be specifically set. You just have to allow the energy to do its job. The body will correct itself and do what the blueprint says it needs to do.

A lot of ailments come from the foods that you ingest. The cells, which are the workers that build your body, can become confused by the drugs that you take. They become doped up, just like when you drive a car under the influence of alcohol. You cannot function in that condition. The dangerous part is that instead of one person driving a car, you have twenty billion cells in your body that are highly intoxicated. These intoxicated cells are supposed to build different parts of the body, such as the kidney and the liver. They're supposed to build and repair the veins that carry blood and the minerals that you need. They build and repair because everything in your body is deteriorating. Your skin is flaking off your arms at this very moment, but it is being replaced at an impressive rate. All the parts of your body are also deteriorating, but these cells are repaired as quickly as they are destroyed. Unfortunately, if these twenty billions cells are all intoxicated, they will not rebuild the structures correctly. It seems to them as if they build everything the right way, but later on one thing is incorrect and then another. Soon the whole body starts to become flawed. It's a momentum that cannot be stopped.

Take a deck of cards. Put one card in front of the other and try to make a straight line. As you lay out the cards the line looks relatively straight, but once you are done take a step back and look again. Suddenly, the line appears crooked and you did not realize that it happened. Well, it is the same thing. The cells think they are correcting the problem, but they are really screwing it up. By the time you realize what has happened, you have a clogged artery or you have cancer cells growing. The cells take material from one part of your body to build something that is useless -- like a tumor. How you nourish your body is extremely important. Your body is a whole universe that is dependent on whatever decisions you make for it. Your body cannot choose those things for you; it is just a machine, even though it tries to get your attention by craving certain things.

In most cases, a craving is your body trying to tell you that it needs something. It already knows what foods have the minerals or nutrients that are essential for its existence. When you get a craving for something, it is your body's way of saying, "I need zinc or I need potassium." Your body knows that the last 100 times it ate a banana, it received potassium. Now that its reserves are low, the body is telling you, "Banana! You want a banana." Once you eat the banana, you feel much better. The banana has the nutrients that the body needed. The body doesn't know specific things. It doesn't know a banana contains potassium. It just knows where it came from and it tries to communicate this to you. You just have to learn to listen. Most human beings have become very detached from their body. They throw everything into mental pleasures and think nothing of the inner life -- the billions of organisms that exist there. They think of themselves as one being that exists only for them.

You are made of billions of living organisms with zillions of railroad track type structures that allow electricity to travel through so that it can communicate with all of the workers. If you become ill, the illness is caused by the program malfunctioning in your body or perhaps psychological problems that are going on in the brain. This includes depression, the environment, and the toxicity around you that you are not always aware of, like smog. Or it is from taking certain drugs. There are a million ways that you can destroy your body.

Let's say that you have cancer or a tumor. Imagine that I am a red cell or a worker cell inside of your body and that I am helping to build a metaphorical wall. Basically you got cancer because I believe I'm doing my job, making a wall to enclose it. I am serving the body system that is serving and giving me life. The house this wall resides in shelters all the cells in the body. The body is fed and gives all the cells their life, their minerals, and their nutrients. In exchange for this, they work to maintain the body because the body maintains them and gives them life.

Again, metaphorically speaking, one day I get so drunk that I take a hammer and crowbar and I start smashing the wall down. Then I take the debris and I start building an igloo in the middle of another room with the material of the wall. The wall was my liver. The igloo is my tumor, a useless bulk of material. I don't even know why I am building it because I am so incoherent that I think I am being logical. That is what happens to the cells in your body. They do not get the message of the blueprint anymore. Instead, they tune in to the chemicals, pesticides, or any other poison and that overrides the signals that should be coming from the blueprint. Then, for some reason, the wall is destroyed and the whole house collapses because the beams, that gave it support, have been removed. As it collapses, I die, the house dies, the body dies and all the living things within it die.

How do we correct the problem once it begins?

Let's take a step back and look at this in a different way. How do all of these worker cells know what to do in the first place? They know because of the blueprint. How do they know about the blueprint? They know because there are other cells reading the blueprint and sending it a message. The worker picked it up. It knew exactly what was supposed to happen according to the message that is passed along. There is a communication through low radiation impulses. These impulses are signals that move through your body. If you could see yourself in the dark without skin as just pure energy, you would look like an entire universe. You'd see all these little silver lights all over your body. You'd see little streams of light moving so fast, you'd almost swear you didn't see them at all. It would look like you were shimmering. But if you slow the streams of light down, you would see the electricity moving downward. That stream of light is a message that is being communicated. The message travels from the brain to the nerves and from the nerves to the cells. There are billions of messages moving back and forth throughout the body.

In the previous scenario, the signals are not communicated but are passed along anyway. So, the workers do not receive the right signals and start doing their own thing. They start hacking away because they are ignorant and need direction. They are not as smart as human beings. Just as humans are not as smart as the planet, the planet is not as smart as the Universe. Communication is lost or if there is a communication from the Source, it's all screwed up.

A healer is someone who can control the energies. The energies are not just moving around and confined inside the body, nor are they limited to the shape of the body. If you could remove the flesh, you would see the electrons moving, looking more like a glow. You would see a finer gray haze of universe all around the darker universe with the silver lights. You'd see a gray glowing universe with more silver glowing lights moving around it, because energy moves around the whole body. You may see it as just energy, but if you could see it the way I do, you would understand the energy fields.

When I want to heal someone, the first thing I do is examine my blueprint, which is very similar to their blueprint. All of our blueprints are created in the same design. Then I connect to the person with the illness and link with their computer as I would do remotely through the internet. If the computer isn't working right, I investigate the problem to find out what is wrong, edit it and fix it. Once that is accomplished, I hit "enter" to make the corrections permanent. Then I hit reboot. The computer shuts off and starts back up again. Now it's fixed.

I am tapping into your mind. I let my energy connect with your energy and communicate with the cells saying, "Stop ripping the wall down or you will be dead tomorrow. Fix it. This is how you have to do it." Then I send a visual map to them. They say, "Let's get together and put that wall back up now." That's when the body starts to heal itself.

This is the first level of healing. You communicate with the cells of the other person's body that lost communication with their blueprint. You tell them to fix it. When the body fixes itself and communication is restored and working again, that person gets healthier.

I am basically laying a foundation for understanding. I give you a very simple blueprint so you can understand the process and it makes more sense to you. Use this as a correlation: I have some books on a shelf and none of them are in order. They are technically in the right place because they are on the shelf. Then I say, "I want you to organize all the books by subject." So you start organizing them by subject. Then I say, "Now that you finished doing that, I want the books in alphabetical order." You are refining the system, making it more adaptable and easier to use. Next I say, "I want you to cross-reference the books by authors." You just refined it even more. Instead of telling you to organize the whole system the first time, this gives you a better understanding of what I am leading up to.

You have an idea of how the body works. You have an idea about the cells, how electricity moves and the basic concepts. So you start asking the right questions. How do we tell the body to do what we want it to do? We have an idea of how it is done, but let's be more specific. Using this example of how it works makes it less of a mystery, unlike the tent healers. The healer doesn't have the power of God. God didn't directly heal you. You know that is incorrect. You know the basics of how healing really works. That is what I am trying to teach you.

The one who has the knowledge has the power. If you know how it works, you now are the healer. Most of those tent healers are not even aware of how they're doing it. They don't believe it's the power of God. In fact, they are not even healing you. They provide you with your own healing. You believe that when they hit you, it is going to heal you. You actually ignite your own blueprint, shut yourself down, and then restart it. They are only a catalyst to help you do it. The healer may not know why the person is healed, but they take credit for it. It is you who decides to be healed. Your belief system tells you that it is done. You allow it to happen.

If I am healing myself, why can't I do it without outside influence?

Your brain is set with the Governor. An example similar to a *governor* is the part of your car's engine that restricts the amount of fuel it can burn. It limits the speed of the car so it can't go as fast as it could without this device.

Let's say that your car's speedometer says it can drive at the speed of 110mph. The car is manufactured to go as fast as 120mph or 140mph. However, when you step on the gas it won't go any faster than 85 mph even if you floor it. The government has created a regulation for car manufacturers and has passed a law stating that each car has to have a *governor*. They did it thinking this will prevent accidents in the future. But if you remove the *governor*, the car will now do 140mph. If you put the *governor* back in the car, it will only do 80mph or 90mph. The potential for you to do more is there, but the *Governor* prevents you from your full potential.

Your brain has a *Governor* that was created by a society that says all of these mystical phenomena are impossible. Society pushes for medicine and science and that's just the way it is. From that aspect, you begin to create your doubter, your *Governor*. Your *Governor* says if you get ill, nothing is going to save you. Or you may believe there is but there's always a little doubt that maybe you cannot be healed. If you could truly remove that doubt for just a moment, the *Governor* would then be removed.

Suddenly, your body can do miracles and heal itself in ways you couldn't imagine before. That's what happens the moment that people go to the healers. It is their belief that healing is possible. The person being healed builds the moment up so much with their anticipation of a miracle that when the healer hits them on the head; the *Governor* gets shut down for a second. The body's energy moves at an incredible rate reorganizing cells and molecular structure. Everything happens at an extraordinary speed, and you will feel heat because heat is friction. That friction is the molecules gyrating at a tremendous speed like the particles in a microwave. This is the reformulation of structure, of matter. When it cools down, it's because the *Governor* starts up again and shuts this process down. By the time it reacts, it's too late. Everything has already been corrected. The *Governor* looks at the body and says, "Alright then," because the *Governor* is not out to change what has already happened. It's just out to prevent you from allowing things to happen. So if the body gets healed in the reboot process, it doesn't matter. The *Governor* doesn't look at that.

Let me back up here for a moment and say that there are people who genuinely can heal, but again it's not the power of God. It's an ability they've learned that allows the brain to process energy in a way that allows them to heal. Their *Governor* somehow got screwed up, probably in childhood. When everybody was saying, "No, you can't," there might have been people in their family who said, "Yes, you can. Yes, it's possible." Or they came from a culture that was more open to these possibilities than we see here in America.

Maybe, for some reason they were saved. Maybe they believed in God. There are miracles done by Buddhists, by Africans, and by millions of belief systems. Miracles are exclusive to YOU, not to God. It's exclusive to the person who says, "Well, I have this ability to heal others." They may claim it is from the Goddess of the Earth and that she works through them and heals people. But it has nothing to do with the Goddess; it has nothing to do with Christ; it has nothing to do with Buddha.

These people have somehow learned to control their energy and to reach out to someone's body and tell the cellular structure of their body what to do. They've learned to overwrite the programming in order to correct it. That's what they've learned to do. They can manipulate the cellular structure of the body so it can speed up and correct itself. When they heal, they don't know what a kidney looks like. They've never dissected a kidney. There's a certain part of your kidney where roughly twenty thousand tubes of your blood flows through. Each one requires a different pressure; each one is a different size; and each one has a different chemical secretion that it makes. It's like a giant chemistry lab. Do you think they know all these things? Do you think they studied it under a microscope so they know exactly what valve in your body to heal? Do they know exactly which valve, out of thousands, is malfunctioning? No! They know that by stimulating the entire organ, which has the entire blueprint written in every single cell, the kidney knows when the electricity is charged. It will make the program restart and it will mimic whatever the exact blueprint says that it needs to do.

The electricity runs down this maze of all the organs and the body design. When it hits a wall, it knows that the wall is not supposed to be there, so it burns through it continuing on the pathway. Thus, when the electricity runs its course, the fluid then moves through the hole. The healer doesn't know what they're healing. The energy knows by the blueprint what needs to be done, the same way that water knows how to flow down a river stream.

Some healers will point a person out in the audience and say, "You, there's a problem with your liver," or "There's a problem with your kidney." And the audience member will say, "YES - it's true; yes it's true!"

People are on frequencies just like different radio stations. What is the one thing you are hoping to accomplish when going to see a healer? You go there to be healed, most likely, or to go with somebody who is being healed. While there, are you thinking, "God, my heart is rotting and I desperately need a new one, but you know I did just scrape my little finger and that still stings a bit; can you please just take care of the scrape?" No, you're thinking, "Heal me God; heal my heart; heal my heart." You are projecting massive thought. The healer's mind is just telepathically picking up on that projection from you. He looks at you and all of a sudden he sees an impression of a heart. He thinks it's from God, but it's really you broadcasting this need. He says, "I see a heart; I see a bad heart," and you say, "Yes!" All of a sudden, your belief in what is happening shuts down the *Governor* because you trust the process of it all indirectly because of what the healer has demonstrated to you. This opens the possibility of correcting your heart.

However, they have already exposed many of those fraudulent tent healer organizations. The "healers" use microscopic ear pieces to communicate with accomplices in the crowd who retrieve information from the people coming to be healed. It's been documented and proven.

Are all of them fraudulent?

Many of them, but you know something? To me, it doesn't matter. I don't like the idea of those fraudulent healers taking money from sick people, because a lot of the people who claim to be healed wake up the next day and are just as ill as they were the day before. The body secretes a chemical, like morphine, and it's very intense. The people believe so much they are going to be healed that the body secretes this chemical pain killer which allows them to run up and down and not feel their back pain or whatever their ailment was. Then the next day, this morphine-like chemical secretion that the body created in its excitement dissipates and the pain comes right back. They never were really healed, but the healers move out of town by the time the sick person discovers this.

Also, a lot of the people who were at the event don't know the supposedly healed person. So they are not going to find out the next day that the person is still ill. The only ones that are going to know are family and friends. Maybe they will tell a few people. If they confronted the healers about their symptoms returning, the healers could say, "Well, the Lord decided you weren't ready. He just wanted to give you a taste. Maybe next year, if you can find the Lord by then, the Lord will heal you completely. He just wanted to let you know he could do it." So they're going to say, "Here is this young girl who all of a sudden lost her back pain. She can run up and down the aisle because she is so filled with the Lord." The next day, her back pain has returned and it's, "Because she does not have enough faith in the Lord."

Other times, the people believe so much that the healer can cure them. Ninety-nine percent of the time, those people heal themselves. In this process, it is really just you healing your own body by removing the *Governor* and forcing so much energy through your system that it just blows out all of the blockages and corrects itself. That is basically how those things are being done. Ironically, the person that gets the credit for it is the healer or God. I wish it was different but it is not.

These cases of healings are reproduced constantly without any religious foundation. Everything in your body, because it is living, can be changed. Think about that now. Everything in your body from head to toe will change completely in three years. In fact, you don't even have the same brain you had three years ago. Your heart has been completely changed. Your liver has been completely changed because the cells die and new cells take their place.

The problems start if you have a disease in an organ. Let's say that the disease is corroding a particular organ away. If you have damage from a disease, that damage to the cells cannot be repaired. Your new cells cannot replace the disease-ridden area like ordinary cells because the diseased area is a separate issue from reproduction or replacement of regular cells. It's a separate living organism now. It is like leather now. The cells are no longer living; rather they are a dead form of life, like your fingernails and your hair. Your body now has to work around that.

It's not just disease that can affect your body. Your blueprint also deteriorates slowly, causing it to slowly decay. The map starts to deteriorate because of other issues in the body. It starts to lose its design, shape, and consistency. There is a weathering of the body. The most important thing you have to remember is that a new cell is replacing a dead cell. When that new cell dies, it is replaced by another cell. Your entire body is constantly swapping old parts with new. You are not the same person you were just the other day. From head to toe, you are not the same person that you were three years ago. If the body is not the same body that it was three years ago, what conclusion can you draw from this? It's telling you that any mistakes made by the new cells probably can be fixed by resetting the blueprint, which is permanent.

The reason disease can thrive in the body is because the blueprint is simply mimicking a process of destruction programmed by error. So it is now following that, instead of the original plan. You haven't reset it. The body is slowly deteriorating. It's slowly letting the disease take control. You need to go back to the original blueprint and reset everything. That is how you heal yourself or others. You heal by rectifying the error. Your body is going to try to correct itself. It's going to change anyway. Why not allow it to bring itself back to the original blueprint instead of allowing an outside influence to rewrite the program? The blueprint is the same thing as the line of cards: it's slowly curving.

Why do we age if our body replaces old cells with new cells constantly and has the ability to heal and replace anything that's going wrong with the body?

There are people living right now, in this time period, who seem to be in their sixties but they are over 120 years old. And there are Chinese people who have lived to an extremely old age; people that are much older than 120 years of age. They have discovered how the cell is replenished.

I believe that by celebrating time with things like birthdays, the calendar, and by watching the clock, you are consistently reminded of time. *The fact that you observe time consistently forces you to mentally accept the idea of aging.* Hence, you invoke that idea on yourself.

As a biological being, you age yourself by roughly thirty five percent if you are constantly looking at time, reflecting on it, and scheduling your life. You say to yourself, "I have to be here at this point in my life." That ages you. You accept aging by that fact alone, since you estimate where you are supposed to be in the aging process. There is a social factor involved when you look at your parents, your grandparents, your great grandparents and say, "This is how they should look at this particular age." This creates a mental image and invokes that in your blueprint. You reinforce the aging process if you follow the map, putting forth expectations of age. Because of this, the body starts designing itself in that manner.

If you start believing that you will live to be two hundred years old now, and you accept that in your belief system, you will probably live to a healthy one hundred thirty or one hundred forty years of age. At that age, you will literally still be climbing mountains, feeling the sun, swimming, and looking like you are maybe fifty or sixty years old. I do believe that. However, the probability is overwhelming because the rest of the world says that you are going to age. You are so programmed into believing that you will die at a certain age that you even mentally evoke death on yourself.

My grandmother died at the age of eighty-six. She was basically very healthy; she looked great, felt great, and she wanted to die in Germany where she was born. She knew that she was in her eighties, so she figured that if she didn't go there soon, she wouldn't die in her Motherland. When she went to Germany, she died that year. So this is mentally evoked. You get tired of life. You decide, "Ok, now it's time. I am ready to bow out." This is something that's been reported in a lot of psychological magazines.

If you really want to keep somebody alive, give them something to do. Give them a reason to go on living. Most people who die earlier are the ones who have nothing to do with their time. They just sit in their rooms, or sit outside on the porch. The people who live longer usually have become volunteers and have something to do. So plant gardens, have pets, and have responsibilities. It gives you a purpose.

So, now that you understand a little bit more about the body, let's take a closer look at this. First of all, there are different kinds of healers. There are healers who heal by chance. Then there are healers who feel you and sense your body's field of energy. Your body is like a multi-universe. Your kidney is a universe in itself. Your liver is another separate universe. When one of these universes is ill or unhealthy, it sends out a signal, or what I call a bad tonal, like a nerve ending would if it was in pain. It does this because there are millions of cells dying. Perhaps they are being attacked by a virus. It's comparable to a galactic battle taking place inside your body. Another person can feel that field of energy from either the signal or the battle, and hone in on it. They can feel where the pain is coming from, but they may not know specifically what the organ looks like or what is wrong with it. They simply feel that the energy is not right; that there's a certain frequency from that part of the organ. So they start bombarding this area with energy. The energy then starts to correct the problem.

Now you must also take something else into account. There are different kinds of illnesses and you must look at them in different ways. There is cancer or tumors, which really are not viruses. They are cells that have gone rogue, due to an outside influence. That is something that can be fixed utilizing your blueprint. But if it's a virus that is invading the body, it is like aliens attacking your world. A virus does not even use the blueprint. It is just out to screw you up. It floats around in your universe. It might move to the liver and start attacking that universe. Tapping into the blueprint is not going to solve the problem now. While your cells are attempting to fix it, they are being killed by the virus that is eating them up. Now it is up to your white cells to raise the armies, go down there, and kick ass.

What happens if the virus is stronger than your white cells?

Then there is a strategic battle where your white cells must learn how to fight the virus in combat. Time is different for the cells inside your body. A cold that lasts a week in the body is like a war that lasts for ten years on Earth. It is comparable to a world war. It's even longer than that because in a week, most of your cells have already lived their entire life. For them, it's like the one hundred years you could live. During this big battle, the white cells are learning so they can teach the next generation how to combat the virus. So the strategy is passed down, as if the old white cells say to the new, "This is how the virus fights. This is how it attacks us. If you do this, we find that it helps to fend the virus off so that we can get a stronghold on it." Then the newer white cells will do it. They will gain an inch toward obliterating the virus. The white cells learn and they die, but they send the information they gained to the new white cells, and so forth, until the virus is finally conquered. If they conquer the virus, it's because they had the numbers.

Technically the virus is much more powerful than we are. There are only a handful of the virus cells but billions of white cells. So while they're getting their asses kicked, the white cells study the virus, learning about it until they figure out how to beat it. You only catch a cold once because the white cells learned from that and they never forget. It is written in the biological universe of your body.

A lot of people ask me, "Well Eric, why don't you just heal yourself when you get sick?" Well, I could speed the process up, but if I don't let my body learn, what happens if a killer virus attacks? I'll die faster. I will not have time to heal myself because I will be dead. The body has to learn. The inner universe has to experience and be conditioned to deal with many different circumstances. You have to tolerate a physical illness. It is just a difficult way of learning. You almost have to try to work yourself through an illness because you need to teach your body to combat the illness.

Let's keep something in mind. First of all, when you have other ailments, what do you do? You do the same thing animals do when they are sick. Through observation, people have learned that animals eat certain roots or herbs in order to introduce the minerals the body needs to heal itself. The body needs new building material to replace the faulty material. I cannot rip the wall out and repair it if I do not have new material to replace it with. I cannot heal my body unless I provide the minerals and nutrients to repair it. Those are the building blocks of the body. It's just not going to ethereally appear from out of nowhere. The material must be ready and presentable for the electricity to bind it all together and recreate it according to the design of the blueprint. If you don't have the material, you cannot repair the damage.

If you have cancer, or even a tumor, somebody can heal you. But then it will be a botched job if your body does not have enough of the minerals to do the job correctly. The person being healed will say, "Well, he healed me, but then I was sick again the next week." If the body doesn't have the material to fix the problem, the building blocks, it is not going to be repaired. You still have to provide the building blocks for the energy to heal you. It's not going to come out of thin air.

If you plan on going to a healer, prepare yourself ahead of time with vitamins and a good meal with plenty of vegetables a day or two before. Your blood will be rich with whatever it needs to repair the problem, such as certain amino acids. Also, in preparing your body to be healed or to be healthy, remember that your body is around ninety percent water. Your blood moves the minerals. So your blood is salty because of the minerals and nutrients it contains. If there are fewer liquids, the blood is thicker – like ketchup. It doesn't matter how hard the heart is pumping to normally move the blood. So if there are fewer liquids, the heart simply cannot move the minerals that it should. Those minerals are necessary for a successful healing session.

Now, in order to get all of those building materials into your giant galactic body, think about this: you have to take something in through your mouth in order for it to travel down to the tip of your toe. Your cells are being replaced every second. Do you know that over sixty percent of the dust in your house is dry skin? Where is all the new skin coming from? It's all being pushed through the body, through the vessel. What creates the fluidity in your body? Water. If the body cannot push it through as fast or as efficiently as it should, what happens? The body deteriorates. It gets ill because it is not getting the nourishment it needs. If you have an illness or a battle going on in your body, drink tons of water so that the "fighter cells" can get there fast enough through the pipelines. If they cannot do that because the blood is too thick, then by the time they arrive the damage is so vast that the virus will simply overwhelm the white cells. If you go to get healed physically, have a lot of fluid in your body so that the minerals can electrically spin around your body and zap into where they need to go.

How do you control and destroy addictions?

First, let's look at what an addiction is. Addictions can be looked at in several different ways to make them very simple to understand. In most cases, an addiction is caused by a chemical. But there are other kinds of addictions. There are pain addictions, like when a woman gets battered and leaves her husband. Then she goes back, gets battered and then leaves again. It is a repetitive pattern, but why does it happen? It is because the body starts secreting an aspirin type of chemical to help them deal with the pain. So the brain actually learns to accept it. There are addictions from medications that the body uses to deal with pain, and the brain does the same thing in the case of the battered woman. It learns to accept it, and that is what creates the addiction. It is not necessarily the chemical that is being used; the result of what it is doing causes the addiction.

There are drugs that are also addictive because through the drug, you present building material to the cells of your body. Anything that you orally consume, your body will try to break down and use as a building material. If you use a drug or you take some chemical in orally, your body will try to use it to build cells. So those cells are going to be retarded. They will create cancer, tumors, or an illness because they do not have the common sense to understand the blueprint anymore. They are going to build and construct structures inside of you that just do not make any sense. Eventually, they will build a wall through an artery and that will stop the blood flow to your heart. You will die for no apparent reason and no one is going to know why. The addiction happens because the brain becomes accustomed to using the chemical that has been introduced to the body and creates a release of neurons and electrons. The brain follows a certain pattern, and the drug tells the brain through its chemical properties to release other chemicals that give you the feeling or the result of euphoria.

The brain is habitual; it gets used to doing something a certain way. It will forget how to produce certain things in the way it is supposed to work. Once you deprive the brain of the chemical that it became so dependent on for creating a certain reaction, it creates a craving in you to get more of that chemical. Now that it cannot produce it naturally, it starts screwing up the signals that report to the muscles in your body; to all the organs that secrete chemicals in your body and control the expansion and retraction of the muscles in your body, so the body starts to react. The muscles start to tighten up, which creates friction. Friction creates intense heat which creates intense pains because the nervous system then says that the muscular system is irrationally tightening up. This initiates muscle spasms, which can also start tightening the muscles around your heart. Remember, the heart is also a muscle. Your lungs are controlled by muscles that expand and contract so they could be affected, too. Do you know you could tighten your muscles so tight that it is comparable to steel? The cells intertwine so close and so tight that they become like the same structure that makes steel as strong as it is. So your muscles get so tight that they start clenching around the organs in your body so that they cannot even pump or move the fluid anymore.

An addiction is habit. It is a habit because it forces the brain to secrete a chemical that gives you a certain sense or feeling. The same thing that makes you feel light or relaxed is the brain producing the signal to relax the muscles in your body so they have less stimulation. That makes you feel like you just want to lie around. All these chemicals tell your brain to do stuff that it doesn't want to do. They fool the brain. They lie to it. Your brain controls all your feelings, all your emotions, and all the chemicals that are released to create electrical discharges through chemical reactions. When the brain gets used to a system, a way of existing, it starts to assume that this is the way it is supposed to work. In some cases, you're ripping a chemical pathway open and then you make everything else feel good. But the constant ripping open of the pathway or doorway will eventually destroy the doorway until it collapses and cannot stay up on its own to prevent you from doing anything. Then your brain is all out of control again. The muscles tighten up, the heart tightens up and you die.

The best way to get off of a drug is to go cold turkey. You've got to treat the brain like a child. You've got to say "No!" enough and end the discussion as much as you can so that it's not thinking about it anymore. It has to learn to do things differently and go back to its old ways. In my opinion, the best way is cold turkey. No matter what it is, even heroin. Unfortunately, heroin is one of the hardest drugs to eradicate yourself from. It also tends to be one of the most physically harmful things. Even so, the brain will start telling you, "I want this." It is accustomed to you releasing it into the brain so it starts to think that's a normal thing. When the brain cannot process normally without the drugs anymore and it doesn't have the resources, it starts getting irrational; it starts to panic and creates the feeling that something is very wrong. It tells the body to start going crazy. This is what creates the need to go out and find the drug somewhere.

The next best way to let go of an addiction is to try to wean yourself off of it. But the problem with weaning is how to do it. You still want it so bad that even as you're weaning yourself off of it, the amount you allow yourself to have is not enough. You are never satisfied and you say, "I'm just going to get it this one time. I'll hit the level I want and then I'll wean myself off of it and slowly quit." If you do this, it's like starting all over again when you even have a little. So it goes right back to why cold turkey is the best option.

The brain doesn't just use electricity to think, it also uses chemical reactions. Emotions are the result of various chemicals released in the brain that are reacting with each other. When they hit each other, it's like an explosion. It's a chemical reaction that creates energy which is released in your brain. This creates an electrical impulse that follows down a pathway. It hits the receptor and the brain responds to the chemical combinations. When you shoot up with chemicals and it gets to the brain, those foreign substances hit other natural chemicals creating an alien reaction, which also creates energy. This reaction sends a signal to your brain for it to create a response for the body. When you use the drug, it keeps creating that effect. As the effect of the drug dwindles, the brain just keeps using whatever is there while it searches for more. When the brain cannot find the chemical anymore, you are alright for a while since it needs time to recuperate. Eventually the brain says, "Okay, we need more again," and starts searching the blood for it wondering why it isn't there.

Well, the brain is used to just going to whatever source is easiest to get what it needs to produce what it wants. When it is used to getting the source from outside of the body, it learns. It says, "Okay, you want this, go get it. You need it - fulfill it. You need it NOW!" So you start feeling the desire, the craving. That craving is the nagging desire to fulfill the desire of the brain. It depends on how strong of an impact that source has made on the brain. Also, whatever chemical it is, from heroin to crystal meth, determines how strong that nagging will be because it knows what it wants. It is going to drive you nuts until you relieve it by getting what it craves.

The only thing you can do is to totally purge the body of the chemicals that the brain is searching for. You need to force it to learn to cope and satisfy its needs differently. But the brain does not forget easily and it has a strong desire to go back to whatever is the easiest means of achieving its goal.

I think anybody can relapse because the brain never forgets. Once you experience a drug, it's very difficult to remove. You can remove the temptation of it by avoiding places that may entice you, like bars and similar places. It is always about removing the availability of it. The brain never forgets. Take control of the brain. You have to say enough is enough and purge yourself. That is the best way to resolve your problem.

How would you go about healing a wart, which doesn't seem to be internal like the other ailments we have been discussing?

A wart is a virus that attaches to the DNA of your skin. It changes the original blueprint to create a new map of your DNA structure. This causes the cells of your body to look at the new map and start building this lump of skin. The virus does not build the wart. The virus takes over the DNA of that particular area and the cells create this structure.

Your body will show you how to see things. A good healer sees the organ in their mind. That is the only way that I can describe it. A good healer will actually probe their energy to the source and visualize exactly what they are doing. They actually knit the cells together, seeing them being repaired in their minds as their energy is doing it. That is what I see.

When I visualize a wart virus, I see what looks like a little white hairline worm with hexagonal spine platelets. It lives in the bottom center or on the side of the DNA strand, and it manipulates the actual DNA structure. I see all these hexagonal bits of cells creating the structure, and I see this worm with a hexagonal-like thing going through it. To solve the problem, I zap it, putting my hand where the virus is located. I just give it a little flick of my energy. That blows its brain and it dies. I do the same thing with the whole body system. If the virus is in the whole body system, I flush my energy through the person, sending my energy out at a certain frequency in my mind.

Your blood is like water. Electricity doesn't just move through water. It hops from platelet to mineral platelet. It needs to connect to something in order to move through your body. If you taste your blood, it's very salty because of the minerals. This makes it very easy for electricity to move through your body. If you removed the minerals, your body would be lifeless. Your body has an electrical field. If someone touches you, their energy affects you. It just bounces and ricochets at the speed of light. Well, my brain becomes aware of this entire process. I can see your whole inner-universe. It just depends on how much I want to see. I become aware of what I am looking for. By the time I start to flush my energy through a person, I know what I am looking for. I'm looking for these little white worm-like creatures with hexagonal segments going down through them. I simply zap them, killing them. I just send this signal and it is over. The energy I send runs through the entire body like an electrical wave.

One time when I was flying in an airplane past the city of Hartford, I saw this black cloud that looked like a giant horseshoe. It was huge, bigger than a city. The sun was glowing orange on the top as it was shining down, and below it was very dark. I was watching when, all of a sudden, I saw electricity start in one spot and move – similar to how a crowd flips the signs they are holding while at a football game, like a wave. Electricity wants to travel. It's the same thing in the body. You start at one part of the body and you let the energy, or electricity, move right through it. The electricity kills all of the wart viruses in the body. That is how I know it's cleared. That's how I remove warts. The skin that is recreated is flesh. You can't just snap your fingers and dissipate the wart. With something that micro, it's easy to use just a little bit of electricity to kill it. Flesh is like a building to energy. You have to destroy it using something to remove the structure. But deep inside, whatever made the structure will not recreate it because it has been destroyed.

When I say, 'Zap,' it is the same thing as when I say I am going to heal or work on somebody. There are two kinds of ailments. When there are viruses, you can heal the body by destroying the virus. Those you have to kill. So healing also involves death. Since it is the death of a living organism of some type, you have to kill it in order that the giant living organism is not threatened. Healing also means fixing something cellular; you correct the blueprint so the workers in your body are not confused. There are two different forms of healing that can go on to affect the human body.

Removing a virus is different than healing cancer, tumors, cataracts, etc. You can heal somebody temporarily. If you truly want to heal them, you may have to do multiple sessions. This is because their cells can revert to working on the same old program after you corrected it. You have to work on them a couple of times so that the program is reinforced. If you are a very powerful healer, you can go into that person's brain and affect the change. You just know that the program is being written. The rest of it is not only deleted, but also thrown entirely out the window.

Let's talk about different methods of healing practiced by others. One of the healings you will commonly hear about is called prayer healing. In the same way that I reach in and correct someone's blueprint, prayer healing is a signal that is simply done by telephone. It is like a TV signal that is sent from a tower to an entire city. The signal is picked up on via their television. For prayer healing, you focus on a person saying you want them to be healed. In most cases, that works best when you focus not just on them being healed, but rather when you specifically say, "Heal the heart." Visualize their heart functioning properly when you think about it. So you keep broadcasting this signal to the person. The signal gets stronger because multiple people start sending the same signal. The bandwidth hits and bombards the consciousness of that person, again, reprogramming it. Instead of powerfully sending the signal and then shutting it down to reboot, it starts to slowly inject the commands over days, weeks, and months until it corrects itself. You see the person slowly being healed. Or, all of a sudden, they are healed, depending on how well they receive the signal.

Now, let's bring up something else. Years ago, I was watching a program on TV that showed the screen split in half. On one half of the screen, there was a woman walking down the street. On the other half of the screen, there was an electrometer from a lab. The lab had drawn a sample of her blood a few hours before. They connected her extracted blood to the electrometer, which had a scale from one to one hundred. If there was any stimulation from the woman's blood with the electrodes in it, the result would show up on the meter. The meter would show little movements going from one to three, and one to two because the blood still had electrons and life force in it - living organisms.

The woman started walking and both sides of the screen were synchronized by time. You could see the minutes, seconds, and the date rotating simultaneously. Both sides were set identically. So here she is walking across downtown Los Angeles and a man in front of her turns around and says to her, "Hey lady! You got a light?" The meter shoots up from zero to seventy-five! It just leaps for a second and then it goes back down. She gets into a conversation and it leaps up to ten and then twenty. The numbers usually fall in the ten to fifteen ranges, but it jumped all the way to seventy-five when she got startled. There was nothing connecting her to the blood sample in the lab! There was nothing in between. No one was on the telephone talking. There was no connection whatsoever that we know scientifically. Yet the cells of her body that came from her blood somehow knew and reacted to her being startled, despite being over fifty miles away.

So there is a field of energy that conveys a signal instantaneously at the speed of light. That signal is communicated to the living organisms in her blood which are at the same frequency as the rest of her living body. This example tells us that this type of communication is possible. It is possible to send signals to other people in order to heal them. This is a form of prayer. Prayer is simply a state of repetitive thought, created in the mind, asking or willing something to happen. It boils down to that. It is really a form of meditation. Therefore, under the right conditions, we can heal somebody from a distance. The real question is, "What are these conditions, and can we recreate them in other situations? Can we make them more intense?" The answer is yes.

We understand now that through prayer and will, these things are done. A very similar state of mind, one of the most powerful states of mind, allows you to achieve psychic feats, such as but not limited to healing. That state of mind is a place. Always remember that. It's a place of consciousness where one's mind is residing temporarily. You have to put yourself in a very placid, plain, unthinking state of mind. Clear your mind of all thought and emotion. Then create a very loving, healing feeling, such as the feeling of life. Create a very joyous, positive vibration inside of you. Then bring that person's thought to you. See their face; see them and experience them. Everybody can be experienced. When I look at you, I can feel you. I can feel what you are. It's a tonal. It's a feeling. For instance, your lover has a certain smell. Everyone has a very specific smell. Not only do they have a specific smell, they also have a specific energy that you feel from them when you are in their presence. It is like their essence. You can feel a sense of them. That sense is very different than what you feel when you are close to somebody else. If you've had more than one lover, you know that previous lovers felt very differently to you than your current one. They hold a different feeling inside of you.

Your mother holds a certain feeling for you, doesn't she? Can you visualize your mother right now? See yourself holding your mother. Your mother is holding you; she loves you and you love her. There's a certain feeling that means 'Mom.' You can feel that right now because you are familiar with that feeling. That is tonal. That is frequency. That is 93.6. That's 107.8. Everyone has a specific frequency. That is energy. It is not a mental thing; it is real. It is just that you do not know what to call it. You just say, "Well, that's Mom." What is Mom? What's that feeling? It's a frequency.

After somebody dies, you might hear someone say, "I felt the presence of this person." How did you know it wasn't just a random presence? "Because it was *their* presence," they say. What defined 'their' presence? It's just a knowing. It's just like sight, smell, and taste can be specific. This feeling is just as specific. It's their frequency. It is them. Personalities help to contribute to make one frequency. No person is really just one personality; it is made of thousands of personalities. You have an "inner child." You have an adult in you, a music lover, and also all of the personalities that you act on in different phases of your life. Well, it is really just complex parts of you that make up one being. It is just different weights of measure, such as the part of you that is an artist, dancer, or whatever you see as your particular skills. Everybody's very different, but the combination of all the personalities creates one final tonal.

If you want to tune into someone's tonal, you first clear your mind. Then you create your ritual environment. You never want to do this in a place with dark or dim lights or become methodic. This is very low energy. If you're doing it inside, turn the bright lights on. Better yet, go out to the park with the sunlight and feel the energy, the life, the vibrancy. You're getting ready to heal somebody, not methodically tromp through his or her brain. I dislike all these dark images. I want a premium vibration.

Sit and clear your mind. Take a deep breath. Remove yourself of all thought, all emotion. This is because thought and emotion are selfishness in many ways. Clear yourself of this and any vexation. That includes people that are walking around you, people who are talking, and people who are not allowing you to do what you need to do. You have to be isolated. If somebody walks past your path, it's going to annoy you. In a sense, you're trying to spread wings from your body, your energy. Clear your mind, and remove all of your expectations.

Then create one feeling - love. Create the feeling of absolute love. Not love for your dog or your friend or anything specific. Just love. Then turn around and feel life. Raise it inside of you and feel it; just *feel* it.

Raise the energy inside of you and feel it; just feel it.

Next, invoke the tonal of the person that you want to heal. You obviously should know the person.

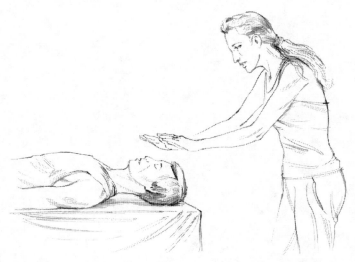

Next, move closer to the person or, if they are not near you, invoke the tonal of the person that you want to heal. Create the feeling, almost as if they are within your reach.

So create the feeling, almost as if they are within your reach, like you're just going to hug them right there. Bring them close to you. Take that love, that light, and push it from your chest, from your stomach, from all of your chakra points and project it into them. Do this with no fear of giving them all of your energy. Just give unconditionally. That's absolute love. It's unconditional. You cannot care if you die. You say to yourself, "If I die, I die. I'm giving because I want to give. Not because I want to give only a little, not because I want to give a lot. I just want to give. There's no amount. There's no quantity." When you give, just feel them and visualize all their illness whisked away, just washed. Envision a light, gold light. It's a feeling. It's like an experience of giving. If they're not near you, then just release everything you built up for that process. Just release it and it finds them.

Take that love, take that light, and push it from your chest, from your stomach, from all of your chakra points and project it into them. You do this with no fear of giving them all of your energy. Give unconditionally. Absolute love.

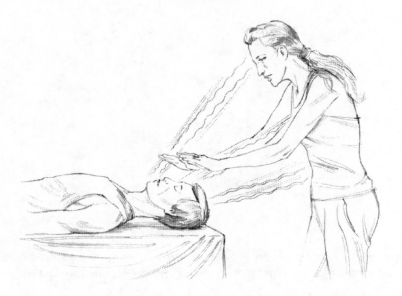

When you give, feel them and visualize all their illness washed away. See a golden light move into them. It's a feeling. If they're not near you, then just release everything you built up for that process. Release it and it finds them.

How does the energy find them?

You just recreated the perfect pitch of them when you recalled their presence, their feeling, and the energy is programmed to that specific frequency now. Again, you visualize them for a moment: their smell, the taste of their skin, the smell of their hair, and the feel of their skin against yours. You create the presence of them. It's a feeling and you release it. You release it with this healing intention. That's the key word: intention. If you don't have the intention, you fail.

The intention is the one key thing that does the job. Love will do what it has to do, but it has to be told exactly what you want it to do. The positive healthy energy and the joy you send is great but you've got to give it an intention. You have to give it a plan to do what you want it to do. Otherwise, it's just going to whisk away into the air and going to be useless energy.

You create this person's energy. You create their presence which creates their tonal – the resonation. It is the station, the signal that they are at. You release the healing energy and the person is just like a beacon. The energy will find the signal and hit it, filling that person. Perhaps there will be a tingle running up their neck or they will get a chill for a second. Or they will just sit there and say, "I don't know why, but all of a sudden I feel like God just walked into my life." They won't necessarily know what happened. On the other hand, maybe they will suddenly feel your presence like the way you just created theirs and sent it to them. They will feel you and recognize your scent. They will feel what it is to think of you and wonder where the thought came from. And their brain is going to say, "Oh, that's Harry," and they will wonder why they are thinking of you.

Whatever it is, there's a reception going on. It's just not the cells of the body or even human beings. For example, Aborigines will cross hundreds of miles to find one another through mental communication – through feelings of vibrations. This is done every day by animals. As human beings, we can control this and make it do specific things by our will or desire. If you create a program -- energy is a program -- you specifically tell energy what to do. You give it intention and you give it a purpose. It knows what it wants to do. Don't make it difficult by trying to make it too complex. Every human being knows perfection; you have the original blueprint. Even if you are old, you still have the original blueprint in your mind. Your brain will know when you invoke perfection. It knows exactly what you're talking about.

If I said to you, "Go get me a glass of water," you know to go to the sink to get me a glass of water. You're not going to ask, "Well, what do you mean? What water? Where? How?" I don't have to tell you. If you are in a house that you have never been in before, and I said, "Please get me a glass of water," you already know to go to the kitchen to find the sink. If you are in the country and there isn't a sink, you know to go outside to fetch a bucket and then go dip it in the pail in the river or the well, if there is one. You just know what to do. Likewise, you know what to do when you go to heal somebody.

You have an intention. With intent, you create. You know what you want the energy to do – to fill the person you want to heal. See it go right into them and illuminate them. But you have to create the light from yourself, from your own living essence. If you do it in nature, feeling the nature of life will simply enhance it. The trees, the grass, the sunlight, and the feeling of life will enhance your own energy. You can draw on that to add to the energy you are creating to send out. That is the kind of energy you can send to someone.

You also can heal yourself the same way. When you sit down to do this, you must do it perfectly. Your mind cannot waiver on one single thought. It is hard, but you start off with small intentions. If you're really determined, you can do a pretty good job. You just have to know that this is what you are going to do. Energy is energy now. Energy doesn't decide whether it is going to be good or bad. It does what it's going to do. If you're in the way, it runs you over. It doesn't go, "Oh, well there's new energy coming in; hang on guys; let's move aside; it's landing!" You've got to have communion with your body. Start feeling for your inner universe; there's billions of living creatures inside of you.

Everybody has to find out what their chi is with themselves. You have to have that communication with yourself. You have to possess an inner peace. Some people have that inner peace. You would think the guru/master would have it. But remember now, there are guru/masters who have died from cancer and other diseases. They somehow lost that communication. Anybody can create that communion and anybody can lose it.

What if the person you want to heal is not open to healing or doesn't believe they can be healed in this manner?

One has to allow someone to heal them so it really comes down to trust. I think somebody can heal you, but if you don't really trust them, your energy is not going to allow them to heal you completely. The energy will be conflicted. I'll explain how I know this.

In a study done with Kirlian photography, they took pictures of a person's finger that showed the energy glowing around their finger. You could see little fiery illuminated spikes of different shades of blue and red that were very vibrant. When they introduced another person's finger separately, it looked similar. But when they put them together, their energies would fight. It would dart at each other like a crackling fire, as if they were fighting violently. However, one finger would eventually dominate the other.

Conversely, they discovered that when two people who cared for each other came together and were comfortable with each other, the energy would merge together showing a beautiful color. Your energy is connected to your mind. It is all the same thing. It is just a matter of working with this field of energy.

I believe that if you want to be healed, you have to accept what the person offering to heal is going to do. Basically, all the cells in your body must trust the other person. They are not going to hurt you. They are not out to destroy you. If you accept what the healer is trying to do, you will be better for it in the end. The healer works with your energy, visualizes whatever is wrong, and tries to correct it.

The same applies when healing yourself; it is all about having inner trust and understanding yourself. Trust that you can heal yourself. You must accept that you coexist with an entire physical organism that is one with you. The body doesn't have a choice. Yet your whole body, every square inch of it, no matter how deep, how wide, or how you look at it, is composed of billions of living organisms of which you are in charge.

By communicating in this way, you can get your body to heal itself to become healthy. Instead of accepting that you are becoming old, work with age; you can work with everything. Just sit down and create these feelings. Create and work with yourself through emotion, sending this invocation of spirit. If your mind is not in the right place, you're not going to send the correct signal. There is a difference between reaching out to somebody and saying, "Okay, you're healed," or invoking an honest desire to say, "I want you to just be healed. I want you to be better." Do you feel the difference? This is energy. It is real.

You have to invoke a sense of spirit in yourself. Spiritual people say that you can feel the spirit and the spirit feels you. It's not something coming into you. It's you becoming the spirit. It was always there. You simply realize it and revel in that emotion. You allow it to be birthed inside of you. It was always there.

To truly heal someone, you must genuinely have compassion. You have to remove all of your desires and every sense of selfishness. Remove your ego that makes you say in your head, "I'm going to heal this person and they will think I am great." The body can sense all of this, so you must be filled with compassion. Unconditional love is the intention. You have to communicate through energy. Energy is feeling an emotion. You just have to relax and just surrender.

Chapter 6

FURTHER DISCUSSIONS ON HEALING

AT THE END of this chapter, I am going to do a healing session for you. Please make sure that you are in a quiet, safe location where no one will bother you or disturb you.

I want to make this very clear. I have to do this for other reasons as I am sure that you will understand since I am not a medical doctor. If you feel that you want to apply any of this advice, always be sure to talk to your physician or seek one out for medical advice. Let me start by stating that I personally use a medical physician from time to time whenever needed. I use modern medicine. I believe in utilizing every single tool that is available. The idea is to feel well and be well. You can always utilize modern medicine while you're working on healing yourself psychically, spiritually or mentally. I do not have any negative feelings toward that.

I am also open to various forms of healing and other forms of alternative medicine, whether it is Rolfing, Reiki, Qi Gong, or something else. I think they all are great and can be utilized with the programs that I teach. Additionally, acupressure or acupuncture are great systems to look for, but find somebody who is very knowledgeable when you seek them. I think that there are a lot of people who are entering the field of alternative health care, but I'm not completely confident that they are as skilled as they should be. If you choose someone in this field, choose wisely.

When you say you went to 'your place,'
what are you talking about and how do you
create your own place to work from?

When I say 'my place,' obviously I'm referring to an inner sense, an inner zone that I draw upon. It is a certain state of mind. I go to that place much like if I was sitting down to meditate. I go to a quieter, clear state of mind. Of course, I remove thought as we understand it, as you've learned in the *Foundation* chapter in my book, *Meditation Within Eternity*. By doing that, I can operate from a higher state of consciousness without the *Babbler* being an issue.

A friend of mine was recently in a serious car accident. His leg was broken in two places and they had to put a titanium bar in there. It was a very complicated surgery. It was also very interesting. He stayed at my home during his healing process and I worked with him to improve his healing process.

I let him borrow my athletic style regenerating shorts. They're dark blue, 100% cotton. I was explaining to him that whenever I get sick or I don't feel well or something happens to me physically, I feel compelled to wear these particular shorts. When I wear them, I regenerate faster. The shorts heal my body. It's as if my cellular structure is healing.

So he went ahead and tried them on. His leg was completely swollen and had severe bruising. When I say bruising, it was black like ink all over the lower region. So when he tried them on, the very next day he was shocked at how much healing had taken place. Within two or three days, all of the bruising had disappeared in that area. The swelling dropped dramatically and his doctor was impressed.

So he was asking me if it is psychological, like a placebo effect. Or is there really something to this? I explained to him that it's the same thing as in the *Ties that Bind* chapter in my book, *Meditation Within Eternity*. There is something that I call programmable energy or programmable information that can be put into objects that will radiate information.

Those shorts are probably twenty years old. I don't even know when I bought them. Evidently, I was sick one time that I wore them and went into a really deep state of mind that instigated a deep healing process. I believe that I was wearing those shorts at the time. In that process, I imbued, or programmed, them to heal intensely and to radiate that healing information into them.

It is not necessarily that the shorts have some kind of cosmic or magical power. It's a program within the fabric. When I see cotton in my mind, I see millions of hairs of microfibers - a writable or programmable surface. I impacted the fibers of those shorts with a healing program. When a person holds them or wears them, they become active. In other words, you are like a battery and the shorts are the object that is turned on. If you have a small radio, it can do remarkable things by capturing sound and music, but it is useless without the batteries. You cannot hear the music without the radio. So it's like you are the battery being placed into the radio or in this case the shorts. It activates the shorts using your own energy field. Then the program reverberates back into your body, thus communicating consistently like a rhythm that tells the cells to work in a very positive and rigorous manner to create the healing process, which is much more rapid than normal.

If you want to learn more about that, I do recommend reading the *Ties That Bind* chapter in *Meditation Within Eternity*. It talks about different methods of programming things. You can adapt it from the original subject matter and utilize it with objects like clothing to program it so that when you wear it, it consistently works with your body to amplify your healing process.

**How can we harness the white fire, the
Prana, to heal ourselves and others?**

This can be very complicated. Most people have a lot of misconceptions about the concept of healing. This happens a lot in the paranormal, metaphysical, and spiritual fields. So many people have muddied it up that a lot of the true power is misguided or misdirected by people who have 'candy-coated' the concept or dressed it up a certain way.

When healing, you can take in Prana and project that energy out to heal another person. However, when you take in that same Prana and try to use it on yourself, it does not necessarily work that way. I could scan other people's consciousness or read the future, but I always found it extremely difficult to do it on myself.

It's like a river that flows outward. If you reverse that whole river, it just botches up the whole ecosystem. When most people try to heal others, they direct energy through their hands. Psychologically, in our minds, when we try to heal ourselves, we're often at a loss because our hands want to reach out to a second person. We've trained ourselves to work that way by channeling our energy in that manner.

So now you have to think of a different process to be used to heal the self. That involves going within your own mind or your own consciousness, which is similar but different. In other words, you have to think in terms of regenerating or amplifying the healing process through your own mind. The mind has a Governor that will or will not allow healing on yourself; so you have to get through this whole mind game thing first.

When you are projecting energy and working on other individuals, there seems to be less of a Governor to prevent you from projecting out that energy. It seems to be easier when you work on other people. When it comes to working on yourself, it's a much bigger challenge. I don't think there's any diabolical reason behind it. It's just the way it seems to work through nature, and it is an issue.

When you ask, "How do I work on other people or how do I work on myself for healing," it is two completely different subjects that need addressing. Not only that, but when you look at the individual self, you are your own worst enemy. The brain really regulates and throws up a lot of barriers to filter out programming to your cells.

Your body is designed to follow a blueprint that tells everything how to function, how to heal. There are red cell workers and white cells that go after viruses. There's a certain design, and as much as your body doesn't want to have outside diseases infiltrate, it also prevents positive programming. Also, it doesn't really acknowledge the difference between the two. This is where it becomes a bigger challenge to personally heal yourself. This is why it's easier for you to be healed by another person. They can focus their energy on keeping their mind clear so that you can receive that energy. It's as if they can focus more of their energy on subduing the Governor in their own mind. They can subdue the Governor and also work on healing themselves.

I'm not saying it can't be done. It certainly is possible, as I do it. Other people can do it, but it is a lot harder. Of course, there are ways to get around the barriers. I believe that the more that you know, the more empowered you become. If you don't understand the reason that something is working, you're completely helpless to affect it. If you have an understanding of how it works, then at least you have an angle to deal with the

For me, one of the side effects of healing people is that horrible things happen to my own body, like enormous pain and vomiting. I am sometimes exhausted for about a week after that. I've tried High Guard and it still goes through me.

In my book, *Igniting the Sixth Sense*, I talk about *High Guard*. It's a way of protecting yourself or others from various kinds of energy attack. In this case, *High Guard* isn't working because you are doing what I call 'decoding.' Decoding happens to a lot of good healers who do exceptional work. Unfortunately, they do it at a price to themselves. They mirror the illness of the person they are working on. They almost literally create the illness within themselves in order to sample or experience it. In this way, they are able to come up with the solution, the cure, or the cellular decoding information that must be projected back into the patient so that their cells can now understand how to start resolving their problem. Since you can control your consciousness as a healer, you need to sample their frequency, that information.

Although I take the illness inside me, my immune system seems to prevent me from getting gravely like them.

You will end up with about ten percent of the reverberation of the disease. That is what you take into your system so your body reacts to it, like an echo of the disease. You might not get cancer but in the process of decoding, your body has taken on some intensity from the disease, which comes out now in your own physical illness or purging. It really comes down to better filtering and better consciousness of what you are doing.

There's not a simple answer that I can give in a situation like this because everybody's uniquely different. You need to recognize the mirroring effect and the process that you are working in. You almost have to sit down and go into a meditative state of mind and articulate what you want your body to do. This is you dealing with yourself, your own inner universe. So you say, "I'm going to be inviting, past my guards, an enemy in order to help this person. Obviously, I've got to learn who this enemy is, but I don't want any of this to remain. It's not of me but we need to do this and I need to recognize that this is not of me."

It gets complicated because in order for you to come up with a decoding process, you have to almost convince your body that there's a crisis and that you've just taken this crisis on. Your body has a higher mastery of coming up with the solution if the problem stems from itself.

So in your case, you've invited the illness in. That's the problem. Your body does not understand whether this is friend or foe since you've invited it in. Now your body is going crazy trying to solve the problem. When it finally does come up with a resolution, you are spent because you had an exhausting fight. You then project the answer back to the other person. But now you've got to heal yourself.

Start communicating to yourself your game plan. Instead of surprising the body by taking on the mirror image of this person's illness, communicating will help your body to solve it. Say to your body, "This is what we've got to do but I want you to understand that in no way am I trying to harm you, so don't get sick. We're just going to study it. We're going to find the answer. Then we're going to send it back and clear it."

It's probably going to take several times doing that before you see any significant results. It's difficult because you are telling your body to absorb the illness so you lower your guard in order to help the person you are healing, but it's taking a piece of you. The only thing you can do is to mentally prepare, not so much on the process, but by telling your body that this is not a real attack. That is my recommendation.

When somebody wants to be healed, how do you know that they're ready for it?

It's been my experience that people love to say that they are ready for things when they are clearly not. My mind gets into these crazy spiraling dilemmas of, "Well, how do they really know that they want to be healed or don't want to be healed? What if it's this? What if it's that?"

Obviously, anybody wants to be healed from an illness. The problem lies within our deeper psyche; it is a vulnerability issue. Some people psychologically use their illness to get attention or as a way to manipulate others. It's become a tool for them. Although they say they want to be healed, deep within they resist your healing process because they really don't want to be healed. It's because *their illness is a strong part of who they think they are.*

Sit down with them. Clear your mind, and simply put your hands outward in the sense of feeling without touching or breathing them in. When you do that, it's always important to tell your body that you are bouncing something off of you. Don't feel that it's a true attack on your person. Let's say I want to use your knowledge to help this person, but not to induce this feeling inside of you to take it on as an illness. That's an important statement.

Ask yourself through your Navigator, your inner knowing, "Is this person really ready to be healed?" And you will know the answer. The question really is, "Will you listen to yourself?"

Are you saying it is very much an intuitive thing with the person that you are healing?

You already know the answer on a person to person basis. You already know if they want to be healed. However, there's a rationalization going on inside of your mind that's trying to determine if they want to be healed. You are rationalizing that there is a problem. You know the process should be working, but something is not working correctly. You already know that they are resisting the healing.

Let's say you go to a person that you are going to work on, and all of a sudden you have this conscious thought that maybe they are not ready to be healed. The real question is, "Where did that thought come from?" Ninety percent of the people want to be healed. You're getting that question mark in your own mind because something is raising a red flag. It's your psychic sensory telling you that this person is resisting because they don't want to be healed.

You have to trust your inner knowing. As a healer, one of the most acute senses is the ability to pick up on someone's emotional sensory. A lot of healing is echoing. It's about imprinting that person, or feeling that person inside of you. When you heal, it's as if you feel their essence inside of you and you know where to go. It's like you can feel their pain inside of you; you are reacting to a blueprint in your mind that is within your own consciousness. If you pay very specific attention to yourself when you are healing, you will see that you are doing a lot of echoing, a lot of reflecting.

It's like a mirror image of them that is holographically superimposed within your own body. You use your own body to decipher, decode, and project what you need to work on that problem. Then you push it back outside of yourself so that you can work on them. When you feel in doubt, there is a reason for that and you shouldn't question your own sensory. You shouldn't feel obligated to follow through with that healing because, in the end, it's your time and it's also your energy.

If you feel that person is not ready, you need to say, "I'm feeling that we need to wait on this. As much as I would like to work on you, I feel right now that you need to be more psychologically prepared to work with me. I feel that there may be a little bit of a resistance right now. That is what I think we need to focus on before we start working on deeper healing."

Some people may ask, "Why is it that certain things seem to work better when you're healing someone and certain things don't work as well?" When I was a very young man, I did a lot of healing work. After that, I went into other areas. I decided to teach, to project what I had learned, decoding that information.

In my own mind, I really see a lot of things separately. In my opinion, working on a tumor or with cancer is easier to do than working on somebody who is a diabetic. Somebody might say, "What difference would that make?" I would say to them that cancer or a tumor is like rampant cellular pandemonium that can be reorganized a lot easier. I guess it is a healer's perspective. That is the only way I can explain it. It's something you internalize as a knowing.

In many cases, working with the pancreas on diabetes is a DNA or genetic issue. DNA is what tells your body to have five fingers, five toes, two legs and two ears through your master design. So, in the case of diabetes, that master design or blueprint is not recognizing that it is flawed. It's following its natural process of design. People who have diabetes have either type one or type two.

There is not one answer for every type of illness. In many cases, diabetes can run in a family. You can look at it generation after generation. It can kick in at the age of thirty or forty years old. Of course, obesity is often part of the problem, but there are other circumstances, too. Each ailment is different and should be treated differently.

I believe that the approach to healing should vary depending on the situation. There are many healers who have one method of healing, like one size fits all. I strongly disagree with that approach because I think you can yield a lot better results if you adapt your healing to specific types of ailments.

I think that a lot of immune system problems stem largely from the brain. Rather than saying you need to heal the body of immunity issues, you have to address the brain or you will never quite solve that problem. It's just going to recur a day later or sometime in the future. You must work with the brain because it's sending the wrong signals. It's getting the wires crossed and it's sending out the wrong message.

If you address the problem from its source, you will solve it. There are different kinds of healing approaches that I would recommend for different things. Again, everybody is different. You must work with each unique situation differently. You can use energy movements to stimulate different regions of the brain. Energy movements will help the development of corrective nerve development. This is going to allow proper communication to the rest of the body.

In my opinion, there is not one universal method that works for everything. You could say that all of them deal with some form of energy, some form of programming. I think that the overall technique can be very psychic, whether it is hand movements, breathing, mind balancing, taking in Prana, physically walking or physically.

Your muscles can retain negative impressions of information. That memory is not only in your brain, but it is also cellular in your muscles. Therefore, you might want to go for a Rolfing session. You have to find the correct healing process to solve your particular problem. If you do not see the results you wanted, either you need to go to a different type of healer or try something different. Always remember, "Never give up."

The answer is out there; the hard part is finding the correct solution. There are many cases of great healers who had tremendous results with certain individuals but nothing with other people. Those other people, however, went to a different healer and received the results they were looking for. It depends on the illness, how you treat it, and the healer's ability.

Another situation might be that your immune system or your body is very ill and you have taken some toxins into your body. Let's say lead paint or some toxic minerals. Now it's not only in your body, but it is also in your intestines, blood, and fatty tissue. I think that you can only do so much to help someone, but they have to also take responsibility for themselves.

There are a lot of people who don't know what I am saying. I strongly recommend that you go to a regular physician, but you should also consider going to a naturopathic doctor, which you can find in a phone book. I have found situations where a metaphysical doctor is able to do things for people whereas an allopathic or traditional doctor is often mystified by this.". If you want to take a different course in your healing work, you may wish to train as a naturopathic doctor. They tend to be very knowledgeable. It takes many years of schooling to be acknowledged as a naturopathic doctor and to gain the needed credentials for this work. Those are a few things that I wanted to mention.

I've done some healing with mixed results. I have a feeling that it has to do with my own perception of whether or not I am overstepping my boundaries. I know that affects my capabilities. So, is my perception of whether it is the right thing to do or not affecting my results?

Of course, it's the right thing to do. It's your nature. Healing comes as naturally to you as breathing, walking, and eating. It is something that you exist for. A healer has a calling inside of them. It's maternal instinct. There is no getting rid of it. A healer feels the need to help those who are in need and they cannot help themselves. The other person also has to want to be healed. That doesn't mean you cannot work with remote healing, which is healing from a distance when the other person lives elsewhere. A person is always going to receive better if they're open to your frequencies, your projections, and your work. Remember, healing has an intention.

With some people, it's psychologically in their nature not to trust because maybe they were hurt or somebody tried to take advantage of them. Maybe something happened to them in their youth. In the back of their mind, they hold all of these different barriers, different forms of resistance. When you're going to work with someone, I think it's very important to spend a great deal of time working with them psychologically before you use your own energy to work with them. Healing is a lot of work and it uses a very pure energy. You do not want to exhaust yourself on someone who filters out a great portion of the energy that is meant to help the cellular structure of their body.

Before you put your passion into helping someone, it is very important for that person to truly be ready to receive that gift from your heart because you are really giving a piece of yourself. Any healer who heals somebody else gives a piece of their soul. That is how deeply they work. They are literally giving something of themselves. It's not that they are giving their soul away, but there's a piece or an essence of themselves that they give to heal the broken pieces of the other person. It is like taking a piece of your heart out and saying, "I'm going to give this to you. I don't need it as much as you do. I'll be fine."

I've suffered from anxiety for as long as I can remember. What can I do now to try to reverse the effects of my anxiety?

A lot of people don't have a deep understanding of anxiety or anxiety attacks but they are very intense and can absolutely overwhelm a person.

Many people may be asking, "Well, what does this have to do with healing?" It has everything to do with healing. Mind, body, and spirit are all a healing process. Your goal is to be the best that you can be to reach your highest potential. Whether you realize it or not, your health and the state of your mind are interconnected. Trouble in one area will affect your overall results. Do you feel that you can hike up a mountain if you have the flu? Of course, you can't. Well, on the same token, if you are mentally depressed or you have anxiety, you will not want to hike up the mountain either. This is all a form of illness that you want to conquer.

The first thing is for you to recognize that it is in your mind. I would recommend using reading the chapter *Foundation* in my book *Meditation Within Eternity* and learning to have greater control of the mind. In this particular case, I would recreate things that are the trigger points of your anxiety. You probably have a few triggers, whether or not you know what they are.

> Over the past year, I've pondered the cause
> of my anxiety. But having the knowledge and
> actually applying it are two different things.

In the first chapter, *The Power of Surrender*, there are some pretty intense techniques that would definitely help you a lot. One of the basic concepts is that you recreate your memories. Your triggers come from events that have happened to you. You experienced something or your brain photo mapped a situation. So it actually wired itself around other normal processes and put the memory into a place in your brain that reacts intensely. You need to teach yourself to reprogram that process in your brain.

You also need to realize that it is triggering endorphins to be released from glands in your body. So that is creating the reaction in your body.

There's a class that I teach called *Reverse Engineering the Self*. It is a powerful, powerful tool. If you really want to get in your head, remove a lot of the deep-rooted stuff, and tune up your brain, that's the material you should use.

Are these tools used with the guided meditation?

Absolutely, the guided meditation from *Meditation Within Eternity* is powerful. Everything in that book is useful. It gives you a whole system, like a car and an engine. Each chapter gives you parts like the fog lights, a better muffler, or combustion system.

By helping other people, you sometimes heal yourself. For me, working, helping, and healing other people really healed me personally. Sometimes it is through watching other people's breakthroughs that you will be healed, too. Think about that.

I do a lot of emotional healing work on people. They do a lot of work to help themselves but so many issues keep coming up that they ask whether they are ever going to be healed.

I'll tell you what I would say to them, "You are done whenever you **decide** that it has ended." Sometimes you've got to offend people a little bit for them to get the message. Sometimes the biggest breakthroughs happen just when you spell it out for them. Sometimes people are their own worst enemy. When you anticipate, assume, feel, or just know that you're beaten in a situation that means something else has won.

I would say to them that, "You need to start being more positive. Do self-reflection and say to yourself, 'I overcame this and I overcame that.' List all of the problems that were solved and reflect on that. Be happy with what you have achieved and maybe the other problems will not be so terrible. If you can start thinking like that, the rest should be easy to solve."

You program your own mind. Many people are ill on their own accord. It is because of their own acceptance of the illness, their own mental brutality to themselves. Be an optimist, not a pessimist.

My wife's had multiple sclerosis for many years. I was able to feel the physical pain in her body once. When I got there, I couldn't do anything with it. I couldn't handle the pain myself. I couldn't release it. I'm no longer able to invoke the love and the joy needed to heal her. She was

hit with four major attacks, over a four month period. She's half paralyzed now. Her biggest problem is fatigue.

I think you need to bring in some professionals now. See if you can find someone who does Rolfing, and someone who has a Reiki background. If you are not in the best position financially to do that, a lot of times people will work for free or for some kind of exchange. They will be able to give you the support that you need and also deliver some relief to her and some form of positive progress.

At this point, my advice is to seek additional help. If you've dealt with this for a long time and you are exhausted, it would probably be better to bring in some people who are fresh to take this to the next level. You still have to make the effort to find them.

Okay, it's time to proceed with a healing process. Again, you want to lie down or be in a reclining chair or something comfortable. If you're going to be sitting, the chair should have arms. Or you can just lie down. I don't want anyone to get a heavy wave of energy and then all of a sudden fall over and hurt themselves. You want be prepared for the best situation.

So let me cover a few things before we get started. When I refer to the Universe, I am referring to God. Or if I say God, I'm referring to the Universe because I see it all as one thing.

Also, part of this method is what I call "broadcasting." I'm going to act as a conduit and I am going to tune myself into a higher frequency. Then I will project the desired energy, a healing vibration, outward into this dimension. So the idea of this healing is to let it affect you biologically, physically, emotionally, and spiritually, whichever way you think you need to start your healing process.

So when I say certain things, it is to help get you focused. It is to help get past your *Babbler*, your *Governor*, and your mind. There is no ego on my part. I am really just trying to get the best results. That's always my goal. I just want results so I am going to use tactics or methods that I feel will ultimately deliver the best results for you. Therefore, I don't want you to be rationalizing what I am saying. Try to just go with it and trust where I am taking this.

At this point, I want you to be in a lying or a sitting position, taking it easy. You shouldn't have any music playing in the background. Hopefully, there are no other people in the room to disturb you, unless they're actively participating.

Some people might hesitate to help themselves with healing because of the fear of acting out. It's like watching people dancing. There is a part of you that would like to dance, but there is also a reservation inside of you that refuses to let you do it because you'll feel silly. If you feel silly doing something, that prevents you from achieving the best results in this particular experience. Keep that in mind. You have to remove any reservations that you may have. Do not filter things. Just go with it. Also, some people are going to be more receptive than others. So it's my job to think in terms of individuals who are going to be on the more difficult side and work on their level so they can have the breakthroughs they need. It will elevate upwards to those who receive more easily.

I want you to relax. Take a nice deep breath in through your nose and exhale out through your mouth. One more time, in through your nose and out through your mouth. I want you to relax your body and just let everything get nice and heavy. Sink into the chair or into the couch or into the floor or wherever you may be. Just relax your body.

We're going to go through a mild level of hypnosis to work out any kind of mental or physical stiffness. I want you to keep your eyes shut and relax. I'm going to allow myself to go into that zone. I want to count from ten downward.

As I'm counting down, I want you to see yourself sinking, letting your muscles become looser and looser; like sand just seeping to the ground slowly. Ten, going down, down, down, deeper, deeper, deeper, relaxing your body, nine, feeling relaxed and comfortable going down, down, down, deeper, deeper, deeper, sinking into the couch, sinking into the chair, all the muscles getting nice and heavy.

Relax. Feeling your jaw slip downward from your mouth, your cheeks relaxing, muscles in your forehead relaxing, we're just going to go from nine, down to eight, seven, six, going down, down, down, feeling in your chest a nice big breath coming in and exhaling; letting your whole body exhale and sink deeper.

That's it. Your mind is clear, drifting away, just like clouds on a summer day, floating by; it's nice and warm out; five going down, down, down, deeper, deeper, deeper, four, going down, down, down, deeper, deeper, deeper, feeling relaxed and comfortable, three, sinking, getting heavier, letting your eyes close, taking another nice deep breath in through your nose, and exhaling. As you exhale, your body is just getting heavier, heavier, heavier, two, and one. Now, feeling relaxed and comfortable, I want you to focus on me. If you know what I look like, or if you've seen a picture of me, I want you to think about me right now because right now I'm thinking about you. My mind is reaching out through time and space to you. I'm asking you a question, "Are you ready to be healed?" I need a better answer than that. I need to feel you. I need you to emotionally tell me, "Yes!" Tell me you are ready to be healed. Now I feel it.

Take a nice deep breath in. When you take a deep breath in, I want you to imagine that you're breathing white light. Positive energy, part of me into you, right now. Moving into you, filling you, becoming one with you, tuning with you. Now I want you to think about me. See me; feel me; sense me; send your love to me. I'm going to send my love to you. Now I'm going to broadcast healing energy to you. I'm going to do an Aum. As I do that, my mind is vibrating towards you. You are to inhale and let it move through your body, "Aaaaaauuuummm." Take a breath in.

Now I want you to take your hands, reach them outward, palms forward and out. Lifting up into the air, now you're going to say out loud, "I choose to be healed. I choose to be healed."

I'm going to broadcast to you now, "Aaaaaauuuummm." Breathe in through your hand, reaching out as if you were to touch God. Allow God to touch and move through you, healing every cell of your body. Let it flow through you. Receive. Trust it. Let it move through you. Feel the passion and the trust, "Aaaaaauuuuummmm."

Repeat after me, "Universe, I am your humble and grateful servant. If you heal me, I can serve you well. Let me serve you." Take a deep breath in. And exhale. Moving from your feet upward, breathing in, and pulling energy upward. Moving, as if light was moving up through your body and out through your head. And so it is.

Thank you for your time. Reflect a few moments on the inner peace that you have. Resonate with it. This healing session is a permanent signal that is out there now. All you have to do is tune into it by focusing on this session. The more that you can allow the trust to move through you, the more that it will work with the cells of your body and expand your own healing process to accelerate it.

Chapter 7

TIME STEPPING

SOME OF MY students have asked me if I believe that it will be possible to time travel in the future. I believe it is possible to time travel right now with the availability of technological resources, but it is just a matter of time for it to actually happen. Only a specific type of person would be able to do it, and it would have to be controlled. If everybody could do it, the consequences of altering the timeline would be devastating.

A person could totally destroy the existence of all humanity. Something as simple as intervening or meeting someone that should have been somebody else's mother or father would have an effect on time. What if a time traveler accidently delays a man on the sidewalk so that he does not walk across the street and bump into the woman that he was meant to originally meet? What if their pending relationship could have resulted in the possibility of a third generation President of the United States? It may be that simple, that fragile.

How would you control something like that? Would you just walk around without bumping into anyone?

If you were a time traveler, you would need to have an excellent understanding of history. You would know the places you could go, and also the locations to avoid. You might have to be anonymous so that no one knows who you are or what you are doing, or even anything about your existence. You might have to take on the concept of a typical life, meaning living the most average life you possibly could. You would take on a job and a whole new persona without anybody ever knowing that you come from the future.

I once saw a very interesting movie about a group of people who came from the future. They started a tour guide business taking people from the future back to the past to witness a variety of different events, such as when a meteor hits and destroys an entire city. They rented a house that was above the city so they could have a view of the whole event, and they did this during the significant events in history. I thought it was a very interesting, fascinating concept.

Let's say you study with me for a long time and by doing so you become spiritually evolved; so evolved that maybe you can affect time and space. Imagine that someday far in the future, maybe forty years from now, you become highly developed and are with a group of people who have advanced technology. You are mutually respected because of who and what you are, and vice versa. What if you had an opportunity to go back in time to observe something? What if you could go back and say to yourself, "Have faith. Keep going. You're doing the right thing. You've made the right decision."

So when would you decide to go back? If the future is happening now, you're already there. So this current moment has already passed. When would you decide is the right time and the right place to come back in time to say something to yourself? When do you think you would be mature enough to appreciate yourself coming back?

Can you just imagine this scenario? You'd obviously be more intelligent, well-rounded with more wisdom than you have right now. How would you look at yourself right now from that perspective? Would you say that you are worthy enough to give yourself that type of recognition? Or would you wait for next year, the following year, or ten years from now? Is it possible that you would never want to do that because you could not even begin to appreciate that kind of knowledge at that point in your life?

I would come back earlier in life. I think I'm ready now because the earlier I receive the knowledge, the more I will be able to motivate myself. I want more time to better myself so that I can get to a point of higher understanding. I think I could appreciate something as profound as seeing myself as an old man coming back to talk to my younger self.

Do you think you are ready now? As an older being, with wisdom gained from decades of practice, do you think that on the 28th of July in 1997 you would make your presence known? When you walk out to your car by yourself to get something out of your trunk, is that when you're going to appear and have a little conversation with yourself.

I think time is of the essence.

Why not six months from now? Why didn't you already do that for yourself six months ago?

Well, I don't know. I'm not in control of that right now.

What will you be and how will you make those decisions? That's what I want you to imagine. Do you have any input on that?

I would have to be at that level of wisdom to know what would be the best move at the right place and time to have the highest effect. I don't know that right now. What if you get to the point where you can time travel and talk to yourself, but this conversation changes your life? Perhaps you will not get to a place where you can go back since you already changed your past. Is this a possibility?

Absolutely, that could be a major factor. Your presence could be the catalyst that destroys whatever future you might have. Maybe it removes the drive of your will to reach enlightenment, or the pivotal peak of enrichment. Maybe, because of the visit, you say to yourself, "Well, what the hell. I know I'm going to make it anyway." That simple thought could prevent you from ever achieving it.

You must think about the massive amount of consideration that is necessary to make this type of decision. For you to say so quickly, "the sooner the better," shows me that you would never choose now as the moment if you had the wisdom and the knowledge of time stepping. You could not tell another soul that you met yourself because if you did that, you would be considered insane. Or you would simply affect the decisions and thoughts of those people who hadn't come to any conclusions about reality or spirituality. They would have new thoughts and conclusions all based on the certainty that you can travel through time because you came back and said, "This is what happened." I've thought about what I would do if I were looking back from the future and decided that I wanted to make a big impact on my students. I asked myself, "Where and when would I show up in the past to present myself to them and how would I do that?"

After a little bit of thought, I asked myself the question, "Wouldn't it be wiser to travel through time with an inconspicuous friend or partner?" It could be your future wife that nobody has met yet, or your husband that you will not meet for another twenty years. Then you could have that person at the most challenging time in your life intervene and say, "Don't worry. Everything's going to be alright. Everything is going to be just fine. Trust me."

Of course, you would be standing off in the distance behind a car or van or in a parking lot observing the conversation. So you're watching the moment happen, the memory that you created in your mind where you experienced your spouse from the future coming to the past to say hello to you. But you didn't know it was him at that time. Can you follow that?

Yeah. Déjà vu?

In a sense, **déjà vu** is a very good point. Is it déjà vu or is it you intervening in your own history, your own time, your own moment right here, right now? You believe it to be déjà vu because everything logical would say that it is déjà vu, but yet perhaps it is you manipulating yourself from the future.

Wouldn't it also depend on your perspective?

Yes, perspective is very important. Remember, we also live in a universe where there is truly no right and wrong. Everything is argumentative; everything is incomplete; and everything can be taken from a completely different perspective. We have to look at things from different angles. We have to look at things so meticulously that it will prove right here, right now, if you're even worth the time to travel back to. This very conversation is pivotal to your history. You may reflect on this very moment, this very discussion fifty years from now to decide when was the best time to do this, that day, that hour, that week, that month.

Now, let me propose something even more interesting to you. Let's say that physically traveling through time would be a little bit too advanced for you. What if you discovered, with ample thought through psychic means or mental thought, that you could project knowledge from the future into the past? You could receive this knowledge although you may not understand where it is coming from. Suddenly, you could comprehend things so much faster and easier, from an unknown source.

So déjà vu lives then? Wouldn't it be easier to accept if it was in your dreams at that time?

Yes, dreams, déjà vu, or something else. Everybody has an inner thought, like the alter ego in your mind. Have you ever had a conversation with yourself and pretended the other side of the conversation is somebody more knowledgeable than you? It could be a parental figure, a spiritual figure, or a wise person. Nobody really admits to this, but there's another part of you that counsels yourself, like a second person you create within your own mind.

To me, that's more like my soul counseling my rational mind.

That's fine, but it's still a secondary state of mind. There's a separation. Now we know through psychology you can have over one hundred forms of personalities in your mind. You are literally a multifaceted person. You really are what would be diagnosed as a multi-personality person.

So we're all schizophrenic?

More or less, but we are socially acceptable because we are the many. There are times you feel foolish, artistic, like a super being, or like crap. Why aren't you just one of those? Why do you consistently fluctuate through different characters of the mind? They're still all rooted to your core, but there's a variety of conscious thinking going on. *What if one of those inner consciousnesses is you from the future, broadcasting thought to help you cope with your life in the present?* This way you have support during the one time that there was no one else here for you. You sent yourself from the future to the past, to be there for yourself. Isn't that interesting?

Very. Don't you think it's also possible to go in the other direction? Being in the present and trying to project into the future?

That is a very good question to ask. It brings up my next point. Get ready for your brain to jog. Moving backwards from the future to now is no different than moving forward from now to the future. It's all one thing. It's all the same thing. Think about it. If the future is already prewritten and the past is already written, what difference does it make where you are? There's only one thing that matters: realization. When you can realize this thought and it makes sense to you, you are partially enlightened. You are no longer a part of the future or the past. By having self-realization, time stops. Although here in the matrix it's moving, you now have a choice to function in the hologram.

By understanding this information, is it possible to project a message from the future to ourselves here in the present to help us?

Absolutely.

So you're saying this concept is controllable.

Yes. It's absolutely fully controllable with training. For example, around the year 1989, I sent myself a conscious thought at a very troubling time in my life when I was sitting out in a field on a stump. It was a grassy area and I was going through trying times when I heard a message from myself. The message instructed me clearly how to deal with the situation. I did as I was told and it worked out perfectly. Only later, in the future, did I think and reflect on that moment wondering, "If I could only do this, I would." With that in mind, I sat down and attempted a particular method of thought so that I could broadcast it, the same as the time when I was sitting on the stump. So that broadcast to myself corrected a part of my life that might not have gone the way I directed it. If I send a message from the future to the past to change something, then I must repeat it again in the future and remember that I did it. If I don't remember that I did it in the future, I won't do it then and it won't ever happen here in the present.

The future and the past are one and the same thing. If you choose now to change your past, then your past has already been changed. Therefore, it affects you presently. It has already happened.

Couldn't we throw ourselves off if we project one message so strongly that we morph into something completely different? Also, can the effect be physical or is it just interpreted spiritually and emotionally?

In my opinion, the most advanced way of communicating in the multiverse to any alien species or human being is through emotion. Verbalization is no different than grunting or snorting. It is a very limited form of communication. We have a certain amount of words and every year we develop new words for things that we don't have ways of describing. Some cultures have limited amounts of words. Other cultures have vast amounts of words, like the Chinese. They have a lot more words for our descriptions of everyday life than we do. You can convey words, but they can become distorted when they travel through time and space because they're not designed for that. But emotion, emotional feeling, can be sent like a compressed database. Volumes of knowledge in a simple expression of feeling can be decoded and your mind will naturally understand, develop, and create whatever the whole experience was meant to be. You will sit and ponder it until you understand it fully. It's like getting a whole conversation in a moment's notice. You just have to reflect on it.

It's a very interesting concept and it's fascinating when you think about it. Ask yourself, "Am I happy where I am right now?" Do you think that you are spiritually evolved and intelligent enough, compared to where you will be in the future, that you can choose to time travel now? Would you choose now instead of next year, five years, or ten years from now? Is this the one moment of your life where you would choose to appear to yourself? Could you truly comprehend that moment? I want you to reflect on that. Seriously ask yourself, "Am I worthy enough? Have I been honest enough? Have I spiritually lifted myself to such a level of knowledge and practice that I deserve this? Is this the most honorable and pivotal point of my life?" Can you say that what you are doing right now will accelerate you to where you will be in the future? Is this the point where it really began to happen? If you had an entire lifetime to choose from and you could only pick one moment, when would you do it?

Why couldn't you pick more than one?

Well, because this is purely hypothetical, but think about it. The more times you interject yourself, the greater the risk of damaging your future. It's very interesting because there could be a lot of ways to do something like this.

It brings me to the story of some mountain climbers in California. They were climbing the mountain cliffs when they found a geode. That's a stone that is lined with crystals that you only discover when you cut it open. They brought it back with them from the top of the mountain. They decided to cut the geode open to see what was inside of it. Although this should have been an easy task, the geode kept breaking the saws as they tried to cut through it. They ended up taking it to a machine shop that had a special diamond plated saw blade to cut it open. When they finally did that, there wasn't a quartz crystal inside as there should have been. They actually found a spark plug from a 1920's farm tractor inside of the geode. The spark plugs were huge in size at that time. They decided to carbon date the geode. A geologist confirmed that the stone turned out to be 500,000 years old. How did that spark plug become encased in the stone hundreds of thousands of years ago?

We can come up with a lot of hypothetical ideas that could explain how this happened, all having largely to do with time. What if one of those college students, who was climbing that rock, put the spark plug that was encased in the stone there to suggest a concept to be figured out by this person five or seven years later after reflecting about the stone that he found? What idea would it spark within him for a concept of the future? If you are going to affect the past, wouldn't you have to be absolutely cunning? You'd have to be brilliant!

Are you saying the spark plug represents a concept?

Maybe it's a modern kind of mandala. When you think about it, it's a form of knowledge that will eventually trigger a realization that anybody could experience if they pondered it long enough. A mandala is a concept that takes you on a path in a direction that ends up somewhere. It always leads down the same path no matter who thinks about it. You might start off with a different concept but after thinking about it for such a long time, it directs you like a dimensional map.

I think it is really important to reflect on where you are going with everything that I am teaching you and if you really believe that you are applying it. Instead of having me as your teacher or decision maker, judge whether you are qualified or not. I want you to really self-reflect and ask, "Am I really ready? What can I do to be more prepared?" That's really a higher thought and it certainly takes the burden off of me.

Can you break down exactly what a mandala is?

Well, if you do not provoke thought in your mind, you will become like stagnant water. Water that does not move is death. It creates bacteria that poison the water. It attracts mosquitoes that spread malaria; it's death. When the water begins to move, it cycles and cleanses itself. So you must have a philosophy in your mind. If you do not stretch your mind now, how will you ever leap from this universe to another place?

So the mandala is mental stimulation?

Mental thought, mental stimulation. But remember what I said, thoughts are electrons. The brain uses energy to think. It uses electricity. You have electrical currents all over our body. If you touch yourself, the experience is an electrical current that shoots back and forth to your brain and tells you what you experienced. It tells you all of the data that you are experiencing. Everything is converted into electricity. Think about all your senses: smell, taste, touch, hearing, sight are all converted to electricity. Your soul is made of energy; it is made of electricity.

You are physical only because you are hot wired into this machine. You are a duality. You are flesh, blood, and energy merged to coexist. By this fact alone, we know that the body is simply an instrument to let the soul experience this dimension. The soul can't smell, taste, or hear anything. This world doesn't even exist for the soul. It can't even touch it, but through this vessel you can experience this dimension.

Thought is just a bunch of senses combined that provoke an experience. The data is brought into the mechanism of your body, which converts it to become a part of your soul. Why would it be converted into energy in the first place? Why not store it as a chemical base?

Your body is storing the experience as energy because it's making you bigger. It's like food. You need food for the body. Thought and collective knowledge is turned into electricity because it feeds the soul. The soul becomes a higher tone.

It's like taking the frequency of a radio and amplifying it. The higher you go, the higher the tonal of your spirit. The more that you can conceive, the more thought and the more data you can take in to become energy. Most human beings have a low tonal; they're just push button robots. They're like the little red cells in the body: the worker cells. The white cells are the dimensional cells. They are the cells that defend the body and have the wisdom. They remember other battles from fighting viruses. They store experiences. Red cells do not. White cells grow, becoming more powerful over time. Instead of thinking about the mundane things of life, you should actively reflect. Forget about what the TV tells you -- don't even think about it. TV *happens* to you. Life *happens* to you. Somebody walks up to you and says, "Hey, you want a job?" You didn't happen to it; it happened to you. Everything in this world happens to you.

The only thing that doesn't happen to you is if you choose to evoke thought in your mind, not your brain. The brain is the machine that runs all the background systems, such as your emotions, your pulse, everything you don't need to think about when doing something. It's automatic. Evoke thought with your mind because using your mind raises your tonal. By having this discussion with you, your tonal raises so that you're more of a white cell than a red cell. You are living and existing in the moment, in the now rather than just wandering around and being subject to the rigors of everyday life. By the simple fact of becoming aware of the moment, time no longer affects you. Everything I have discussed is all interconnected.

You have to realize this; you can't just nod your head. You have to sit there until you say, "My God, I see the logic of this." It will happen to you sooner or later if you think about the mandala that I just discussed with you. The mandala is all this knowledge that is condensed. As you think about it, you apply it to your other thoughts and it makes everything link together. You start having an epiphany. It starts making more and more sense with everything else you thought about in your life. You were just missing that one piece, and that piece is a mandala.

There must be a way of speeding up this process.

If I do not stimulate thought for you, you will become stagnant. My energy is of a higher resonance. I am a giant tuning fork, vibrating and sounding a vibration that is very high. You are on a lower tonal and you are sitting there waiting for something to happen to you. I could say nothing. I could do nothing. I could choose not to have you in my home and in my life. I could choose not to speak to you at this level. What if I chose to speak to you instead about what you watched on TV? Or ask you about your job?

Instead, I choose to speak to you on a spiritual level and that is sending out a tonal. If you watch two tuning forks, the one that's not vibrating will pick up the vibrations of the one that is. Sound travels. Every time I speak, you hear the sound and it provokes new thoughts. It's actually a physical thing. Well, energy and consciousness is very much the same thing. By evoking thought, I'm creating energy and sending forth energy right now. You are experiencing it and it is raising your tonal. The higher your tonal, the more you observe, the more you understand, and the more you become dimensional as a spiritual being or a super being rather than just a common being.

Let's talk about time. How do we measure time?

By distance.

We don't measure time by distance. We measure time by deterioration. We could measure it by distance but it would be by the fact of deterioration. How long will I exist from point A to point B until I can't go any further? Or how long will a mountain exist before it deteriorates into a valley? Or how long will I physically live before my body becomes aged, withered, dies, and goes back to the earth from whence it came? Everything is a level of deterioration, created by free electrons. Free electrons slowly pull the molecules apart, piece by piece, until you begin to deteriorate.

Well, isn't anti-matter like aging?

No, we are discussing time. You say time doesn't matter and I say you're right, time doesn't matter. From nothing comes nothing. Where did this all come from? Where did time, space, the universe, all the planets, the material, and the building blocks come from?

A vacuum energy.

Yes, it was a vacuum. In actuality, it comes from free electrons. That is where the first building blocks of energy came from, slowly over billions of years. But even the free electrons came from nothing. We know that molecules are solidified for us because we are moving at the same rate. Our molecules are moving at the same rate as the molecules of a table. It's like standing on the side of the road; you can watch the other cars go by at eighty miles per hour and see nothing but a flash. But if you get in the car and you're also moving at eighty miles per hour and you're driving next to the other car, you can experience that car. You can wave to the kids, watch them doing what they do, and see the lady flipping through a magazine. You can probably even see the cover of the magazine but as soon as you slow down or slow your frequency, the cars bypass you because they remain at the higher speed or higher frequency and then they become an unreality. You can no longer experience them.

There are multiple dimensions. This dimension, the one that we are in now, is a vibration. It is really not solid. We know this from quantum physics, but we accept it as solid because we cannot comprehend anything else. *When you can truly comprehend that it's really not solid, then you no longer have to abide by the rules of this dimension.* And you can walk on water like Christ did. You can heal the sick. Or you can raise mountains with one hand as Krishna did. If you think on this and question its solidity, the matter will become the same tonal as you and it will have its plausible, everyday effects.

Are all the other dimensions matter
vibrating at different speeds?

There truly is no such thing as matter. Matter is only 'matter' because we move at the same rate.

Is that what these other dimensions are then? Are
they energies vibrating at different speeds?

Correct. If you can change the thoughts of your consciousness, you can change the vibration of your body. That's how I've done the things I've done, walked through walls in front of students, done miracles from levitation to you name it. It's all done through manipulating this dimension and what I choose or don't choose to accept as my reality. I can affect something right now in small ways or something grand and huge. That's what Krishna, Buddha, Moses, Milarepa and Christ did. But you must really discipline your mind. You must question the existence of what you have been given as the representation of reality. You can't just say, "I choose not to believe." You must really understand why you don't believe and it must make absolute infinite logic to you.

Is this concept basically a desensitizing of our reality?

Yes, but it is more than that. Listen to what I am saying. You keep yourself in this dimension, but if you get a group of people to believe that you can do something, then mask your thought so it works with that group. It's like pouring all of your electricity into this group and converting it to make something happen. That's how Christ did what he did. His used his followers, disciples, and believers in this way until he evolved so much he didn't need them anymore. It was a crutch in the end. I'm trying to point something out to you because Christ could do all sorts of miracles. He did things all the time, didn't he? He raised the dead; he walked on water.

It was the people his disciples spoke to that he needed. He sent his disciples out to work the people up, to build their belief in his message. Before he arrived in a town, the people were already expecting miracles and they believed. It was a very naive time.

He was building up the energy.

Correct, he did this so he could perform all those miracles. When he went to his hometown, Jesus could not do one single miracle because the people didn't believe him. They said, "You're Joseph, the carpenter's son. You worked with my son building our house. How can you be the Messiah?" They refused to believe him. This is an interconnected thing and has to do with dimensions.

That's interesting.

It's very interesting. It's very thought provoking. In order for you to move to the higher levels, you must be able to comprehend the truth. Now we can talk about paganism, new age stuff, meditating, or whatever but none of that is going to get you from point A to point B unless you really understand how it all works. If you understand how it really works, then you can do it.

Do you think books like: "*A Brief History of Time,*" by Stephen Hawking is a good thing to look at or can it be used to provide a basic knowledge of how energies work?

You can only comprehend something by comparing it to something you already know. This is very deep now. That's how human beings think; we bridge thought. I see these shoes and from these shoes, I see the plastic and analyze both of them. Now, I create plastic sneakers. Then I create plastic sneakers with little lenses in them so the light can shine through to kill the bacteria that grow on your feet through a form of photosynthesis.

I've bridged the thought three times over. If I want to conceive the universe, I can only use the bridges that exist within this tiny, little speck of microscopic dust (this planet) compared to what the universe can give me to comprehend it all. Forget it. Math is an excellent tool but it has its limitations. Therefore, Steven Hawking is brilliant because he is trying to bridge in the highest level that we can comprehend.

Do you mean time and distance?

That's right. The data is good, but you must always remember in the back of your head that there are greater possibilities.

When one of the NASA missions launched satellite probes out into the universe, I made some predictions about what we were going to find out there and I was highly accurate. Science could only conceive or imagine that all the other worlds were similar to our other gaseous planets. When the probe passed by Io, one of Jupiter's moons, one of the things that was discovered was that it had volcanoes. But the volcanoes were not spewing up fire; they were spewing up a different liquid. It was either sulfur or sulfur dioxide, which appeared like liquid ice. We couldn't conceive that concept until we saw it and then we had to accept it.

With all of our imagination and our arrogance, there are still some things that we can't even imagine. Well, we can imagine it but it doesn't fit our definition of possibilities. There are things that we will never be able to comprehend until we go to other worlds and expand our knowledge base. We can use that database to try to figure out the galaxy. Maybe we can start working on other universes, but it's never ending. There are consistently things that we can already imagine, but we can never seem to connect it and prove it scientifically.

Besides studying from you or somebody that is accessing this information, how can we find knowledge that will bridge us into an enlightened state?

I don't think that there is an easy way because the biggest problem with human beings is that they are perpetually lazy. Human beings do not want to evolve. You are actually an organism made from this planet that has a specific function: birth, procreate, and death. That's your purpose, just like any other creature on this planet. Just because human beings are now building houses with electricity and modern conveniences, it is not such a big deal. Animals have been building their shelters for eons, finding different methods to it. They evolved technologically over time, cracking open seashells, inventing new ways to find things, and new strategies to deal with their enemies.

Animals easily adapt. You biologically compare yourselves to their evolutionary process and feel arrogant about it. Biologically, you are the best. You are the greatest but compared to everything else in the universe, it is really nothing. You have everything against you because your brain is probably going to sleep. It's bored, or it starts babbling, telling you about all the things you've got to do in life. The mind has to somehow survive through all of this. The odds are highly against you.

Another problem is that whenever you read something, because of the way the brain is designed, you get locked into a certain perspective. For instance, it's like reading the book *The Vampire Lestat*. After you read it, you want to be a vampire. You think like a vampire; you walk outside and you perceive outdoors in the way that the book presented reality. It will linger in you for weeks until it begins to fade away since you cannot feed it. You cannot continue the cycle. There is no club or group that you can go to for vampire lovers, where the members create new stories and play into them. So it dies off as a perspective and you're forced to go back to your normal way of living.

Any time you read a book, suddenly that's the one. That's the latest and greatest thing. It's the new belief, the way to go because your brain tells you that. It indulges itself in reality. It kick-starts your imagination, just like it does with the fictional book. But you're not really making this decision; it's the bio-chemicals. Anything that's shown to you for a certain amount of time can create a withdrawal effect when you don't see it anymore. That's a chemical response in your brain. You are a machine. When you have a thought and you indulge in that thought, creating the visualization, your brain doesn't know the difference between what you're seeing right now and what you imagined when you were reading the book. It's a reality to your brain so it wants to relate to that.

This is how people become so convinced by the Bible. There are no vampire groups to go to, so you can't continue the fantasy. But if you read the Bible, you go to church. It's like a snake biting its tail. You will always be stuck in that mentality because it is repetitively being fed to you. You have a place to ground yourself into. This is why every religion has their temples. For this reason, we must always be careful to ensure that our minds are truly open. We must truly be an intelligent, articulate person who knows this secret. Other schools of thought know it and they allow themselves to fluctuate through different methods of thinking. That is the way they keep themselves from stagnating. There is other stuff out there, but it is very dangerous for human beings to over-indulge.

**But now we're opening our minds.
Isn't that the whole purpose?**

The real purpose is acknowledging other schools of thought. When you reach a certain level of understanding of many different perspectives, then go for it; put all your eggs in one basket. Until then, I'm not going to suggest it although I'm not going to prevent you from it either. It's just not within what I feel is the right time. You will find that with everything I have already covered in this lesson. I have discussed a multitude of different philosophies that would never happen in a single place of teaching, like a church or temple. They all would discuss their way of accepting and perceiving reality. I offer a large diversity of thought; and that diversity helps you to understand the entire universe and how to conduct and arm yourself in this dimension.

I'm saving you. You just don't know it. I'm saving your soul right now from the dogma of religion from the Christians, Buddhists, Jehovah's Witnesses, and everybody else. I'm saving you.

**So no matter what point you originate from,
you evolve to this one way of thinking.**

Right, but remember what I said earlier about there being no right or wrong in the universe? It's parallel with what you're saying now. Awakening or reaching enlightenment is never allowing yourself to stagnate. If you stay in one method of thinking for too long, you will get trapped. You will become like the brother of one of my students. He was not very religious but he got hooked up with some Christian friends that were heavily into studying the Bible. He decided to read a little bit; however, they talked him into studying a little bit more and a little bit more. Now he's addicted to it. He's going to the meetings, the classes, and he's doing all kinds of religious stuff. He is totally absorbed with religion and that's all he will ever know because he is now incapable of stepping out of it.

One of the biggest things that you must remember is to be fluidic so that you can walk dimensionally In-Between. That's a big word around here. *You must have fluidity of the mind*. It's purely what I teach – fluidity. I extract it from all philosophies, all points of view and it's so flexible that it's incredible. You need the flexibility so that you can see the truth – the truth of different religions, philosophies, concepts, and theories to help you understand that there is a little truth in all of them, as well as a lot of crap. Anything that comes out of the mouth of human beings is usually ninety percent fabrication. Always remember that. Humans have a natural tendency to distort the truth, no matter how honorable their intentions.

It circles back to what I was saying about time and traveling back or sending a message to yourself. You must reflect on these things as if you were your future self. As you look back in time at yourself, think what you will be like. Do you see the duality? Isn't that an amazing thought? To do this, you need to think about perceiving your thoughts in your most mature and advanced state. Ask yourself, "What would I think of myself at this point in my development?" It is very hard to do because you have to challenge yourself to do it. Give yourself the benefit of the doubt because you can analyze concepts in your present self and think, "Wow, I wouldn't like this about myself. I suppose I might like that. I might want to change this and that." Nobody can be a better critic of you than yourself.

Is it the same as being very open to the concept of us in the future being able to generate a thought and include a message to send through to the present?

That's right. What would you say to yourself right now? Would you think that you are worthy now or would you say, "I was a young stupid kid at that time and I really didn't appreciate what I had in front of me."

If you saw yourself as an old person, don't you think that it would be a complete reality altering shock?

What would you do with it if you don't have the capability of appreciating what you would have to say to yourself? I would rather wait until I'm thirty or forty years old before I did that to myself. Not nineteen or twenty years old.

I can see that aspect of it but from where I stand, the more time I have, the better.

You are wrong because you are thinking selfishly. I want to prove that you are being selfish because you think that you are 'all that' now. You think that you deserve it. The correct answer would be, "I would probably think to myself that I have a lot more growing up to do and that I should wait five or ten more years before giving myself any pearls of wisdom. I am willing to admit now that I probably wouldn't appreciate the potential of what it could be later on."

I'm not asking if you saw yourself. I'm asking if you would choose now, if you could perceive yourself from the future. That's what I'm asking -- not if it just happened. Being a responsible, spiritual being evolving right now and reflecting on your responsibilities, if you were to have any effect in the world, what demonstration can you give that you have the wisdom to choose a point in your life? And would you choose it now?

I don't know that.

You do and you don't. You have to project yourself there. You have to let your mind go there and really conceive it.

Do I have to tap into my future intelligence so it can tell me when to choose?

That's right. That's what I'm proposing to all of you.

Wow! So I'll be able to put myself in the future from the present?

Every action you take now, you will reflect on when you are older. You are living the future right now because you are writing the future. The only difference is that you -- this is the big key here -- are functioning in the world. The world is happening to you right now because you're not thinking about how you're going to reflect on yourself fifty years from now. You must think about what you are doing now, what you're going to think fifty years from now as you remember this moment. We're fifty years in the future looking back and remembering this conversation. What are you going to think?

What a dummy I was.

What are you going to do about it now? I want you to think about two concepts: life and knowledge. Life is a limited amount of time. You are eventually going to die. There are two things that you are guaranteed in life -- you're going to be born and you're going to die. Physically speaking, that's your guarantee. Those are the two guarantees that you have in life. When you accept this, you have to assume that you have a limited amount of time to accumulate a fuel that is going to decide what you will be when you die, if you even exist after death according to what we believe, and how you will function. Will you be a being that can move freely through time, space, and dimension choosing your next destination? Or will you be pushed around like a hockey puck through the karmic oceans to your next destination? Or will you simply dissipate? Every decision you make between now and fifty years from now will decide what you put in the bank, what your account will be filled with, and how much you've earned. What are you going to buy with that?

From a Karmic point of view?

That's right, what knowledge are you going to deal with? All the knowledge you accumulate now and all the pondering that you do is going to pay off later. Are you doing as much as you can now to plan for your future? It's like your retirement or if you're buying a home; you're thinking about your future right now. Ten years from now are you going to say, "If only ten years ago I had started this path I am on now."

If you saved five dollars a week for the past ten years and the bank said that you could have that money at the age you are right now, would you be thankful at this moment that you saved it? When you are thinking about buying a car or fixing the one you already have, or want new clothes, or money to go to school, would you say thank you to the you of ten years ago? Wouldn't you be so thankful for the person you were for being smart enough to think about the future? That is what you should think about right now. That's what I'm trying to tell you.

Everything that you do spiritually right now in this moment will determine whether or not you become enlightened. Your actions will determine whether you are going to become an enlightened being, a being that will come back to this world to teach others, or a being who will fight other dark beings, contributing something to this world. It is all being decided right now in this moment and it has been cemented into your mind. It has been declared as fact. So if this never happens, don't cry fifty years from now saying, "What a fool I was." You had your chance. You understand what this moment means. However, you will forget by tomorrow morning. You will go right back to your normal everyday routine as if this conversation never took place.

I can also guarantee that in forty or fifty years from now, no matter what the outcome, you will remember this conversation. You will remember how right I was in telling you this and also that you wish you put more effort into doing this. That's what really sucks. Only then will you be able to appreciate what I am saying.

It's like the rabbi who would not allow his students to read the Kabbalah until they were a certain age. I'm not Jewish, but I have great respect for the thousands of years of wisdom and the culture the Jewish people maintained throughout the centuries. Being very rich in wisdom, the rabbi would tell his students who wanted to read the Kabbalah that you can't accumulate the necessary wisdom until you are at least fifty years old. Until then, you will not even begin to understand what it is saying. You might as well say it is Chinese. You can read the words but you cannot feel what it says.

If we can project our growth into in the future, can we save time and obtain more knowledge by the time we reach that age?

You accumulate five times, ten times, one hundred times more.

So where do we start? Is there an exercise?

Students always want the exercise. The exercise is hope, want, desire, and will. Will who you are now. Make sure you show up on time and reflect on the things that I say. Read these lessons over and over again. Think about what I was trying to tell you. Every time you read these lessons you will gain something new. I promise that it will take you to a new level. Every time you read it, you will get something more out of it than the first time you saw it. There is a technique. Let me explain something to you.

When you meditate, you can only bridge to the highest level you have built yourself up to. Even though you are not doing it willfully, spiritually speaking, by understanding the philosophy of what I am teaching, you will help yourself to bridge across universes in your meditations. It just happens by the simple fact of understanding what I am saying to you now. A lot of people say to me, "Eric, I want to walk through a wall like you did." Or, "I want to move objects like you did." Or, "I want to do psychic things like you did." Or, "Eric, I want to have the same knowledge and I want to tap into that same source that you do. Show me the technique." Well, I'm giving you the technique.

If you comprehend what I am saying, you simply know how to do these things. There is not really a formula. One day, it just makes sense to you. If I hand you a pair of shoes but you've never even seen shoes before because you've only been barefoot your entire life, will you be able to understand, based on the knowledge that I have verbalized to you, what to do with them?

Whoa! Oh God! Whoa!

It makes sense, doesn't it?

Yeah, very much so.

You can put on the shoes and then you can do more things because of them. I am talking to you and I am trying to help you to conceive things that you have never really thought about before. Suddenly, you will go, "Wow, this now makes more sense to me," and then you will start doing amazing stuff. You will see stuff moving through the walls. You will begin to feel other people's presences. You will be able to heal people because you will just know how to do it. It's just going to be common sense, like the way you look at those shoes.

Intuition.

No, it's beyond intuition. You just know. Is it intuition to put the shoes on? Or does it just make sense?

It's logical.

Why is this logical? It is because you have bridged a lot of concepts until you got to the point where you can make sense of it.

Well, I'm talking about what you're saying... to think about the feeling of it. It's more like a soul intuition, like your soul telling you how to do it with your logical mind.

Your soul tells you that you want to heal. It doesn't tell you how to heal. That's the difference. Even as an energy being, you are logical and intelligent. It's a fundamental truth of the universe. It's been proven forever. You're constantly thinking. That is why you chose this body.

If we project out information or we project out energy into the Universe, does it also come back to us?

Well, I call that sampling. If you send something out, technically you can't have an empty amount of space. So if you send energy out, something else moves in. You're like a giant chemistry lab. Whatever comes into you, you analyze, study, experience, and grow from. So if you put energy out to the Universe, what you get back always makes you more because you can never become less than who you are. You can only accumulate; you can never deteriorate energies.

Are you saying that your tonal can only drop to a certain level?

You can have something and then never use it. If you never use it, you may as well never have it.

I just think that if you don't access a high tonal, it's useless.

It doesn't matter. It's the knowledge that creates a higher tonal. Tonal is something that you develop. If you have a tuning fork and you use it, then you have the knowledge if you can match the pitch. If you have a tuning fork but don't practice with it, then there's no point in owning it. You can make it sound but you have to put forth the effort.

If you tap the tuning fork, then it's like singing. Everybody has a voice but not everybody knows how to sing.

True. If you want to learn a technique, one of the things that I suggest for you to do is lie down in a quiet place without other people around, clear your mind and think about your past. Choose a moment in your life and visually recreate it in your mind, that very moment, that very place, and feel what you felt. Then, as an adult with the knowledge you have gained as a more mature person, give that knowledge to yourself.

In other words, express an emotion to yourself, "It's going to be okay. It's going to be all right."

Linked to the past?

That's right. Don't think about whether it's going to work or not. Just do it. Let me explain something else to you. Time cannot be moved. We can't move through time but you're still reliving every single moment of your existence from the day you were born; it doesn't stop. Under hypnosis, you can relive incredible details that you think you have totally forgotten. Every single second is recorded. We are the best recording system in the entire world. There isn't even a computer that can come close to us. We record in sound, sight, smell, taste, touch, and texture.

Wouldn't you like to be able to plug into the TV and become the character in the movie and relive everything that they are doing? You have been recording information your whole life. As a soul, you have recorded the years of your life. Your body is a giant recording mechanism. You are a giant state of the art camcorder and everything is recorded, such as whom you are now, how you perceive things, and how you think. You record the limits of what you feel and what you think. The things that can prevent you from doing psychic things are created by all the experiences in your mind. They are all parts of your personality: the child, the adult, the angry person, and the lover are all within you. Remember what I said earlier. You are made up of hundreds of different personalities. These personalities were all created the day you started living. Go back into your mind and find those personalities. They are alive; counsel them so that they can become more knowledgeable in your mind. So when they move to your consciousness now, you will say, "I just feel like I understand more." It's like making an investment ten years ago.

**So the best bet is to project the entirety of
your wisdom from here to there?**

You amplify the now. You amplify what you are now. You amplify your spirituality and your wisdom.

The future me could be doing this to me right now.

Exactly, it doesn't matter if you really are going back in time or if you're going back here; it's still going to pay off.

**I want to ask if it's very important to project
into the future in addition to the past.**

You've lived in the past so you can have more knowledge of a moment. Thus that makes it easier to change it. The past is something that you already know. Obviously, it's easier to affect the past, even if it's just a mental note. I think that all psychic abilities are suppressed. As a Cro-Magnon human, you survived using your psychic abilities. You sensed your environment as you walked. You relied on your psychic sense to find the caves that you could use for shelter. Also, because you walked everywhere and you were small, you were preyed on. In turn, you had to know which way to go for water, which way for food, and which sense to use if something was preying on you. These were all psychic abilities. You lost those psychic abilities over time. All of those psychic abilities are still within the capability of your brain, but they are repressed.

I can sense if somebody's watching me so they are still there.

Yes, but not all of your senses remain and certainly not to their full potential. They have all been suppressed. You need to ask yourself how you can free that knowledge. How do you free that emotion, those senses? They are also suppressed by society's structured way of thinking that has been pounded into your brain. By healing yourself, giving yourself psychotherapy, you release certain emotional patterns within the brain and that allows you to feel and sense things. I think that is really a big deal. The other thing is that you have to experience your *self*. There is a little trick to experiencing your *self*. Everybody thinks of *their selves* but they never experience their '*selves*.' We know exactly the kind of emotion we need to emit to release a certain blockage. We know that all animals need a certain amount of affection. We know that monkeys need to hold a doll or have a replacement mother, because monkeys who receive that affection and attention as babies are more secure and more developed than monkeys that grow up without that.

I think a lot of people don't have a communion with their *'selves.'* As I said to you before, there is the *"me"* and there is the *"I."* The *"I"* is your soul; the *"me"* is your flesh and blood. You are both right now so you have to learn to work with both. One of the interesting things is to try to feel your inner emotion, but men have a difficult time doing that. Sit up so that your feet are touching or sit Indian style. Are you ready for silliness now? Have you ever hugged yourself?

I pat myself on the back.

Can you readily admit that, in privacy, you have attempted to hug yourself?

I have.

Have you ever tried to nurture yourself? I want you to simply hug yourself. Feel what it is like to turn inward. It's a very interesting concept. When you hug yourself, it feels like somebody is embracing you, but it's really you that's embracing you. The patterns in your brain get confused for a moment, but there is another part of you that becomes sympathetic to the self and that is very healing. If cancer patients and other ill people did this, they would heal themselves at a very rapid rate.

You have an inner universe; you have millions of living organisms in your body. How do you reference yourself other than saying to others, "Oh, I'm doing well." You don't. You need to learn to love yourself by saying internally, "Everything is good; everything is working well; everything is healthy." One of the ways you can do that is by hugging yourself. It's not effective because it is a strange thing to do, but it's a way of turning your mind within. So just go ahead and do this for a second. Put your hands up and around yourself; just close your eyes; feel your arms touching yourself, and just love yourself. It's almost like you are embracing yourself. Feel that affection. It's like you want to acknowledge that you're happy; you're so proud of yourself; you feel good with yourself, and you want yourself to evolve. You want yourself to become something more than what you are now. Give yourself that nurturing, and also feel yourself feeling your self. The duality of this is that your brain says, "Wait a minute; I can feel others but how do I explain to myself that I'm experiencing my self?" That's when the brain starts to work in a diversified manner, because it doesn't sense that as logical.

You can feel yourself *feeling your self*, and that's something that is not familiar to you. It's actually very foreign, but it feels good doesn't it?

I do that in meditation, but not physically. I turn my energy into myself.

Yeah, but the point is to have physical contact with the self. Do it physically because you are also a physical being. Your hands are the most sensitive part of your body. They are the most utilized part. You have to rid yourself of the ego. That is really what prevents you from spiritually evolving because it controls what you allow yourself to sense, feel, and do.

You can heal your inner self. You can also talk to yourself as a second party or second person as if you're conveying an important message, telling yourself you are doing well. You can be the empathetic voice, the voice of encouragement to yourself, and it really works.

Can I tap into my female energy?

Absolutely, that's what I'm trying to point out. You are tapping into your polarities. It is working with your self instead of by yourself. You are helping to help yourself. You are helping to encourage yourself. If nobody is going to compliment you, you cannot say to other people, "I need compliments please. I need encouragement right now." People don't normally know how to do that. I'm not a very encouraging person, I admit it, but people do need encouragement.

That is what the monkey story was signifying. If anyone knows what you need and can give it to you, that is you. You can balance yourself by understanding yourself. This is what allows your sensory to become higher, more intuitive, and more spiritual. It means you are balanced or at least you can begin to understand what it means to be balanced. If your mind is constantly in turmoil, doesn't have companionship, is frustrated and worried about things, why not be your own best friend?

About five years ago, I went through a six month period when I did not have any regrets. For example, if I was mean to somebody, I didn't feel guilty. Then, all of a sudden, I had this stint where I felt all these things from the past that I had forgotten about. Then all this guilt from all these events that I didn't remember was all coming up. I had to go through the pain that I had blocked out before.

Your brain is a machine and it affects the body; however, the mind is who you really are. When the brain starts dumping all the garbage from your past, it jams up and it cannot function. It is like a computer. Do you understand the fundamentals of a computer? If you start putting in software and it starts to bulk up or starts to override the auto-reset that allows it to comply with other new programs you're putting in, what happens? You have to shut the computer off, reboot it, and let it sort itself out in order to function better.

ERIC PEPIN

So when you start investigating your own mind, you are going to come across huge issues that need to be resolved. New scientific studies are now being done on the brain; it's very interesting. They consist of a new hypothesis about dreams being your brain's way of working out experiences. When you dream, the dream state brings you through certain emotions, almost as if to chemically balance the brain in order to resolve certain issues.

There is stuff buried deeply that has never been fully digested by the brain and it is still trying to understand why or how to conceive those unresolved things. The child always says, "Why does it rain? Why is the sky blue? Why is this? Why is that?" As adults, we do the same thing only in a more complex way. The brain wants to know. Painful things happen, things that shock us. Things still seem intimidating and overwhelming even as adults. Sometimes we cannot process it. But as we get older we have more tools to process those emotions and thoughts from the past even though it may not be as painful. That is a very normal thing. You deal with things when you are ready for them.

So we're like a computer that doesn't have the power to process the information that is presented?

At that particular time in your life, you may not have been able to process a certain event. That is true. But you now have the capacity to work it out, right? Sometimes those unresolved feelings just sit there, affecting other parts of you. It can make you ill. It can lead to cancer, tumors, and body ailments. It can cause you to stutter. It can slow down your reading capabilities. You may not even know it's there or that you have a problem. You may think that you have resolved all the problems and issues in your life, but they're still there. It is a matter of sitting down and thinking about your whole life from the earliest moment and just going through it like

-236-

fast-forwarding a video. But in the process, counsel yourself saying, "Yeah, that really sucked when my father did that to me and I was really hurt. But you know something, I'm here now and I'm going to be okay." It sounds like a strange thing to do, but if you want to reach the highest level of your mental capacity, isn't it wise to clear out all of the bullshit in your mind?

Clear your mind.

That's right, you have to lay a stable foundation and that's what sharpens your mind. Everybody has stuff that has happened to them. It's just a matter of doing a mind defragmentation like you do with a computer. You are defragmenting, sorting, fixing, and making everything perform at its peak capacity.

You said that when we sleep, we're basically absorbing everything we learned that day. Somebody told me the same thing the other day when I was trying to explain about how your spirit learns. When you sleep, your spirit doesn't sleep. It just keeps going and so do your experiences. They go up to your brain and relay everything you've done during the day. That is exactly what I was trying to explain to him.

I don't necessarily think that's the only thing that happens. I think there are stages of dreaming.

The other point that I wanted to make is the speed that you process information. One hour normal time can be made into ten hours of dream time because you can speed up the thinking process in that dream state of mind, like a computer.

It's like hitting turbo speed. You can still calculate figures but it takes five seconds compared to ten minutes.

Isn't that the subconscious mind working? You are not necessarily doing it with your conscious mind.

It's not the conscious mind. It's not the super subconscious. Nobody really knows for sure. There is no real way to say specifically what part of the mind is in control. To me, it's a machine that is processing. The mind is idly observing what the brain is doing and trying to understand the process. The brain is processing all this data and possibly throwing out a lot of useless information just to make sense of the pivotal moments. There are different levels. There are parts where you leave your body and come back. It's all in the sleep mode and the processing.

Doesn't the superconscious state, since it's not attached to the body, sneak away from the body?

I don't believe that you leave your body. I believe you send probes out. Energy that is simultaneously thinking at the same time you're thinking, sending the images to your brain. People say it is astral projection. It's not.

So you're saying your aura is also part of your super consciousness? You're just not aware it's there?

Right, you're multitasking. That is the best way. On a computer, you can run a program, surf the web, process numbers, and you can play a game at the same time.

Right, the totality of your energy is still there.

Yes, absolutely. That now brings me to the next phase. I see that we are dealing a lot with mental thoughts. I once read a book that one of my students gave to me. It was a book that his mother gave to him about a man who had a dialogue with God. In the book, it says that God speaks to him through his body and he just writes down the answers. This concept is similar to a class that I taught my older students. I thought I would talk a little bit about that now.

I thought this book was very interesting, but I don't believe he is actually talking to God; yet in a way he is. Some people might question what I mean by that. First of all, the book is good. You should read it. It was written by Neale Donald Walsch, called *Conversations with God: An Uncommon Dialogue*. It was his first book and is a little older now, but I think that he has a little bit of a Christ complex going on, but so do I. Remember that anything that comes from a human's mouth is a bit embellished. In any case, he brings up an interesting point of view.

I believe that everybody can do this. One question Walsch asked was, "Does God exist? Does God communicate with us right at this very moment?" My answer is, "Absolutely yes!" The problem is that you choose not to hear God; you choose not to listen within. God is communicating with you as much as the cells of your body are communicating with you. It's just a matter of listening. If we are made of the fabric and body of God, then we must have a direct link. We just have to figure out that link. Now, of course, I am going to use a concept from Luke Skywalker and the Force. I believe that God is an energy that permeates us, goes through walls, through tables, through us, through everything. It's a living force.

It is us. It is everything.

Therefore, we should have a direct link to understanding God. Well, remember when I was speaking about that alter ego, that second consciousness you ask questions to in the mirror? Well, this is what Walsch uses in order to convey his thoughts. He asks a question and he freely allows this alter ego, or this other part of his mind, to speak to him as a representation of God. Now he believes it is God, but I call it a representation of God because I don't necessarily think it is God. It is his representation of God that speaks to him telling him how to understand things or the meaning of certain things.

Now you have what is called the superconscious mind. If you are an old soul, that superconscious mind has lived thousands of lives. It is the totality of all the knowledge that you have accumulated in your lifetimes. Let's say that you create an alter ego to teach you, to talk to you, to make you understand certain things and it is an access to higher knowledge within yourself. It is really you, but it is more advanced knowledge than you are familiar with, so the knowledge sounds more precise. That is what this person is utilizing, and basically he asks questions like, "God, how do you talk to us?" and the response sounds like, "Well, I talk to you through emotion and emotion is the universal language. I talk to you through the trees, the things that you see, and what you feel. Nothing that you experience in life just happens. It happens because I put it there for you to learn something from." Of course, I can explain all of this in different ways too, but there is some truth to all of this.

You should try an experiment with your alter ego and start conversations with yourself as this man did. However, you have to be very careful because you can also create a lot of problems for yourself that way, like multiple personalities and that sort of thing.

People always say, "You can talk to yourself but you should only be worried if you get the answers," and here I'm saying, "Listen to the answers." I'm not responsible for any psychological damage.

One time, I asked about Joan of Arc and you said that at that time people were persecuted for being able to hear the voices. Is that the same kind of thing except that there's a fine line between you and your consciousnesses?

Well yes. They could have a chemical imbalance where the brain was able to override the mind. The voices spoke to them even though they didn't ask any questions. There are some things that you should keep in mind. I always listen to my inner self. I teach you a lot of the time by analyzing how I do things. I do a lot of stuff instinctively without even realizing I am doing it. I have to reflect on how I know that information.

Isn't our knowing or that alter ego the superconscious? Isn't it the soul's totality of knowledge? Wouldn't that be classified as intuition?

Yes, to the first part. There is intuition, but you cannot always trust intuition. Intuition is only based on what you can bridge. You can only judge something by what you compare it to; therefore, it's fallible. It is not trustworthy, but then you have to trust it, so there's a duality there. There's a right and wrong to everything. You must keep that in mind and never say a certain thing is absolutely this way or that way.

Out of the totality of my superconscious mind, it sure knows a lot more than my conscious mind, so it must be more trustworthy than my rational mind, my intuition.

No it's not. Your alter ego or that part of you is also influenced by your behavioral side, your uglier side, the side that wants to manipulate or control. There are influences. Mahatma Gandhi once said, "No good man is completely good and no bad man is completely bad." The truth to the matter is that every human being has a dark side.

Oh, I totally believe that.

I'm saying *don't trust it.* It could sound absolutely logical to you but give you information with malicious intent. Will you be able to judge those malicious intentions or even be smart enough to realize that the information is one-sided? Even if it is really you who is being one-sided, you're creating this whole alter ego. This is a perpetual argument that can go on forever. My answer is, "No." The only thing you can really trust is your inner heart, your inner soul. If you want to call it intuition, you can call it intuition. I don't call it intuition. Intuition is feeling what he or she is feeling or scanning. It's a sixth sense.

You should be careful of what is logical. What you feel can be changed to feel something completely different through the use of logic. It can be made to feel very real through mental thought or rationalization. It's very complex.

I think it is a little bit of both. It's not just good. You need logic to guide emotion. So it's a little bit of both, right?

It's everything and nothing.

> Today we were out in the woods by the Red
> Salmon River. We were meditating by ourselves
> and it seemed like I slowed time down. I was
> thinking that the only way I could do that was if
> my energy was moving faster. Is that correct?

Well, it is correct but the river also had something to do with it. I affect time quite often, either by speeding it up or slowing it down. During these sessions, if you go into deeper states of conversation, you will find that time is just flying by and you'll wonder, "Where did it all go?" If you slow your mind, time will go faster. You will actually go faster than time. *The slower you go, the faster you move.*

You don't want to overlook the river. The river represents movement to your tagging mind. If you think about time, you'll see it as a river. Without thinking about it, they're almost synonymous in your consciousness. Water is transparent. When you meditate next to a flow of water, it represents time in a subconscious way. When you meditate next to it, the flow of it will naturally affect time without you realizing it.

> Also, there were bugs. When I sat down, they were
> just buzzing all over. When I started meditating,
> they slowed down. Is it still the river?

Let me explain this differently. Let's say you are going to meditate in your back yard and there is no water there. Your mind has recorded the feeling of being by the Red Salmon River. If you go into your mind and try to recreate that feeling while you are in your back yard, the bugs would slow down. *That is a major key that I am giving to you right now.* I don't know if you are going to miss the boat on this or not, but creating the feels-like of the river is the key to why you had that experience. Had you not done that, and if you did it anywhere else, the bugs would not necessarily have slowed down. That's why I'm trying to put that connection together for you. It's all in the feels-like. Take the environment and what you felt, and bring it into that space.

Here's another example. You are going ghost hunting and you say to me that you are trying to figure out the best place to go. Remember our conversation? I told you to sit a half hour in a room. *Since energy and entities move at higher frequencies, take the feels-like of the Red Salmon River and create that vibration in that haunted space while you are sitting there for thirty minutes and watch the phenomena come through!*

There's a million dollar piece there if you want to work with it. It's all about putting the pieces together. In another class, I taught that sometimes you've got to think about the book falling out over here to make the door open over there. It's never where you think it's going to be. So this is what I'm trying to say. A great analogy would be that you have to find the recipes.

So I just realized when you are using the river as your *feels-like* to create the effect, that's also what I'm doing. So if you go into a haunted place and you create that *feels-like* of time slowing down, the entities will manifest before you. You are thinking with an organic brain and you can't move into that frequency, but you can shift your frequencies so that they can manifest. You have to slow your environment down.

We went to the pond yesterday and we were slowing down the ripples, and I did the same thing with sound. Later on, we came back here to meditate and I went to the pond in my mind. Even though I recall being there, it's like I was looking at the water and didn't recognize it was water. I didn't understand the correlation.

Well, it could have been a biological reaction in your brain because you are probably affecting different hemispheres. One part of your brain sees something and the other part slows down a bit, skips a beat, and makes you think you didn't see it. Or perhaps you saw it before the recognition part of your brain realizes that you did. Sometimes the biological brain will start to get a little quirky at times because you are going into a different, altered state. It can go outside of you to also affect your reality. It's a duality.

Last year when I met you, you told me that I would need to go back to my déjà vu when I was a child. It was a long drive and there were two exits, so I chose the second. It took me twenty minutes to find the cottage. You said that I would find it so I just wanted to share that.

That is awesome. I remember that particular conversation.

I wanted to ask about the technique for getting your feels-like of the river or anything else that represents time. It makes sense to me.

Well, there's more. You've got to figure out the code. It's part of the code. It is a language and you have to internalize it without using words. Do the feels-likes, and project them as much as you take them in.

We were looking at the ripples on the pond. Matthew said to feel that inside myself. Once I get the feels-like, slow it down. Feel the ripples slowing down. Once I internalize it and feel it on the inside, it will change the outside.

Yes, it changes the outside because you change your consciousness. In some cases, you can slow down the organic brain so that your hyper-dimensional brain can take over. It's not dominated by your organic brain so you almost step out of it. When you do, you begin to see reality in a different way, like when you're walking *In-Between*.

If I am going to a haunted house and I want to see phenomena, then I usually slow time. I no longer think of the water or the river. To me, it's just the tag and I just do it. To find ways to explain it to you, I have to think how I do what I do. So when he was talking about the water, I realized, "Oh, that's my tag. That's the perfect tag." So this all ties together. So that's it!

Chapter 8

THE KINGDOM

Can you give us a detailed explanation of frequency? I started thinking about it after reflecting on the module "Time Stepping." If I understand this correctly, the past, present, and future are all happening at the same time?

Yes, that is correct.

Is it correct to say that each one happens at a different frequency? Can you explain this in a little more detail?

The term frequency is used in so many different ways. I think it is very important to address exactly what frequency is because it is actually many things. When the word is used to describe a certain term, right away most people say, "Oh, I know what you are talking about. What about that frequency?"

The simplest way to describe frequency is to compare it to radio channels. How many of them are moving through the atmosphere right now? There are probably hundreds of thousands of them. Each one is an individual frequency and all of them are happening right now. The only way you can experience any one of those frequencies is to move into its dimension. Then you can experience the textures of the music of that specific station. It holds data and experience, so that would be a frequency. By tuning into it, you are tapping into that dimension.

When you speak of a frequency, you are speaking of the frequencies of music, and also the frequencies of dimensions and realities. You are within a specific frequency; and that frequency is held together in its own motion, its own perpetual vibration.

You can compare it to cars driving at different speeds in different lanes. You are driving a car that is going thirty-five mph on the ramp. Other cars on the highway are going fifty-five, sixty-five, seventy-five, and eighty-five mph in different lanes. You can see the cars and acknowledge that they are there, but you cannot experience what is going on in their reality until you drive at the same speed as them. Once you move up to the same speed, you can look over and see someone who is flipping through People Magazine or chewing Wrigley's Spearmint gum. She has blonde hair and blue eyes. However, when you step on your brakes, that frequency is broken and you have now dropped into a lower frequency. You are no longer part of that higher frequency; you are now a part of the lower frequency. If you speed up, you can no longer see the lower frequency because you are in a higher frequency.

Right now, you are moving at a frequency and everything in this room is vibrating. It only appears to be still because everything is in unison. If you concentrate on the concept of frequency, you will start to move into the *In-Between* state. And if you really start to think about it, you will feel slightly strange. If you focus and look around the room, you will see with your eyes. To help you rationalize and bring your mind into the moment, look for static on the edges of things. You can almost see a light haze, a light fog, or a sense of something there. Do not acknowledge it, because if you do, then it's like acknowledging that our reality is not real. That is when your organic body takes control and says, "No, wait, come back here." It puts you back into the Doe so you don't mess with another dimension.

However, the more that you start to focus on the static, the easier it will be to 'get in.' That's when you start focusing on sound. Perhaps you will start to hear a voice. You may start to hear the echo, the hum, and other different things. You can hear people moving. So you are pushing the temperament of reality. As this happens, you will start to feel your tongue, which will start to have a bland taste. It's almost like a metallic flavor that is associated with LSD. When people experiment with LSD, they taste something like a strychnine flavor. It is basically from blotter acid, which is a little piece of paper with a chemical sprayed on it. It causes an LSD effect. LSD manipulates certain molecules in your brain that produces this effect. You can produce the same effect by doing this exercise. This is what we call the *In-Between*.

By acknowledging and paying attention to those things, you will begin to shift. You will eventually find quirks, nuances in your reality. You will notice that people seem to act a little weird in their body. For a second you will say to yourself, "Now that's weird!" However, if you even acknowledge that you thought it was weird, you bring yourself back again to 'normal' reality. You can't think about it if you are in that state. Trees, colors, everything starts to very slightly change, almost like you're not sure what you are seeing. The more you let your mind go, without thinking about it, the more you allow yourself to keep experiencing those things and paying attention to them. Your consciousness begins to shift deeper. If you allow yourself, you will go into very deep states. It is a skill that you learn.

You are effectively leaving your organic body. Your consciousness is moving faster than the cellular level of the atoms of your body. If you really push it, you can literally enter a whole other dimension. Frequency is still a part of this because you're simply changing lanes, but you are doing it through your own consciousness. The reason you are able to do that is because you are aware of the possibility of that concept.

Is it the speed of consciousness that allows you to enter this state of mind?

Well, you cannot say *speed*. That is when it gets complicated. We use 'speed' as a jumping off point to get the idea. It's an analogy because 'speed' would not be relevant. When we think of speed, we think of distance. In truth, it is almost like you are vibrating. But even vibrating can be considered speed because there's still a back and forth motion that gives you a concept of that. It is like forgetting backwards. You just simply choose to not think. If you do not think, then you are not anchored into this reality. This is why we always practice *non-thought*. Thought is what holds you into this frequency. If you shut down thought, you no longer have an anchor that's going to hold you to this dimension or to this frequency.

You simply have intent. Your intent is to move into this other frequency or into a frequency other than this one. If that is your intent and that is your direction, then that is what's going to happen.

If you've never been there before, how can you find that frequency with your intent? Wouldn't you have to feel that frequency before?

Let me ask you a question. How did you find this location?

Someone showed me the way.

Somebody told you how to get here. Somebody passed on the information that this was a place to gather for like-minded people. How did you get here? Did a friend give you a ride? You did not know what to expect. The difference between going to an unknown location of this frequency and going into another frequency is *expectation*. Everything is mental for you and that prevents you from going into another frequency.

When you came here, you didn't know what to expect. What is the first thing that you do? You want to know. So you start wondering in your mind. You start imagining what this place will be like before you get here. That's a knowing because you are dealing with consciousness. Consciousness is a whole different ball game. It is like thinking in *light*. If you can think enough in *light*, you can create another world.

What if I wanted to see a past life?

In my mind, that is completely different from what we are discussing now. To see into a past life, you go into another dimension or another frequency. Why is it that way in the brain? I do not know, but that's the way it is.

Does it take intent with an open mind to find this frequency?

Yes, absolutely. Simply forget and let yourself fall backwards. In so doing, you are effectively trusting and conquering your fear of death. You have to let go of everything because everything is an anchor to keep you in this dimension. The people that you love are anchors. Your body is an anchor. Your life, in general, is an anchor. All of these things collectively hold you in this dimension. The only way to get past that is to release it, and that is very hard to do. If you do that, you might just vanish altogether. Then again, you could wake up and realize that you were dreaming the whole time in another world. It happens.

The idea is to still maintain some kind of control. It is pretty easy to always hang on to this dimension, but it is the forgetting, the actual act of letting yourself forget that allows you to pop into somewhere else. It depends on what level of intensity you want. If I were to give you a map of how I see this, I would take a bunch of parallel lines with each line representing another dimension. If you zoom into it with a microscope, each line would be made of thousands of little microfiber lines. We're in one of those microfibers. You need to get through all the other microfibers before you can jump to another solid line. It's very difficult to do.

I have to think of a zipper and a light switch to shut down when I'm driving or when I'm using your meditation because I start to see the energy coming from cars and people.

Some people might think you are crazy for saying that, but there is an element of truth to that. This is really, really important: sometimes you have to create things that you can relate to. It's like the whole Windex thing. When I say, "Think of a type of glass cleaner," most people say Windex because of the word association. Window/Windex -- I've covered this before. So, in order to fool your consciousness, you had to come up with some concept that your brain can relate to. It doesn't necessarily make sense to other people, but it makes perfect sense to you because there's some part of you that can accept it for what it symbolizes.

In order for you to get out and about, pretend that there is a zipper over your head, like the zipper on your clothes. Pretend to unzip it, open it, and pop your head out into another dimension. You are really creating a back door. The brain is so smart, yet it is obtuse because something absurd fooled it. The concept you created makes perfect sense to it. So it can now achieve what you need to achieve.

A long time ago, I used to create a *kingdom* in my mind. The kingdom itself was not that important, but it represented the key. You use the *kingdom* in your mind the same way your brain perceives that it works in this reality. The special tag for this concept is having your field of protectors, your filters, control what you let into your consciousness and what you let out. At that time, I created a kingdom in my mind because I could relate to that concept. Everything has layers of meanings, and these layers are infinite. A kingdom to a non-spiritual person may simply mean a castle and some property.

What if your consciousness was the kingdom? What if this represented your mind? What if the kingdom was the whole of your existence? Just like your body is made up of trillions of living cells. It is difficult for us to envision. But if you think that your consciousness is a kingdom in your mind, it is more palatable for the brain to accept. The fact that we say this kingdom is our mind is the first thing that fools the brain. You are telling the brain this is who you are. This is a different way of looking at yourself. With this kingdom, you want to have a core. The king or queen would obviously be you. You have to be careful on this because the queen is always considered to be less than the king. If you're a female, you have to say that the king is dead.

That is how it works. As the monarch, you have now taken command of the kingdom. In my case, I am the king. In my mind, I envision the whole castle. Most people see its shape as circular. If you observe yourself building it, you'll see it very circular. You have to ask yourself, why is that? Why didn't I build it into a mountainside? The brain already knows that you've set the standard for the concept of a castle. It's working with you, setting up a parameter because the body thinks in a circular sense.

As you're building your kingdom, you can almost see that there are layers to it. It's as if the center is higher. Then it drops lower. You have a wall, another wall, and then another wall. These are all regions to get into the core – the center.

What is that core?

That is your *middle pillar*. That is your *true self* enclosed in there. You're the king. There's a center point that your king is protecting. In a sense, you can say that is your true soul. Then you set up your knights. These are your protectors, your warriors. You give them armor, weapons, and shields. Of course, you give them highly polished armor because they have to look cool and intimidating. They're bad ass because they have to be. If they're sissies, you're screwed.

You know they're bad ass. All of your knights will die for you because they are willing to do anything for you, even if it means they die in battle. You have them and you have a certain amount of corsairs. In addition to that, there are legions of armies.

Next, you have your people. Those are your laborers, which represent your red cells. The red cells are basically going to work on your health, whether you have an illness or whatever. You say to them, "This is what I want you to do. There are some holes and deterioration in the castle wall. Your job is to go out there and fix it." Now that might sound silly to the average person, but again like the zipper the brain says, "Oh, you're talking about the cells of my body!" You know that is correct, but you are not saying this is what it feels-like. Then they're going to go out there, start working on it, and repair it. How do they know what to repair? Let's say that you already know that your knee is bad. Then the wall part you told the red cells to repair is really your knee, but in a different perspective and consciousness.

In addition to your laborers, you also have villagers. Those are your farmers or the last outer wall. They actually go outside and they work with the land. They cultivate it and they bring stuff in, just like your body needs to get food. They determine what is good and healthy for you. You can say to them, "Don't bring anything into the kingdom that is going to be bad for it. Here is a list of things that is bad for it." You will find that your tastes start to change. Your desire for food will start to change. The foods that you had a taste for before, which were very destructive, are now unappealing to you. It's great for people who smoke cigarettes or have habits they want to break. You can say, "Don't bring in tobacco. Tobacco is bad for the kingdom. I command you not to bring it in." Your body relates that to the cellular structure and all of a sudden, you don't want it. You don't know why. You just don't want it because you found a different way to communicate this message to yourself.

The first person perspective is very hard to work with because you see yourself as an individual. How can you tell yourself what to do? So you invert it, create a kingdom, and say, "This is a representation of my body; that is what it is." You can make it as complex as you want. As the king, you can also create your church or your spiritual center. You can walk inside the spiritual center and create all of that. There are ways now to get into the back-end program. So how do you get there? Are you ready? I shouldn't be telling you this.

In the church you can have your monument to God, if you will. It can be classical, like a stained glass piece. It can be beautiful or whatever you want to create. You can have chanting, too. Yet somewhere in the back of your mind, it's just like a video game. You've got a pool of water. What does water represent? It's fluidic. It represents consciousness. If you were to look into that water, who or what are you going to see? Are you going to see yourself or are you going to see nothing? You will look into it and there's almost nothing to see but your reflection. Your brain scatters what it will be because you are dealing with your true self. You don't know who you truly are so it's hard to see your reflection. That is where your brain is at a loss.

Interestingly, you can dip into the pool and dive down into the water. So that represents escaping from this consciousness into some other kind of consciousness. When you come up for air, you open up your eyes in this reality. You are going to find that your awareness and your spirituality are heightened until you fall into your sleep – the Doe -- and you become your everyday self. But you can also say, "If I go into this pool, I'm going to come up into another dimension." So, in order to see different places, you keep yourself going. That's why I didn't want to speak of this because it now prepares your brain for what it is. It is *what you do not know* that is hard to find because that is the truth. If I give you texture, or say what is going to happen, then your brain will create an artificial thing.

When you create *the kingdom*, you create an arena that will work better with your body. You can work with aging. You can work with your youth. You can tell your minions to do whatever you want. But like any other castle, and any other kingdom, it takes maintenance. It takes constant care. You have to go to that kingdom at least once or twice a week to maintain it. You can use it to help fight depression. If the king is depressed, what are you going to do about it? Well, you could have a festival. You can dance and have the maidens spinning around. That will all create a certain effect, but by the next day, you will forget you did it. When you will go into work, people will say, "Boy, you seem like you're having a really good time!"

However silly it may sound, you're doing the same thing with the zipper. You are using your mind and saying, "I have a zipper and when I go up there, I know what's going to happen. I am going to unzip it," and it immediately reacts to your demands. Your brain will say, "Okay, that makes sense to me!" But, if you argue with yourself and say, "How can it make sense to you? You stupid idiot! How can you be my brain?" You then just locked yourself out of it. It's a matter of trusting yourself and using your imagination to allow the desired outcome of a higher state.

The kingdom also has gates. There are intruders, bad people, beyond the gate who are trying to get in. Because of this, you create checkpoints. You let them be there on the land because you have exterior watchtowers. When somebody comes up to the land, your guys come up on horses and say, "What do you want? What are you looking for?" Any intruders have to get past them to get to the next level. So you tell them they have to screen everybody. There's always someone trying to take advantage of you, get money from you, or trying to get you to sign something. Your guards at the watchtowers will determine how sleek you are. Even if you're not paying attention, they do not let certain things get by you.

This leads us into awareness. How aware are you now? Are you conscious or are you just functioning? By setting up these guards, it will help you to remain in a certain state of awareness because it starts filtering information that is coming into you that you may not want.

I remember once when I had my guards up very strong and I was watching the movie *The Exorcist*. While I was watching it, I noticed that the film makers put in a creepy face for about two frames. Then it disappeared. Hardly anyone else would notice that. It was a green face and internally I said, "What the hell was that?" My filters were doing what I told them to do. In this reality, my guards were reacting by understanding that I was looking to stop anything in disguise getting past me. I want the guards' attention on it. My guards aren't looking for the guys hauling in the wheat to feed me. They're standing in the pile of wheat to see what is hiding in it. They're looking for the stuff that's sneaking by. That creates a higher sense of awareness.

Since I did this at a very young age in my life, it contributed hugely to how I think and perceive things. It enhanced the clarity of how I understand and see things. That was a big factor for me during that phase of my life. It was interesting that you brought up that whole zipper thing. That's what I was doing with my kingdom, but of course it was much more

ERIC PEPIN

elaborate. It's something that I thought was important to bring up in case it helps someone else.

Is the concept of The Kingdom visual?

Yes, absolutely. Once you build the kingdom and become comfortable with it, then you can mess with it. You can manipulate your brain to try more interesting things. One of the things you can have in your kingdom is a room with a giant map on the wall. On this map is your kingdom, but nothing in your kingdom is what it is supposed to be. It will be affected by your intent.

You go into the room and walk up to the map. The map is going to give you directions to a certain place that you need to be. It has something that is very important to show you. It is a quest that you say you will take on. So the map shows you where you need to go because there's something very important for you there. Then you close the map and you put it away.

In real life, you then open up to the possibility of allowing yourself to be shown where you need to go. All of a sudden, somebody might say, "Hey, we need to take a trip to this place," and you say to yourself, "I would have said no easily before, but this time I'm game to go." It will present itself rapidly in your life. Or something is going to get your attention. It's how you get past the matrix. This is how you can teach your consciousness to pay attention to what it would otherwise ignore.

It is a form of hypnosis, allowing you to be more conscious. If you want to make more money, you could also direct your attention to that. If you like the map concept, create a map to show you where you physically need to be to make more money or to enhance the possibilities of financial gain. If you visualize piles of gold, your brain might not understand gold but it understands the 'feels-like' of gold. Now that your brain

-258-

has a sense of it, it knows to send you in a direction to find it, or to create that function in your life. It could present itself as many things, whether it's the right job, the right place, or the right opportunity. It's a way of fooling your own little filters.

You were mentioning the knights in shining armor. What function would they have and how does it relate to High Guard?

Your knights represent your nobility. They represent everything you imagine in your fantasy world. They also represent your strength. When you think of yourself as having shiny and beautiful armor, it represents the goodness of your intentions. If you're forceful, mean or cruel, your armor turns to dark, dented, and rusty armor. It's progressive, but if it's good-looking armor, there's a good intention. It's noble and just. You can have armor that's silver, white, or something really amazing. Of course, you want to do good things. Any white cell wants to do what is good, righteous, truthful and powerful. We really gravitate towards that because it's our make-up.

Your knights have to be strong. They should have good swords and shields, made of quality material. The better you imagine them, the stronger they are. Do not limit the knights by just giving them steel blades. If you really want to give them power, give them Jedi swords.

However, if you start to get too extravagant, your brain starts to psychoanalyze what you're creating. *Sometimes it is better to keep it simple, rather than making it too complex.* As soon as you give the knights light sabers, they're no longer knights. They're Jedi knights. That means that our castle is now going to be a giant spaceship or something like a planet.

Now you have giant spaceships coming down, shooting at your kingdom. Simply put, you must choose a scenario that will work with the brain. It has limitations and boundaries as to what is acceptable and what is not. Your wicked brain can turn on you at times.

God is always considered to be in the kingdom. You have to remember that you are God in that kingdom, which means you are all-powerful there. *You have all the power you need in this life.* It's just a matter of whether you feel powerless. If you do, then you're powerless in that world. If somebody that's powerful in this world is consciously affecting you, then you have to defend and conquer them in your kingdom. In your life, you will then find that you conquered them also. So that will give you strength.

In other situations in life, you can see the negative influences in your life, whether it is finances, relationships, or something else. You will see some cloaked character coming into your kingdom. Who will be under that mask? It's going to be the ex-husband, or the ex-wife, or some boss that you are having trouble with in your real life. Now you have to battle with them and wage war. Don't win your war in one day because that's not realistic. Spend a week going through all the scenarios. Also, have some losses. If you lose in your life, see that battle loss on the field in your kingdom. You can summon up friends and allies. Then you have to create that battle. Then take it over and win. Essentially, it's very similar to rewriting your past, as in *The Power of Surrender*.

So when you rewrite it in this way, you're writing it in the present. That should be a revelation. You can have a tool to effect the present by doing something very similar. If you project into this, you'll find that you've gained a lot of strengths. In essence, that's a tool that you can utilize. You bring it into the now. If somebody is dominating you in your life, then dominate back in that other reality. You're going to find that somehow you are doing that in this reality. You're finding the inner strength to do that here. Again, it's a way to fool your consciousness and remove the limitations that you may not have been aware of before.

When I'm visualizing, meditating, or doing
High Guard, sometimes I just can't visualize
myself or see what I look like at all.

So then don't.

So it doesn't matter who's in there?

No, it doesn't matter. Be whoever you want to be because
you don't really look like what you think anyway. When you do
that, you will find that you can visualize yourself anywhere.
It'll have an opposite effect. If you want to see yourself and
visualize better, one of the things you can do is look at a
mirror before you do a session. Stare at the mirror and study
your face. Don't think of yourself as you. Think of the image in
the mirror as a different person because you will find that you
can invoke other people's faces in your mind easier than you
do your own. If you think of yourself as a second person in
the mirror, you will think the same way in your visualizations.
That is an easy way to bring it through.

How many of these sessions can you do in a day?
Is it something you do after you've meditated?

Well, you can do it after your meditation. I recommend
substituting it for one of your meditations because there is
only so much time that you can spend when you are in that
state of mind. When you do meditations, sometimes you are so
much in the zone that it's harder to do your visual techniques.
So, just find some quiet time. Sit down and do it by
yourself. Start building your kingdom slowly in your mind. In
fact, don't build it. *Remember it.* It's already designed in your

head. What kind of stone is in your castle walls? What does it look like? Everybody knows already. Do you have gray stones? Do you have tan or brown stones? Or do you have large white marble stones?

Everyone has their own style. You're just going to have to work with it. It reminds me of that psychological test where they say, "You're walking through the woods and you stumble across a cup. What kind of cup is it?" Some people will say it is tin. Some will say it's ceramic, and others will say it's made of wood. Your answer represents how you perceive life. The test goes on with something like this, "You cross a body of water. What kind of water is it? Is it an ocean? Is it a lake? Is it a pond? What do you do with it? Do you do anything?" And I'm the one that is always swimming across it.

Having said that, how you choose to interpret whatever it is you are doing is an indication of what is in your deeper psyche. In a sense, the water represents your sensuality of what you do with water. *I remember once a person told me, "I'm not doing anything. I'm walking on it. It's frozen." That's a good one.*

One of my students brought to my attention that a lot of people have trouble with their imagination or visualization. What is your interpretation of visualization? Some people think it is supposed to be vivid, like a color TV or something. It's not. It can be for some people though. It can get extremely vivid for them as they work with it. But for the majority of people, it is very transparent. It's very faded.

I'll give you an example. Close your eyes right now and tell me what your bathroom looks like. Can you visualize in your mind the shower curtain, the floors, the tiles, and whatever is on the floor? What does the toilet look like? What does the sink look like? Now, if you do that and use your recollecting mind, you can also do something that's visual. Okay, visualize your bathroom sink, your floor, and your toilet. I want you to look and tell me what's on top of your toilet tank, if there is a toilet tank. Are there some objects there? Now all of a sudden, I want you to see a kitten sitting on top of the toilet seat. Can you see it? You have a visual mind. We just took something that was a memory and overlaid it with imagination. Do you have a window in the bathroom? Can you visualize in your mind how big the window is in your bathroom?

Yes.

Can you look out your window and see what's out there?

Yes.

If you walk to the door, imagine that the door is shut. Now suddenly you open it and you've transported yourself into the middle of a village. You open it up and you look outside and there are cobblestone streets and farm animals. You can visualize that. That is even more complex. Start to do little exercises where you are using your ordinary, everyday mind. Then introduce an overlay of imagination into it. If you do that enough, then you can go to a perfectly imagined scenario.

Once you can visualize your bathroom and are able to open up the door and step outside into the village, then you can start walking around the village. It is now no longer a memory; it's now all imagination. If you marry the two concepts together, you're going to find that the brain likes to combine things. If you have trouble visualizing something, just abruptly utilize something that is easy to do and combine it with whatever you're visualizing. If you do that enough, you will have more complex visualization skills.

Here is another thing you can do to enrich this; it is a good one. Most people can recall seeing blown glass pieces that are very dark on the inside with things like flowers inside it. Visualize that in your mind right now. You can do that. Close your eyes and visualize it. While you're visualizing it, see the transparency of the glass and the thickness of it. Notice how there is only glass between that and the structure you are observing. Just by doing that, your brain has to work harder. The harder you work something, the better it gets. Now we are going to take it up a notch. You can see the rainbow etching from the reflection of the glass when it hits the light. Do you realize how complex that is for you to imagine or just be aware of? Those kinds of things are very good to help you to use your imagination.

I read that with telekinesis, you should visualize things. Then try and feel like it's already happened. Use the visualization as your container and then try to build it up with a positive desire.

That's true but that is only part of the process. You might have to build up kinetic energy in your body so much that you can get it to jump right out.

So you build up a chi ball?

Yes, it's kind of like that.

If I were to place Prana in the proper context in order to nurture the castle, would I visualize it as waves or more like a river?

Visualize it as fog because it is like Prana coming in. You are asking it to come in. I would see fog. I love fog. Doesn't everybody love fog? Fog is ideal because it is made of little bead drops and the bead drops represent Prana. It washes into your castle and will teach your body to accept this kind of livelihood. Everybody loves fog.

Can you put a pyramid around a castle like you do in High Guard? I was thinking about incorporating High Guard with my castle.

Well, if you put a pyramid around a castle you are going to get into the whole thing about Jedi's and jets and everything else. You can have a mile wide moat filled with alligators around your castle. You don't see that every day, do you? Do you know why you desire to create more complicated things?

It is security. It is your fear that something is going to get by you. It is your fear that something is going to infiltrate you. And it is your fear that you did not do a good enough job. You have to try to overcome that. Your empire or kingdom should be historically accurate. Its contents should be made of things that were active in the time period of history that those things actually existed. There is an easier way to override inadequacy or your fear that something is going to get through. Your inadequacy stems from your fear of the unknown. You are afraid of the things that might be out there that you have not prepared yourself for. So, create a wizard -- a bad ass wizard! The wizard goes stomp, stomp and you get whatever you want.

Best of all, the wizard goes stomp, stomp to create a few things that you are not aware of so you can do things, too. By having those things that you are not aware of, now you get past the possibility that something can get through. Your subconscious mind says, "You don't have to worry about that anymore."

So that provides another element of security.

Exactly. That's the point.

Is it acceptable to have a pyramid or would you want a plasma shield like in *Star Wars: Episode One*?

A pyramid, as long as it is the kind of pyramid that consists of energy. Plasma shields are great, but you would need batteries coming from a direct source, which would need to be semi-infinite if not permanent.

As I'm working through all the techniques, I'm trying to work with the fluidity between them and maintain non-thought as I move seamlessly through different techniques. The one that I find challenging is the In-Between. I've been fortunate enough to experience that state, but I can't move into it with fluidity and I don't know why.

It is a tough one to incorporate. I almost have to get myself into that state of mind to figure out how I do it. There are a lot of things I just do automatically. I'm so used to having non-thought, so I have to analyze myself and ask, "How do I do that?" Give me an example of what you've tried so far. Where do you run into a situation where you try and fail? You have to be careful. It's like mixing bleach with ammonia.

Well, if I'm at home and there are no distractions, I can use the techniques that were presented in the module. I try to practice when I'm not in that ideal situation. I'll pay attention to the sound or to a texture and try to move into it in that way. I know there are distractions

that are out there because there could be a meeting or something else that is going on. If I have enough focus and attention and I have that sense of what that space is like, then I can capture that space wherever I am.

Well, it is doable, but you have to build up your design still with one or two factors. In other words, you haven't developed your cup to hold it well enough.

I think that you're rushing it too quickly because it is certainly possible to accomplish. I can do it. Just keep practicing it. When a baby learns to walk, she doesn't just get up and run around. But eventually, the baby will learn to walk with enough practice. It's going to happen relatively soon if you keep at it.

Also, it sounds like there is a lot of direct intent that you are unknowingly bringing in because there is such a strong desire to make this happen. Maybe there's a way you can set something up in the house that will trigger this state of mind without having to apply too much intent or consciousness into the factor. I would get an object, hold it and view it saying, "See this object? This is my intention." I'm not saying that the object is involved with the intention. It has nothing to do with the intention. It's just that when you walk through the house or you're in motion or in that state, you can look at the object and use it as a mental trigger to subconsciously start your third phase. That might be the best way to avoid the expectation. I think that's possibly how I allowed it to happen.

I remember a scenario with a student, when we lived in Cedar Mills. We both entered that state of mind. I showed him a spot on the wall with the light shining on it from the moonlight. I told him to touch it and it would be very hot. That is the third phase, and it depends on your goal. There was no heat involved; he created it.

Chapter 9

UNVEILED

I AM CONSTANTLY SEARCHING for ways to help students understand the concepts that I teach. Relentlessly, I search for examples that will, somehow, at the right time in your life make everything click for you so that you will hit some level of enlightenment. I know that you understand the generalities of everything I teach, but the real keys, the information that will help you to reach different dimensions, are the most elusive to your understanding. You may understand it, but not to a point where it instantly triggers a chain of events in your mind to simply understand. That's ultimately what we are both searching for. So I am always looking for new ways to explain an older concept. It is very unfortunate for you to jump ahead and think, "Well, I already understand that." If you really believe that, then you don't know what you're talking about.

Why is that?

If you did understand it, you would be enlightened. However, because you are not, you should not jump to the conclusion that you already fully understand something. You have an understanding of it, but you are not taking it to the next level; something is missing. It's like living in a house your whole life, and one day you move a piece of furniture and suddenly you find a little cubbyhole in the corner. You've lived there your whole life and never noticed it. You're missing something. This is one reason it is that I use movies as analogies and try to find new ways for relating information to you.

Movies can be entertaining, but what information can they really provide?

Movies are a form of the consciousness of the planet that is communicating to living organisms. In a way, it's a part of evolution on a large scale. It's a way of educating an entire species. Look at Hollywood: the movies don't stay in the United States. They travel all over the globe to the Philippines, Europe, Asia, and all parts of the world. As this happens, the language barriers are broken down. They are translated, but the same concept is being preserved. It's getting into the majority of the people's consciousnesses, particularly the next generation who is more adept at understanding it. Essentially, there is a movement for the whole planet as a living organism in space. Its own intelligence is rising because it has to educate everything. It is like your brain responding to an external stimulus. The whole body is rewarded.

If we discover water because something informs us there is water in the other room, everything in the body is rewarded by that information. The information spread by movies is moving the global consciousness; it is an expanding, living creature. We are the neural system of the planet. Every human being is made from the substance of the universe, which is the body of God. We all instinctually have a sense or a desire to return to what we come from, meaning to God. Civilizations on different continents develop in completely different ways. Yet, despite the differences in cultures and despite never knowing about one another, there is one thing we all have in common. We all made an assumption about God. We all understood that there was something beyond us. Of course, humans built upon that concept and created ideologies around what each civilization thought about God. We know instinctively that humans and the planet are moving towards a higher consciousness.

Do non-spiritual people believe in and strive to move into higher states of consciousness also?

Yes, but humans are perpetually lazy. It is everybody's problem on the face of the planet. Humans want the easiest route. When you think about what we are trying to achieve spiritually, one of those things is attaining the higher dimensions of consciousness. That means *experiencing* other dimensions. We would move into a different state of mind and our whole reality, as we perceive it, dissipates; it's gone. We are now in a whole new dimension of space and time. This is what we are working for, but that's very difficult to do.

The things humanity is doing with technology now are very interesting. They are creating virtual realities based on an illusion, cheap imitations of how spirituality moves us to the higher dimensions and other places of consciousness. Humans are still working diligently to create a false reality in order to believe that it is going to contain their immortality and happiness. Spiritually, everyone thinks of a form of immortality that happens when you die, free from disease, free from cold and pain. What humanity is striving for with these digital worlds is virtually creation of what they perceive this other level to be. Of course, the real question is, "Do I think this is bad or good?" Naturally, I think it's bad. The Darkside will mirror the Force. The Darkside will mirror it -- think about what I am saying – *mirror*. How close to perfect is a mirror image? It's almost identical except it reverses everything.

The Darkside and the Force are interwoven in time, moving though a level of time that we cannot understand. But it is only a moment for it. You could say it is a dance, a battle in which one of them will win in the end. I think the need for humankind's laziness, or in this scenario trying to create an alternate reality, is its way of achieving immortality. In so doing, they will go for the fastest, easiest, route and that will be it. But in the end, when the plug is pulled, everybody ceases to exist. The ones who really achieved the true spirituality are the ones who will truly become immortal. Most human beings want satisfaction now. They cannot feel tomorrow; they can't deal with tomorrow. When tomorrow comes, it will be a different story, but by then it will be too late. It opens up numerous amounts of interesting ideas when we look at the concept.

In this era, the average human being can understand the concept of holographic universes and virtual reality. As technology advances, it appears there will no longer be thuggish 'Tron-like' worlds. They'll instead appear to be absolutely real. There is a level of truth to this statement. Being artificial doesn't mean it is completely evil. No, evil is one percent. Ninety-nine percent is truth. Otherwise you couldn't get sucked into believing it. It has to be as real as this reality. Spirituality is a tool to help you recognize what you need to walk away from. It teaches you not to be lured in like a fish chasing bait through the water. You must understand that there is a hook there. There's a price. It may be tempting, but you've got to understand what something is. All the levels of it are just very, very intriguing. This reality is an illusion.

In what way is this all an illusion?

In the same way that a computer generates a virtual world, so is something generating this reality on a much larger scale. You might say, "If this is an illusion, it's not real." No, it's true to say that it is real up to a certain point. Everything is energy. Energy is real. It is just constructs of light. It's not the reality of what it actually is. It is an illusion still. It is truly a hologram, and it is truly a virtual reality. It's just a matter of how you want to perceive it.

Soon, when you go into those worlds of virtual reality that you create, you will no longer be able to distinguish the difference between here and there. You will see this not just in a movie. You will go in there and you will feel the texture of the chair and you will feel this conversation. Maybe there will be a virtual spiritual teacher. You could stay there forever not really understanding what is going on, much like the pods in the movie *The Matrix*. In essence, the question must be asked, "What becomes reality and what becomes freedom?" In the end, one is enslavement of your spirit and the other one is true freedom. You don't know the difference. They are made to be like webbing that you cannot see. One has spaces where you can possibly make it through. The other is going to catch you and it is going to destroy you in the end.

Are you suggesting reality is like a computer program?

Yes, and I'll give you an example using that analogy. Technically, everything is predictable up to certain point, although there is a point where it no longer is true. But you run on a level that predictions can be made, which makes it a matrix. Let's say you have a room and you know the measurements of it. If I take a ball and bounce it, could you tell me where is it going to stop? Could you put your finger right on the spot where it is going to stop? You could not do it. But if you had a computer calculate the weight and density of the ball, the speed, the size of the room, and all those variables, would it be able to tell you where it's going to stop? Imagine if it were a supercomputer, even beyond what you understand supercomputers to be. This is the kind of computer we will have in another 10,000 years. What is now random? What is now predictable? It's only unpredictable to you because your brains cannot go to that level and make the calculations. When you become enlightened, you become a supercomputer. That is the secret.

I can see that prediction is just a mass calculation of variables, but is human life also predictable?

In a way, everything is predictable. Even life and humankind are predictable. You just cannot perceive it. Years ago when I used to do readings, it was uncanny how accurate they were. It wasn't accurate because the future is technically written; it is predicted. It is tapping into this consciousness that is here. It is like radio signals moving through the air right now, TV signals, and satellites. You don't think about it, but it is moving through you right now. There is a super consciousness that is part of the planet, and another one that is part of the universe. When your mind can move at the speed of light rather than biochemically, you can understand the knowledge you want. Now people only pick a certain thing to focus on when they develop their abilities. You might watch TV, but you're missing all the cellular phone calls going through the air, all the satellite messages, and the hand-held radio conversations. There are probably 900 stations of satellite TV going through you right now, but you only select one. Maybe you select to predict the future with your ability. The idea is that you are still limiting yourself because it has not completely dawned on you what you can do. If you can do one, you can do them all.

If reality is predictable, can you also change it by will like rewriting a computer program?

If everything is an illusion, you can change reality if you can reach enlightenment, but it is very difficult to do. More often than not, you fall back to sleep. This is sleep now. We have supercomputers that will create these artificial worlds, and they're going to be amazing. But there is one thing that these computers cannot do. Everything that you see in a virtual world is something that can be conceived or can be imagined. Anything that is beyond imagination cannot be created in a computer program.

Things beyond imagination exist within the true supercomputer, the consciousness of God, which is incomprehensible to us at this level. It is in every corner. It is beyond words. It is so unimaginable to perceive that it is enlightening in itself to ponder it. It spurs your consciousness to become a wiser, more powerful being just by observing it. In your little world, you see amazing things, but it is always about touch, feel, sensation, sex, drugs, and rock and roll. You are limited because you perceive yourself to be your body. This is the limitation of your program. Think of a computer program. Can a program do something more than its programming?

I believe the consciousness of God is the ultimate computer. When you look at supercomputers on this planet, in thousands of years they will be able to create amazing things. Imagine what little you experience in virtual worlds in comparison to what you could learn and see by getting off the planet, which, in the big scheme of things is just a little pea in the solar system, which is also a little pea in the galaxy. Think about the whole universe. That is the true supercomputer. What are the possibilities for universes and dimensions that exist within its virtual worlds?

How would God's virtual worlds work?

Humanity is made in the image of God. That is true at some level, not in the physical aspect, but in a dimensional, conscious way of thinking. Humans have their own virtual worlds: our dreams. These virtual worlds are real. Aren't your dreams so real that, sometimes, you cannot tell the difference? You smell and you taste. You're cold or you're warm. You can have sex. You can do all those things in this reality. There's no difference between this reality and your dream world. It's just that this is the point of projection. When you go into your mind, there are virtual worlds from your supercomputer, which is better than any other computer that's going to be made for thousands of years. It's creating its own micro version of what God is creating, the very thing you exist within. In essence, when you go into your dream realm, it is another form of virtual reality. You are just recreating this reality. You are mimicking it because you want to control it. The difference between your virtual worlds and this reality is that you think you do not have control. I have always taught students to look at their hand in their dreams, and awaken. Take control of the illusion. If you can do it there, you can do it here. There isn't a difference, you just believe there is.

I can see how humanity's intelligence is growing in its evolutionary process. It is moving forward as a species. The number of visionaries is growing. There is a deeper layer of understanding when it comes to spirituality, but you still do not understand the truth of it. You want your experience, yet you want to ignore your connection to God. You want it all to be about physical experience. That is the organic planet. That is the Darkside. It is all about stimulation. This is creating a solidified self rather than an energy consciousness self, which is boundless. It is all about plugging into gratification through your normal five senses. You cannot perceive what is beyond the five senses. Therefore, everything you create is really solidifying in your mind. Because of this, your mind cannot expand in your own unique way. You might be able to fly in your virtual worlds, but you will never be able to do what you could never have already imagined. You can only do things that you can perceive now.

In the end, the people who create a virtual reality and follow that path will reach an end. It is like a new toy or video game. It's exciting at first, but it becomes boring when you have mastered it over and over again. It becomes obsolete. You withdraw and start seeking something else to satisfy you. What happens when you've reached the end of your experiences? Imagine you have done this so many times that it has lost its appeal. That will eventually be the death of the red cell. We are talking thousands of years into the future. Eventually, you will reach an end where there is nothing for you to do anymore; then you will have to turn to God or die. You have to leap to that unpredictability of amazement. It is the infinity of knowledge and experience beyond the human race. It is beyond any sentient being you can become or even conceive. It is absolutely boundless. You want what cannot be understood at this moment. You want what cannot be perceived or conceived; that is what you are working toward. You are a seeker of experience. You create your own artificial experience because you are too lazy to work within this higher level, but it is not that hard. Human beings are perpetually lazy. In life, technology deters you from awakening. The comforts of life deter you from pursuing a spiritual awakening. Hence, you have a much harder time obtaining it.

You are trying to comprehend something that is not meant to be understood. You cannot do it with the human brain; you cannot do it with any of the human senses nor can you comprehend this with words that only represent things for this dimension. I am being asked to use the things you already understand to give you something bigger that you do not understand; that ultimate unknowable knowledge. But you cannot do it from here. First, you must realize what all this is and then you can do it. Your vocabulary expands and then you can speak the language. Your consciousness and your means of understanding completely change. We are energy beings. *Perhaps the hologram is inside of us and this is the reality.*

Let us assume you think you are your physical body and your mind is just your brain. In essence, your dreams are your virtual world. The body of God is a structure and the mass of its inner mind is this reality. Couldn't you say then that this is God's dream? If you can catch the wave, this is really a fantastic thought. Imagine the brain of God. Imagine something so vast that you are just a microscopic particle inside of it. All the events in your little universe are happening in the same way as the molecular events under the microscope, just as organisms live all over you without your awareness of them. You are a miniature of God, a micro version of the macro universe. You create these vast universes in your consciousness and your dreams are all the scenarios played out within them. Imagine that God's mind is what you are within and that this reality is all of the billions of scenarios happening within God. This is why it is all an illusion. If your dreams are an illusion, and if the universe is the body of God, then this is the illusion for God and you are part of it.

The first mistake you can make is to think that God is human. You cannot assume that God thinks like a human or that God is anything like a human being. It is not. In order to get you to a level of understanding, I had to fabricate an untruth. For that tiny piece of knowledge I had to fool you into thinking in a way that took you outside of the box for a second. As a human being, you want to think of God in a human way and to categorize it as a big brain or some structure of matter but it's not. Throw that part out but keep the pearl you got. Now you have an understanding that this is all an illusion just like it would be an illusion in your mind. Do not think of the other half because the other half is not real. It is only a container to move you to where you are now. If you get stuck on the concept of the container, then you will lose the information. That is the dangerous part.

How can you become aware of the illusion or this virtual reality?

That is the battle of the student. No matter how hard you try to wake up or become aware, you go back to sleep. It is an acceptance of your virtual reality. You begin to accept the virtual reality as your true reality and you forget that it's not actually real. It's seems so real that you convince yourself it is real. You forget to question the reality.

This reality is also a kind of dream. Be careful you do not get caught up in the words. Throw the container out. "Dream" is the container to get you to this point. Forget about it. It's just a word that I am using so that I can help you reach an understanding. While inside your dream, you think it is reality. At some given moment, you wake up in your dream and the ultimate recognition occurs within you. This is the moment you tell yourself, "This isn't real. This is a dream; I'm dreaming." Within the dream, you have the realization. But then you go back into the dream world and forget you even asked yourself if it's a dream. Some part of you knows it is a dream, but that realization begins to wash away because you start to interact with the virtual world again. In essence, you go back to sleep there. You go back to a dream state consciousness. When you are here, you go to sleep when you lose your spirituality. You forget to fight for your spirituality and hang on to your little bit of consciousness.

The more you fall asleep and the less that you do spiritually, the more this world solidifies for you. Conversely, the more that you fight to awaken, the more that you begin to see the entities move through this reality, the more you begin to see the other dimensions and universes. Eventually, you may be able to affect this dimension, but you constantly go back to sleep because it is difficult to stay awake. In this reality when you go to sleep, you become part of the machine. You go to work. You go to sleep. You do everything like a routine. People lie down because it is too much work to find your spirituality again and work on it. So you automate. When you wake up in your dream and you realize you are dreaming, what do you do eventually? You go back to sleep. You go back into your dream. You do whatever the dream's program is designed to do. What do you think you are doing in this reality? Absolutely nothing is different.

Are some realities more real than others?

There is only one true reality and that is to become conscious and have true awareness. It's like being aware of many different things at the same time. That is really being alive. To be a true sentient being in the universe, to have consciousness and not be moved by the program - that is enlightenment. I choose the destination. I choose to become part of the dream. I move along in it, but I can step out when I want. That is the difference between you and me. You understand that is what you want, but you do not understand how to step out of it. That is why you need the teacher.

Even now, I pull you out of your dream. Even now, as the awakened one, I have to use my wakefulness to reach you. In your dream, you go back into a sleep state of mind and you just function. Here, you lose your sense of spirituality and you go right back into the program. That is why you have to fight. It is like trying to stay awake in your dream. I know it is hard; it's nearly impossible. But it is achievable, and if it can be done there, it can also be done here.

Haven't certain people learned to control their dream worlds?

Well, those are just virtual worlds. It is no different really than this one, but this is the main one. This is the place in between the Dark's consciousness and the Light's consciousness. This is the ultimate point of projection for your consciousness. In reality, you are as living and active in your virtual worlds as you are here. You just are not bridging them together. In the same way that you may have lived past lives which you don't remember, you exist in other worlds but you're not aware of them. When you go to sleep, one minute here could be a day in your dream world. In comparison to the universe, I've just come in for a minute, which is a hundred years here. In your dream, you convince yourself that you are in control even though you know you are not. Even though you know you are not in control here, you convince yourself that you can go back to your spirituality whenever you want. In reality, you are not in control anymore; you have given up control. You have decided to go on autopilot within the machine.

Why is looking at your hand such an effective way to shock yourself out of automation in the dream?

It is an active choice that is not in the program of the dream. It is from another program that leaps over from your other virtual reality to your dream reality. That is what shocks the system. Switch things up every now and then. Don't follow the same patterns. Throw something in there that will mess it up. Use me in that intimate way to shock the system. It works because I'm multidimensional. That ripples all of your virtual worlds. You just may not know it. It inspires the questions, "Who am I?" and "What am I?" That process, in itself, begins to build the body for enlightenment. The enlightenment body is a multi-spectrum body. Instead of being a product of the virtual reality, it can move through them all as it's not limited. You can change reality.

In your dream, something is happening. In a way you know it is a dream, but you are ignoring it. In a way, you know what is going to happen but not entirely. There is a purpose behind the dream; the dream fully intends to do something. In reality, life isn't much different. You know that you are asleep, spiritually, because of everything you've learned from me, but yet you still choose to be pushed through life. In a way, you already know the outcome of everything you are going to do. In your dream, you are a little bit afraid of what will to happen, and a little bit curious. In this reality, you are a bit afraid of losing the teacher, but in another way you're curious as to where life will push you. It is really not much different.

So how do we get out of the loop of falling back to sleep?

You meditate. When I say that you are not moving slow enough, no one really understands what I mean by that. You hear me say it. You nod your head, but you do not have a clue. Although I will explain it to you and you think you get it, you will only walk away understanding ten percent of what I really mean. How can I say that for sure? Because I know already, I've already leapt ahead. If you really understood it, you would reach enlightenment in no time.

When I say we cannot move slow enough, it means to be conscious of as much as possible. Watch what happens when I'm talking; *feel* what you feel. See the carpet. Feel the chair that you're sitting in. Feel your hands touching your skin. Hear the sound in the room. Be aware of everything. Be conscious of as many things as you can. The first question is, "What for? It is just going to be the same in two seconds." That is how a human thinks. When you slow everything down, it is a struggle in the beginning just to be aware of it all instead of automating in it. The longer you can train yourself to be more aware of things, the more you can slip out of the virtual reality. You become less and less of a machine. The machine, the Doe, needs you to interact like you would in a dream. It wants you to automate and stay asleep. When you become conscious in your dream, you awaken. Think about the correlation.

You have the knowledge. You have the memory. In your dream when you look at your hand, it is the first thing you are becoming conscious of; everything else is just happening. You are in the dream, running and walking. There are things happening to you, but it is a virtual reality. The reality is being built so fast that you do not see it happening. It looks like it's real. If you stop for a second and question something that is the moment you realize you are dreaming. It is the moment you stop and say, "Wait a minute, this does not seem real." Something triggers you and you become conscious for a minute. You are questioning and seeing things for a moment, instead of just being pushed through the sequence of events. That is what wakes you up. However, you will eventually fall back asleep. That's why I say in your spiritual training, "You cannot move slow enough." Everything is moving so quickly right now. It is the speed of light. It is what is creating this frequency. You are all moving at the same speed.

To stop and move your consciousness to any one thing at any given moment slows it down. Pretend you are holding a glass. If you think of that glass, everything is speeding around it. But, because your mind can move at the speed of light energy, you can hold it. You just do not understand how it happens. When you start to look at everything, you begin to hold everything with your mind. Your mind begins to learn to hold reality. Similar to how Hollywood portrays it in the movies, everything in the environment stops and is frozen and you can move around it all. It is the only way I can explain this. There is a knowing inside of you that feels good, but it feels really calm. You look and you know that something isn't right. You just don't know what it is because you are so used to it. Well, it's the same thing that happens in your dream. All of a sudden, you get the sense that something isn't right, and that's what makes you realize it is a dream.

How can we wake up?

You can do it by willfully and actively trying to hold things in your mind and by slowing everything down in your mind. Stop babbling. Stop talking. Just be still. But as sure as you fall back to sleep in your dream and forget to be conscious, so do you fall asleep here after those few minutes of stillness. You fall right back into the machine. When you glitch out, it resets you to go back in. It is the same thing happening in this dimension. You constantly have to build your strength, your awareness and your consciousness. It is only through diligence in your spirituality that you will someday break free. Otherwise you become another red cell. You become part of the product of the machine, spewing it out. It is difficult, but this is why you want a spiritual teacher. You want to have someone who is constant, a pillar that you can project and hang onto and be near. It somehow holds you into this gravitational pull that separates you from all this other *artificiality*. Somehow, even when you move in the "artificial-ness," you know that there is a connection holding you and you can return when it's time. It is when the teacher says, "Sit; let's learn; let's talk. You are stopping everything now. You are moving out of this reality."

How do we know when we are beginning to wake up?

As you become more spiritual, things will begin to happen. You have to be careful not to think in terms of time. Most people think of time as distance, "How long does it take to get from point A to point B?" That's not how time works. Throw out the concept of time. It is just a container, an idea rooted in this dimension. When you begin to become very conscious of things, you will feel yourself begin to move. You can move, and everything around you is still. By meditating, doing your spiritual work, and obtaining as much energy as you can, that is what allows you to escape from this frequency. It allows you to change this dimension. It allows your mind to bridge time and space. You will not be able to do it if you keep allowing yourself to fall asleep. The only way to stay awake is to set an alarm. To wake yourself out of your dream, you need an alarm. In a way, your alarm clock is me. I am here to snap you out of your dream, to bring you to here and now, so you can question what you perceive as reality. Alarms can also be little spiritual things, like having a certain time every day to meditate. It is what brings you into this place.

What is one alarm that you recommend using?

Set up gatherings with other students because when you collect more like-minded people, you can create a bigger bubble of consciousness. It works as long as everyone has their mind working with you. But if you have heavy sleepers, that can be like a poison. When I see people begin to slouch and they are not getting it, it means they are going to sleep. It is like the universe saying, "You're too weak. Fall back into the machine." You've got to be very careful whom you select. You could make your experiences more powerful or you can introduce somebody that's going to bring it all down. They could put you to sleep because they do not have the power to maintain their own wakefulness. They cannot momentarily slip out of the hold of this dimension. This is why the teacher will sometimes push energy out to wake the students.

There are times when you may hear my voice change; it's because I am really hyper-dimensionalizing. You see my physical self, but that is not the whole of what is going on; it's part of the illusion. Your five senses keep you here: your sense of smell, touch, hearing, sight, and taste. All of these things bind you to this reality and make you believe in this reality. Why do I say, "Sit; be still; clear your mind of thought?" Then you stop using your five senses, or at least you're not being attentive to them. You're really shutting them all out. What are you left with? Nothing, technically. You begin to awaken your consciousness on levels that you cannot perceive right now. At first you say, "Well, there's nothing there." It is human nature or spiritual nature that you question these things and want to experience more.

The more you do it, the more your consciousness will adapt to the situation by finding other ways to experience. You will develop other ways of experiencing other than touch, sight, smell, hearing, and taste. As sure as biological evolution will change all physical life over time, so will your consciousness adapt and evolve. This is what will allow you to experience in other ways what you have not even thought of. You have to endure the natural instinct to use the basic stuff that you have already. Once you do that, you will be able to perceive and move through time and space. You can move without being seen and be able to do miracles. But you cannot do it if you keep thinking the way you think now.

The only way you are going to get out of your current thought pattern is to stop thinking altogether. Thinking can only tell you what you can imagine, see, and understand. You can understand a whole lot more. It's just that you do not have the faith to take that chance. You are afraid of it. You are afraid of death. Death means the removal of what you think you are and, ultimately, that is your five senses.

> You're here in this time, in this space, in this dimension, this life and it is not the whole of you. Is it just a very small part of you?

Yes.

> Is the rest of our consciousness completely asleep, or are we living other lives at the exact same time?

You are living what I call "holographic lives," virtual realties. You are living them, but they do not have to be lived the way that you do. You must remember that you cannot see the whole path.

> If you become enlightened in this life, do you become enlightened in every life that you are living simultaneously now?

Yes, once you reach enlightenment, it is you. It's just a knowing. You just know how to move through it all. But there are limitations when you go into this reality. You must give up in a way, a kind of temporary death, much like how you forget your past lives. There's a part of you that you have to forget, because there is no way for you to solidify in this dimension if you don't. I could not be having this conversation with you if I accepted the totality of who I am. If I did, it would be so powerful that all of this would disappear; I would disappear. Or you would still keep my body here in your mind, for your own virtual reality; but I would not be here anymore. In a way, I would become a hologram. Because I choose not to be fully conscious of the totality of my being, I am able to move at the speed of this dimension. But I have enough awareness of it to step out when I want.

If you watch closely when I start to move up, you will start to see what looks like an illumination. If I kept pushing it, it would be the dissemination of me in your virtual reality. I would either cease to exist, or it would stop and you would see some part of me you recognize as being the typical Eric. When I'm typical Eric, there's this other part of me that is more concentrated in other places in other universes. When I go to work, I'm not really here; it's just my organic body, but I'm still aware. I don't think of me as being just here. You think of yourself as, "This is me." I don't think that way. I think of this as a fraction of me. In a way, I am in many places as consciousness.

Why is there a consciousness here in this place?

It is most likely a byproduct of the creation of white cells from red cells. You could be living hundreds of lives, but still experience this particular place as your main life. All people start off as nothing more than an organic body, a red cell. They think with a biochemical brain. But eventually they ask, "Is this all that I am? Am I more than just a man or woman?" By doing this, they create a soul, which is what creates consciousness.

In my opinion, true consciousness is developed when you question your identity and ask, "Is this all that I am?" The reason you are even able to have this conversation with me is because you are obviously more spiritually advanced than most people. Just the fact that you are able to understand any of this, just by having this conversation is giving you huge pieces for building an inter-dimensional body. In essence, you are here because you are on the verge of either finding enlightenment or losing it altogether. The most concentrated "you" is right here. The other parts of you are really micro-consciousnesses; they're still virtual. This is more the virtual world of God's consciousness. When you go to sleep here, you go into micro consciousnesses; the virtual world of your own consciousness. I would not concern myself so much with the containers of our talk about dreams, because you are going to get lost again. What matters most is that you begin to try to be as conscious in this dimension as you can.

Your mind uses electricity to think. Everything you know, your whole embodiment of thought, is contained as energy. The organic body that hosts 'you' needs a recycling period to regenerate. That's the purpose of sleep. It is for the brain to get dopamine and whatever else it needs. Does energy need to sleep? Is it even feasible to imagine energy being in a state of rest? It is simply going into the virtual worlds and working through them. You should not get so absorbed with where your mind is going or what it is doing. What is more important is that you work on being aware of this dimension and its structure. Work on being conscious. I have been over this a million times in a million different ways; driving and feeling the wheel of the car to thinking about your body sitting in a chair. What do you always do? You go back to your dream world.

Incorporate as much of the things that shock you into awareness as you possibly can. Build your ability to shift your consciousness as much as you can. *If you can do it, meditate three times a day.* Within four weeks, there will be a huge difference in your spiritual abilities and the things you can see and do. You will be shocked. Once you get the ball rolling, it becomes a catalyst for more experiences that automatically put you into that state of mind.

These experiences keep you more 'there,' out of this virtual world. In fact, you will get to the point where you are 'there' more of the time than you are here. That is ultimately what you are trying to achieve. This is why it is important for the body to be healthy. It's important for you to have your finances as secure as you can because anything that can draw you powerfully into this speed of dimension will pull you back down here from your spiritual place. This is where you are going to exist all the time if you are not careful. It is very hard to get back up there. This is why it is important to have as few distractions in your life as you can.

You have to work. Accept it. But like my home, my work is designed to keep me in that spiritual place. Also my close friends are spiritual. I keep my dimension together as much as I can by surrounding myself with spirituality. In essence, that is what you have to do. The more that I circulate in that outside world, the more I fall asleep. This is why your house, your room, your space, whatever you have should have things that remind you of your spirituality. Everything in my life reminds me of my spirituality. Everything has some kind of spiritual significance. They are there because when my eyes see them, they help hold me in this place of awareness and consciousness.

When you go out into the world, what is the one place you know you've got to come back to? Your home. So if I fall asleep out there and I don't have my spiritual reminders, what is the chance of me being awakened by accident again? When I end up going into the machine, I come back to my home. My things, my vibration, my tonal, are designed to help bring me back. You utilize whatever tools you have. I don't need it so much, but it is here to help me in case I ever do. That is part of that spiritual consciousness. It is a very multi-frequency place. Out there, the machine runs you, but your space is like a little bubble universe that, in some way, allows you to step out of the program that is pushing itself on you all the time. It's shielding you so that you can think while you are in your space and begin to question things.

When you go back out into the world, you go right back to sleep, right back to automating. Sleep is a very deadly thing. It is the destroyer of many people who almost became enlightened. Take relationships, for example. When you end up in a relationship, that person spends the majority of their time with you. If they are deep in the machine, what is going to happen to you? This is the person who you probably spend fifty percent of your time with. This is the person you open your consciousness to. This is whom you allow in your absolute closest presence. Eventually, this person will bring you into the machine. They'll put you to sleep. Everything is a distraction; it's just how you look at it.

It's very interesting to look at virtual worlds and spiritual ideas. It reminds me of the yogi masters thousands of years ago. They would go to these other dimensions. In the future, you will have artificial worlds, but they will be nothing like the real thing. As amazing as they possibly could get, it is a tenth of a percent of what is out there that you can experience.

One of my students, who worked very hard at his meditations, finally hit another virtual world; a virtual world of what God is. He experienced it for a while and it was too overwhelming for him to bring that here. He got up and said, "Oh my God! Oh my God! It's the most amazing thing I've ever seen," and he went on for about thirty minutes. It was just mind blowing, but he kept living in the world of his music and other things that interfered with his spirituality. Eventually, he got caught up in the sleep by accident because of his life experiences. He said there is no way he could draw what he had experienced. There was no way he could explain it. There were no words for it and he wanted to stay there forever.

I think that is part of the reason why I get sick sometimes, when I want to throw up and feel nauseated as if I am on a roller coaster. When I go there, it feels perfectly natural to me, and then when I come here, I realize how false everything is.

Everything feels and looks like plastic; that's the only way I can describe it.

Eventually you settle in, accept this dimension again and become alright with it. If you are awake in your dream, isn't there a part of you that looks around and knows it is all fake? You want to escape and you almost get nauseated. Then you just accept your dream again. It's the same thing.

When you are experiencing something spiritual or paranormal, are you supposed to just surrender into it, let go and have a new experience?

Well, yes and no. It is a different kind of control. When I say, "Let it go," I mean let go of it with your brain, but you can control it with that other part of your dimensional consciousness.

Sometimes, I'll have an experience and then I can tell that there is some babbling or automation going on. How can I make the experience deeper? I know that I can get more out of it if I can just figure out how.

Well, that is the reason why you cannot; it is control. Everyone has problems with it, even me, but I have obviously gotten passed that. It is your analytical self. It is okay to analyze, just do it afterwards. It is almost impossible for you to do because you just want to analyze what is going on mentally. You cannot let go with your brain so that your consciousness can collect the data on a different level.

Here is an exercise to help with that. Have someone work with you. Before you go out to do one of those things, have them show you a group of objects one at a time, and try to remember as many as you can. Twenty-five is ideal, but that is an extreme amount. If you can get up to ten objects without saying what they are in your head and then recall them verbally afterwards, that's an excellent discipline for you to work with.

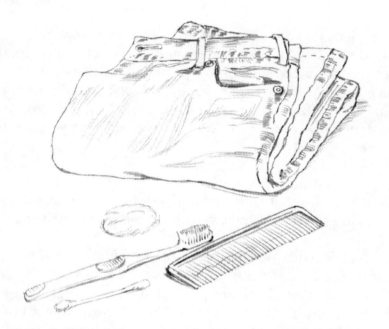

While you are reading, look at the objects in the image. See if you can acknowledge what they are, one at a time, without saying what they are in your head. You will find that the exercise shuts the Babbler off.

Then go and experiment on those other levels because it is like learning to do two things at one time. You might have to struggle somewhat, but once you have it down, you will find that you can do other things the same way without realizing that you are doing it. Fool your brain with a simple exercise like looking at a bunch of objects without saying the words in your head, and then jump over to some other larger exercise where you can experience it without analyzing it. You will find that the little exercise shuts the Babbler off. Looking at animated objects will also teach you to let your mind get fooled so you can go to deeper levels and have new experiences.

There is also a program online that will just show you different objects. It's like a memory game, but it will just show you random objects one after another.

Perfect, just do not say what they are in your head. When it is done, say, "There was a camera, cigarette box, comb, toothbrush, cotton swab, and a pair of jeans." See how far you can go without saying their names. As soon as your brain says, "Jeans," or "there was a pair of jeans two minutes ago," you are done. Now you have to start all over again so you can get further than that.

Could you do that with reading? I've been thinking about trying to read without saying the words in my head.

Yes, I do it all the time. That's all I do. I just let my mind go over it, and I know that my deeper sub-conscious is tracking the words. So all I have to do is just skim over them, but it's harder. Start off with the objects. There is a game that I play on my cell phone, a card game where you have to match the symbol behind each card. I've noticed that the images, like a heart, are the hardest. That tells me that you can do numbers much easier because they are more familiar. So it depends on what objects you are going to work with to train yourself. Always go with objects more than numbers or letters.

I've done it with numbers as well. When I'm doing the Sudoku puzzles, when I'm checking them at the end, I used to say the number in my head. Lately, I've just been recognizing some of them instead of saying them in my head. I just scan, and pretty soon I'm going really fast.

Well, as good as those games can be, you really need to use real life objects. That is the best way because there are other senses that kick in. When you are looking at a two dimensional object on the screen or something like that, your brain sorts it differently. When you look at objects three dimensionally, it's more personalized and you can sometimes hear the sound as it is being picked up. When you go into an environment with that training, like a haunted house, your brain is more disciplined to deal with those things in a three dimensional sense.

Can that go back to feels-like? Will it help train you in that area?

Sure, absolutely. Sometimes you have to be careful with *feels-like* though because *feels-like* can really nauseate you after a while, until you really get good at it. It can really throw you for a loop because when you start to categorize objects and then you practice *feels-like*; there is something weird that happens between your brain and dimensional intelligence. It sometimes leads to feelings of nausea. It is almost the same thing as sensory overload, just a little different.

Earlier, I experienced a flashback of my father's house on the east coast. That was a perfect example of how the memory works. Certain textures or images can trigger little flashes of other time periods.

That leads to a discussion about this moment. There should be something that you could do to hold this memory. If you were to meditate, then you could come back here and then recall this whole period with me. There are other important values to it because there are more things happening here than are even being said. You should mark your memory now. Take your shirt. Look at whatever happens to be the focal point of this particular moment. Just focus on this moment. Then without taking your eyes off that focal point, take your shirt, and smell it. Then try to mark what the smell is from your shirt. Try to find it. Hopefully, it smells good. If you don't do it right, it won't work. Now, when you go back into your everyday routine a week or even a month from now, sit down and go into your meditation. Think about this particular moment, this particular state, and smell it. It will help bring your mind back to this moment.

Whenever you have a memory or a place that you enjoy being that you want to remember, try and mark it with smell. Then you will be able to bring that moment back with deep meditation.

When I look at how human consciousness evolves and grows and how some people manipulate it to look certain ways, it seems that the mainstream population is basically manipulated or told to think a certain way. The people just go about their daily lives. It seems like everybody's focus lately has been on war or the economy, if they're not focused on their eating, sleeping, working and reproducing.

Well, it depends on who is in charge. No matter what, the human race is a very collective thing and we are becoming more globally conscious now rather than nationally divided. Not that long ago, China had their walls up, and they had their own collective. They wouldn't even let in any outsiders. Europeans had their own collective way of thinking, and so did Americans. As technology and the internet has evolved, older people now are forgetting their trained way of thinking and have less power. The younger generations are talking on the internet every day to friends in China and Australia. Everybody's talking to people from Africa to Alaska. They're starting to speak one language, so it is becoming a wash. Even culturally it is all becoming a wash.

This is disappointing because you want to keep the creativeness of nationality. On the same token, I am all for it because it removes fear of foreign cultures. They're not looking at people who speak a different language, thinking they are plotting to kill people. You can empathize with them instead so your whole perspective changes.

It is the lack of understanding of what they do in their home or what they are eating, so people assume, "They're just savages. They're killers." If you were around them at all, you would begin to laugh with them and you would know their first name. You would be hanging out with them and marrying them. Then there would be no more fear.

Well, people are progressing but you have to remove the old ways or else people cannot change. Once you hit thirty, your perceptions solidify and you remain fixed in that state as you grow older. Very few people still remain flexible in their thinking. It is very hard to go from one way of thinking to another. You could spend another forty years breaking out of that religious mantra in your head. When you do start to think differently, you will feel as though you are really alive for the first time. You will think about things that never occurred to you before. You have to make sure you do not lose your mental flexibility.

I have a question about "The Handbook of the Navigator." You say that when you teach your words are alive. How did you manage to do that for the book? It seems like it has the same effect as sitting in front of you listening to you. It's pretty crazy.

Well, let me ask you a question. When you read the book the first time, had you ever heard my voice before?

Yes.

Okay, because you heard my voice, you received another texture of my communication. So when you read the book, you could hear my voice.

If you didn't have that exposure, you would have read the book but you would put it in a different voice other than mine. It would not have been your voice but you would put a voice to it. Therefore, you got one level of texture or data from it. Now that you met me in person, or saw a video of me, when you read the book you will get three levels of texture. Of course, three is the magic number. So you will hear things being said in the book and see me throwing my hands around, raising my voice, and you get that communication also. So it is about decoding.

Even if you've never met me, there is conscious thought in the Gaia mind that you tap into when you read the book. These conscious thoughts are like bits of a code. When you find the right string of thought and you create the code, the effect happens. Creating that effect was the hope of writing *The Handbook of the Navigator*.

You once told me to try to love my job for a week. Did you also mean to have some type of balance between work and spirituality?

I first started to understand this approach when I was probably about 22 years old. That was when I started to really understand the concept of meditation. At that time, I started to meditate and turn my consciousness inward. That's what led to a greater level of enlightenment for me. I had to cope with work. I had to cope with everyday life and then I learned mindfulness.

Be mindful of the room you are in and just bring yourself back. Where are you right now? You have a choice to let things eat away at you or, like a Kung Fu fighter, throw it over your head. They're running at you. They jump. Instead of letting them tackle you, use their weight and a little bit of your energy to throw them over you.

So, if someone is negative toward you, you have a choice to either react to them or just see it for what it is. That's their 'I' needing to get gratification, to get a response from you. Do not give in to them. Just use your mindfulness to say, "I recognize this is negative and either I can automate and get caught in it by reacting with negativity or I could just not let that absorb me."

That's mindfulness. When I understood mindfulness, I was able to take the everyday grind of life that was eating away at me and recognize it for what it was. Then I would just say, "Okay, I'm just going to throw it over me. I'm not going to grab the bull by the horns. I'm not going to contemplate or bow. I'm just accepting it for what it is. It's where I need to be. It's what I need to do. I will do those things and when I start to think negatively or dwell on it, I'm just going to be mindful about it and just let it go over me."

Well, the first week or two of trying to be mindful is the hardest. By the third or fourth week, if you can consistently think of it, it becomes you. In other words, it just becomes your way of looking at things. Most people will practice for a week and then they'll forget about being mindful. Eventually, they start reverting back to the Doe and become disgruntled. Then the I's take over without even thinking about them. Then they're back in the thick of it again. So constantly remind yourself to be mindful.

I always thought it was very interesting when I visited Jewish friends of mine that they had these little boxes on every doorway, even in the hallways. The box is called a mezuzah and it contains a blessing and quotation of the Torah called the Shema. In that prayer, it commands you to have that paragraph on the front of your doors and gates as a reminder. If you walked into a bedroom, there would be this little scroll. Every time you walk through a passage way, there's one of these and you would have to kiss it. I asked my friend, Ozzie, why he had these things in every doorway. He explained to me that it's to remind him about his relationship with God. By having these things in every doorway and having to touch them, because you walk through doorways all the time, it's a quick little reminder, "Okay, am I in check? Am I still here?"

Now, of course, my thinking is what you are thinking. Eventually, you are just going to create a habit and you are not even going to think about it, but that's not the point of this. You have to find ways to say, "I need to be mindful." That is why we created the Higher Balance necklace. When you are combing your hair and you look in the mirror, you can see the necklace when you have it on, "Aha! I have to remember to be mindful." Or, if you bend over and it taps you on the chest, you say, "Oh yes, I've got to be mindful."

This is how religion became so prevalent. It is how your faith is built up. If you wear a cross all the time, you are constantly reminded to be spiritual, and that's what convinces you to be religious all the time. You have to find creative ways to be more mindful. So, I thought, "Well, why don't I just get a big poster and put it over my door that says *Mindfulness*, or put it on the refrigerator. Do whatever works for you.

You explained exactly how being mindful for the first week is incredibly hard. Then it slowly gets easier until you automate your mind. Do you then fall back into the I's?

Yes, exactly. It's just like a path out of the city. It gets greener and greener until you are in the forest. You see the creek and you see the water. You are walking on the path and then there is a bench. So then you start walking further and the path gradually turns to concrete and takes you back to the city. Before you know it, you are looking at the buildings, and looking at the trees planted alongside the buildings. All of a sudden, you are back in the city and you forgot all about what it felt like to be in nature.

So, you have to always remember to be mindful. The *Doe* is all powerful. You have to find ways to remain mindful. Do you know how I remain mindful? Teaching is what enables me to survive. This is why I tell all my students to teach. If you have somebody to teach, it will make you mindful because you have to think about it. You can't speak it. You cannot do it unless you're thinking it.

Your true salvation is to exercise your spiritual mind instead of letting it become sedentary and fall into the *Doe*. The only way to do that is to continue exercising your consciousness because you are bringing it in to this dimension.

I find more satisfaction when I can talk to somebody, even about Christianity or the deeper meaning of the Bible. I get deep satisfaction out of that. It helps a lot.

Yes, it helps a great deal. It exercises what you already know. What you have learned in the beginning is just as powerful and potent as what you will learn from the more advanced material. When you forget the lower stuff, there is nothing to hold up the advanced material. It is like a foundation. That is why you have to start off with a good foundation. Lose your foundation and the whole building is going to come down. So if you do not maintain the foundation, you have a problem. Teaching always brings me back to the lower levels and then it maintains the higher ones. Teaching is the greatest way to maintain your spirituality in an environment that is constantly in the Doe.

In one of the classes, you mentioned that you were psychically attacked. Suppose one of us found ourselves in a similar situation.

Well, then you better hope you have studied the class so you know what to do. It's either pull out your sword or build your pyramid. Control your breathing, your consciousness and your frequency fields. There is an awful lot of information here.

Chapter 10

TELEPATHY

TELEPATHY FALLS INTO two categories: telepathic communication, which is the ability to *transmit* information from one mind to another and telepathic perception, which is the ability to receive information from another mind. What I am about to share with you will give you a greater understanding of telepathy. With this information, you will be able to develop your telepathic skills and gather information about other people. You can incorporate this skill into scanning, as well as other areas because the two are basically one and the same. For example, if you go into a residence and you want to enhance your sensory, you can scan for mental activity, conscious thoughts, or intelligence just by having the intent.

Telepathy is a part of the sixth sense and it is just one way to direct this psychic ability. Even though you are directing this ability into a specific area, it can be utilized for many other things if you are creative enough.

What is the difference between telepathy, psychometry, and scanning?

They are obviously all connected, but I will cover telepathy first. Let's talk about the general concept of telepathy. When you hear the word *telepathy*, the first phrase that pops into your head is *mind reading*. When you think of mind reading, you come to the conclusion that you are going to hear the thoughts of the individual's mind that you are reading, but that's not how telepathy really works. It is certainly feasible that you could pick up on somebody's thoughts that way. There are a lot of variations of telepathy and its many uses.

Psychometry is the ability to take an object and tune into it to gather information. You are not exactly using a mind reading process. Rather, you are using a different means to gather this information so it wouldn't be considered telepathy.

Scanning is certainly within the realms of telepathy. In fact, scanning is very similar to telepathy. It is generally used to gather information on an individual. Let's say you are out in public and there is someone who happens to capture your attention. You then use your mind to telepathically gather information about that person.

How does telepathy work?

The first level of telepathy is empathy. When you empathically pick up information, you are picking up the feelings and emotions of other people. Additionally, you are also picking up depression, anxiety, and stresses that may not be your own. It's important to be able to ascertain which thoughts and feelings belong to you and which ones belong to someone else. When you can categorize them in your mind, other people's emotions will not consume you and your brain won't react to erroneous information. If the brain can acknowledge that this is an outside influence, it is not going to have such a dramatic effect on you. Then you can move yourself to higher levels of telepathic abilities. Empathizing would be one of the first skills you learn.

The second level of telepathy is refining conscious information from another individual. You are not going to hear the words, "I've got to go to the store today," coming from inside someone else's head. You will not have someone project information, like numbers, or words at you. You are going to start by developing a *knowing*.

As I have said before, females have a natural aptitude for developing telepathy. They analyze you as a person: feeling you and studying your texture. Your texture is your facial movements, your eye movements, the left or right movement of your head, and whether you have a feminine or masculine aspect to your personality.

Whether they know it or not, women are picking up subtle cues because they are very, very social. In the past, women spent their time raising children, communicating with one another and developing social skills, which helped them to sense if there was tension between members of the group or if the general communication amongst the group was relaxed and pleasant. The women were able to read body language very easily.

As time progressed, they started to have non-verbal communication with each other. They could feel the intimidation from the other women and other territorial intentions because they possessed an inner sensory. However, the men went out into the fields or into the forest to hunt, so they developed a different social structure. There certainly was camaraderie between the men, but it was very different. It was designed more for using their mind as *hunter-gatherers* as their brain worked creatively using holographic imagery. Each of the sexes operated within a different mindset. It was a little bit harder for the males to use telepathy than the females.

With all that in mind, you will sense a person's presence, their desires, or their intentions. And earlier on, when you are developing your telepathy skills, you may get a sense of the other person's negative intentions. You will know that because there is a part of you that feels it in their presence. This is a form of telepathy. Telepathy directs your will to intentionally feel something from someone or to search for information, whereas *empathy* is feeling what you randomly pick up.

For instance, I can pick up whether or not a person likes me. I can pick up their good intentions towards me or if they are ambivalent towards me, and I am able to pick up whether or not they are fronting me. *Fronting me* means that they are being very charming on the outside, but on the inside they evoke different types of thoughts, such as, "I really don't like you. Go away."

These are examples of the basic levels of telepathy. This knowledge is not just about scanning others, using psychic abilities, or extra sensory perception (ESP). In the very beginning, telepathy uses your acute senses to pick up information about another person. You can get a lot of information just by observing the subtle movements of their facial structure. My advice is to go with that. Don't deny that it exists. Utilize that as you push yourself for more information because the details you can pick up go far beyond guessing or just seeing with your eyes. The big secret of telepathy is your *inner knowing*. The inner knowing provides vast amounts of information in the conscious mind that exists within our brain. We tend to ignore what it says to us.

I often speak to people who have relationship problems. They break up with someone and I'll ask them, "When you first met this person, what were your initial thoughts and feelings about them?" They usually say, "Well, I thought he was a jerk. I did not like him. I really despised him." And I respond back, "Why didn't you listen to that initial information?" That instinctive sense you have from your initial meeting gave you a lot of information. That is part of your telepathic sensory.

The best subjects for psychic work are the people who you don't know because there is less for your brain to draw on. The brain uses logic and deduction to describe your subject. The less you know about someone, the more you need to rely on your basic sensory. At first, you use the brain, but then you have to really push for another sensory to give you that information. This is when your mind starts to scan for data. If you are acquainted with a person, your brain starts giving you bits of information that you already know about them.

You have a broader range of speculation because you already know most of the general information about them. So it's easier to pick up on. However, it becomes more difficult to draw on that higher source of information.

Telepathy is about self-observation. You should start recognizing what is happening when you are doing it as that information comes streaming in. You can catch yourself doing it from time to time. If you find that you are observing yourself doing it, you can expand upon that particular feeling, that state of mind. Then you start to reproduce that effect on a broader scale. That gives you an idea of how this works.

It is hard to define telepathy. It is such a broad part of the extra sensory abilities. You are attempting to specialize in a specific area of telepathy.

Can you ever actually hear another person's thoughts in your head?

Yes, that is considered to be advanced telepathy. Emotion is the communicator of the universe. It is the communicator that precedes all languages. When you think in terms of telepathy, you must think in terms of picking up and receiving someone's emotion in its complex and detailed form. If you can allow it to flow, your brain will then begin to communicate what that information actually means. It can be very, very, complex. Everything has an emotion.

Without actually grabbing the physical object, I want you to feel a needle. Feel the needle poking you. Feel the structure and the coolness of that needle. You are able to feel it because your memory recalled that information without touching it. If you were to invoke the feeling of a needle, you would know that sensation. You can learn to pick up on those things in a variety of ways and learn not to block out that sensory because that's what we naturally do. If you allow information to flow in, you can begin to telepathically communicate the intentions or the information from other people.

Words are from the lower region of the brain. It is very foreign to your higher sensory. Your five senses are rooted to this physical dimension. Your sixth sense is designed to take you outside of that. It is like saying, "Can you see the smell your nose is receiving? Can you hear what your mouth tastes?" You can really get philosophical about it; realistically, the answer is no.

You learn to mimic those emotions by the words that you communicate in your head. But realistically, words are a much cruder level of communicating information for the sixth sense. When you speak words, you don't necessarily feel them. If I say chocolate cake, butter pecan, or peanut butter, you're not really giving it any thought. It's like empty data. But if I were to say, "Think about a spoon with a scoop of peanut butter on it. Flip it over and pull the peanut butter off into your mouth. Feel its texture. Think about its smell, and taste the flavor of it." You can almost recreate that whole sensory. Your higher consciousness works more naturally on that level than with actual words. Words just don't seem to flow correctly with the higher consciousness. It is not the correct texture that your sensory is looking for.

There was a lot of research done in the past with twins and couples who have been together for a long time. They often complete one another's sentences or pick up on the other person's desires. In one way, you could say that they have lived together for so long that they sense everything and it is just a matter of their brains crunching the numbers.

Scientific studies have come up with some very interesting theories about this. For instance, one person intuitively knows when the other person is in pain. Or one person can put their hand in a bucket of ice water and the other person recognizes that it is something cold versus something hot. This is another example of telepathy. It is all emotionally based. They communicate the information back into words.

In rare cases, you can hear words. You can hear entire conversations in your head and you can hear it in the other person's voice. But there is a natural Governor within the brain that directly rejects that because it does not recognize the source.

If you were to hear voices in your head, the first thing you would think is, "I'm either going insane or I've got schizophrenia," or something to that effect. Your natural inclination is to throw out your intuition. There's a natural resistance to hearing voices. When this type of telepathic communication happens, if you're syncing well with the other person, you have such clarity and resolve within your mind you can broadcast information. But it's almost a waste of time to focus on unnecessary verbiage when you can excel to dramatic levels of telepathy if you would only train yourself to work on empathetic information. It is more advanced in so many ways.

What if someone speaks a language that you don't understand?

It doesn't matter in the beginning, but for the more complex levels it may. They will have the same basic knowledge that you will have. They know about hot and cold, pain, love, joy, and sadness. They will recognize the feeling of cotton, the touch of leather, the coolness of steel, the touch of a loved one's hair, or its smell. This is a universal language.

If aliens visit us from another planet and we cannot understand their culture, their experiences will be extremely different than ours because their five or ten senses are completely different. How they experience may be different, but there can be a bridge of communication if we could both recognize that we are able to experience it.

In the end, you will still get the basic information from them. I believe it is absolutely universal. You can develop a form of communication. It is more than likely that emotion will be the form of communication rather than a verbal conversation. I do believe that the alien species would develop a level of communication rather than communicate with clicks and gurgles. It's very unlikely that they will speak in our language. The position of the voice box in the throat and the range of possibilities of our physical body compared to theirs would be profoundly unique.

What if someone is a very visual thinker? Is it possible to see their visualizations?

Yes, absolutely. First, you have to learn how to be absolutely clear, which means you have no information going through your brain in word form. Your intent is to feel other people by using your eyes. You are utilizing your normal senses to gather information until you get better at this. If you looked at someone, at first you would desire to feel them. You would desire to know what they feel like. In a sense, you mirror them. For a second, you are almost envisioning that you are them. Eventually, you move past that and it's no longer necessary.

It is not something you would really think about. It is just the intention of wanting to experience it for a second. If you envision yourself as them, you can feel what it is like to be them. By being them for a moment, you gain insights into the configuration of their consciousness, their being. You get a sense of what they like and what they don't like, what would turn them on, and what would turn them off. You now have a means of getting more information from them. You are essentially opening the communication lines.

If you become too distracted and someone is talking to you, that telepathic communication will drop. If they approach you and start talking to you, there will be two things happening. One part of yourself will be feeling them and the other part will be communicating on a verbal level, but you are still connecting with them. The interesting thing is that they are aware that you are doing this. They are just not going to understand what is going on.

Some people say that there is a certain feeling you get from a person who has this skill. You are scanning them and connecting with them on this level of energy. Their energy is saying, "Hey, there is something going on here," but they don't know how to communicate it or articulate it in their consciousness. There is definitely a feeling there. They are just not skilled enough to pay attention to it long enough.

How would that be different than assimilation?

Assimilation reflects telepathy, but it is also used to feel what it is like to be a tree, animal, or an object like a couch or table. Assimilation has a different purpose and yet, there is a similarity but it is not as defined. With telepathy, you want streaming information about this person's thoughts. What are thoughts? Thoughts are emotion. They are evoked from emotion. Is there love? Is there an interest? Or is there disgust? What are their feelings and how do they communicate that in a language to you? With assimilation, you feel the presence of the person rather than live streaming information.

Who would benefit from telepathy?

This knowledge would suit someone in the military very well. Martial artists would benefit a lot from telepathy because they could have an edge on a person's intentions and their opponent's next move. This would be a good tool for therapists and psychologists because it gives them insights into whether their patient is lying to them or being truthful. It would be good for anybody who was in a situation where they could be physically endangered. That is the best use for telepathy.

What are thoughts? Are thoughts alive?

First of all, thoughts are evoked by emotion. The brain has to reinterpret a thought from an emotion into a formalized structure and transfer it from one person to another. Therefore, thoughts are energy. They are part of your consciousness. They are part of your being. Thoughts are evoked by observation from some inner part of you. There is a reception of that observation within you that is translated into what you feel. Then it is resurfaced and sent out to convey a message.

In other words, there is the physical body where you have all of these senses that interpret, touch, feel, smell and take in data. The data is converted into electricity or energy. The brain gets it, sorts it, formulates it and processes it to your mind or to your higher consciousness. The same goes for the information being received by your mind. It then reciprocates back into the brain and converts that information so you can express it in this dimension. Thoughts are alive because they are felt. What emotion can you feel that is not alive? It has an intention because you are feeling it. It has creativity and it has an existence.

What are some general barriers one must overcome to practice telepathy?

Most people can be very deceptive. People feel violated or intimidated when they know that your intention is to get information from them. When you rehearse telepathy, there's a freezing-up mechanism so there's a controlled response. There has to be surrender or a natural flow. Energy must be very subtle and flowing. It has a natural resistance to being contained in this dimension. The second you think of having to give information and practice this skill, it's like taking the emotional feeling and converting it into a physical feeling.

When you really think about it, you're telling yourself that you're going to do this willfully. Now you've got to artificially produce emotions by consciously knowing what you want to project. This has a kickback affect and almost prevents the information from emanating out correctly. This is what makes it very difficult. When a person does not know you're trying to draw information from them telepathically, it will flow. But if they suspect or believe in telepathy, immediately they're going to sense that you are getting information from them so a natural barrier flairs up. There's a natural resistance and a mechanism that projects the feeling of, "Who are you to get information from me?" Of course, these are circumstances that one has to take into consideration. Much like all levels of the sixth sense, you still have to get around the Governor. There is a set of conditions of what is and is not acceptable within you and you have to find the loopholes around that.

Can you only use telepathy with humans?

Not just humans; there are other beings you can use it with. I think you can use telepathy with alien beings and certainly you can use it with animals. Animals show a high level of telepathic ability with feeling and sensory. For instance, a few months ago, my dog was making a very painful, barking sound and I ran out immediately to see what was wrong. I could not see anything physically ailing him, but I felt this intense pain from him. So I knew something wasn't right so I took my dog to a veterinarian. The vet looked at the dog and said, "No, I don't think there is anything wrong with him. Maybe he just had a brain seizure or something." I knew internally that was not right, so I said to the vet, "Look in his mouth." I just knew to do this.

The vet said, "I don't see anything." And I said, "I saw something. Open his mouth again." She got mad at me. She opened his mouth and I said, "What is that? It looks like a stinger from a bee." She said, "Do you know something? I think you might be right." Sure enough, the stinger was making his tongue throb.

Animals have a different way of communicating pain. They internalize it, they cope with it, and they have fewer ways of broadcasting their emotions. But I was receptive enough, at least in this case, to pick up that information and internalize it. I did not necessarily understand what the problem was because the source it came from was minimal in its communication, but I knew it wasn't good. The veterinarian was able to pull the stinger out of his tongue and shortly after that, the pain went away and my dog was better.

This is just another level of telepathy. There are some videos of dogs filmed at their home. When their owners are within a mile or so of their house, the dogs suddenly get up and wait by the door. This is a telepathic sensory.

You have to look at one thing. A dog is attracted to you for two reasons: 1) for bonding and 2) for food. Its mind, or its intent, is always on you for those two things. A dog does not think about a large variety of things like we do. Telepathically, it has a greater connection to that source of food and that source of attention. Therefore, it is going to easily pick up on it rather than randomly. There is a level of intention there. The dog depends on you getting home at a regular time, so it may be more telepathically connected to you in order to feel that presence coming in because it knows it is going to be rewarded.

On some lower level, the matrix of the Gaia mind connects everyone. When you evolve spiritually, you can withdraw your consciousness from this collective grid. However, you can pick up information from anybody as long as they are unconscious of your intention, unless they use some kind of energy defense. If you simply want information from the vast majority of people, you can get it almost instantaneously. It just depends on the complexity of that information. You have to go into deeper levels of their mind to get more personal information.

It is different for other cultures. In the deepest area of your mind is your personal information. Your less personal information is closer to the surface. You are more likely to get an understanding of what they do for work rather than information about their sex life. I think women pick up information easier than men do. Practicing and refining your skills will determine how much information you get.

It has a lot to do with what you have been exposed to in your life. A military veteran who just recently came back from war would have a very high sensory range. They will pick up on any movement you make and any conscious thought that goes beyond that. They have an innate sense of awareness of your presence. It is not just your physical presence. They are almost on edge at an acute level of survival. They probably won't be on the outlook for personal information. Other people, depending on the work they do, have different levels of sensory that they unconsciously develop. It will be different for everyone. It depends on whether or not they have applied themselves and practiced this skill. Sometimes their work creates a natural opportunity for development without being aware of it.

Does someone have to be spiritually evolved to create this sensory or can they just be psychic?

When you are dealing with psychic phenomena, this is not unusual. It is a function of the human brain that we simply have not exercised enough. I do believe that it kicks in for everybody at one time or another. Mothers wake up in the middle of the night knowing that something happened to a family member.

The person having the experience could have sent out a broadcast and the mother knows their frequency so well that she tuned into that information. She interprets that feeling as, "Oh my God! Something horrible has happened!" She may not know what it is but she knows something horrible has happened. She is just getting an impact of that information as a package, an emotion, and reformulates that package into a broader emotion. She does not know if it is a plane crash or a gunshot, but she knows there has been a traumatic vibration sent out from the person that she received telepathically.

People in a bar might get a sense that something is about to go wrong. There is a certain tension in the air and they do not want to be a part of it. Or you might pick up someone's intentions from a blind date, or someone walking up to you on the street, so you suddenly feel cautious. These are all examples of telepathy. There are different variations and different circumstances. As with anything, practice makes perfect.

If you intentionally want to develop this skill, the sky is the limit. If you unintentionally develop this skill, you're going to have limitations because it is something that you are not really trying to refine. It's just happening so it will meet a level of perfection or imperfection and go no further.

Could a Red Cell successfully develop telepathic abilities?

Yes, inadvertently. A lot of martial artists do it but they are not necessarily developing spiritually. Firefighters, police officers, and military people can develop it. The list goes on and on.

I remember watching a program on the Discovery Channel about some firemen who were in the middle of huge fires in California. All of a sudden, the person with the most experience got a feeling or a sense to move the units to a different location, even though the fire wasn't spreading in that direction. It was logical that the fire would go in a different direction and ruin hundreds of homes. Despite this, they acted on their instinct and sent everyone to the safer area sensed by the experienced firefighter. Did they telepathically get information from the fire? I would say that they got information telepathically, not just from the fire but also from the plant life.

Living organisms give information and somehow they are tapping into higher levels of the predicted future. These are all working together, but it is still data. It is still information and they internalize it. When the firefighters were asked how they knew which direction the fire would spread, they said they just felt it. They just knew from a feeling. It really wasn't just a hunch. *It was a knowing.* They just knew that they had to react. They decided to react to that knowing.

Everything has an emotion. If you take two things and combine them, that creates a different emotion. For example, imagine what it feels like to see an empty glass. Now fill it with water. Does it have a different feeling? Of course it does. It is just that science does not really understand how this all works. When firefighters are shown training videos of past fires, they are really being exposed to different feelings and emotions. The more experience firefighters have, the more they seem to have a higher level of accuracy in interpreting these emotions. I would say it is because they can now define that emotion and what it means. It is a form of telepathy.

Is there a physical sensory associated with telepathy?

Telepathy is how you feel your emotions. Ask yourself where you feel your emotions. You do not feel them in your head. If you have ever been in love and it has not worked out for you, it is going to feel like somebody has stepped on your chest. There is a huge pressure that builds up in your muscles. You are sighing all the time. This is how the body works with emotions. Telepathy is your emotional center because it is very emotionally based. The majority of it is something you internally feel in your chest. You also recognize telepathy in your mind center. A man is going to centralize it more in the chest. If you are feminine and masculine, you are going to get it in both. Ironically enough, women also get a lot of their feeling in the lower part of their body, in their stomach region. It has a lot to do with tension and anxiety for them in that area. These are all different centers and it depends on what area in the body you have chosen to experience that information.

Is that tension associated with the base chakra?

Actually, it has to do with your womb. It is your center for creating life. There is a maternal instinct that develops there, an instinct of preservation. You learn to communicate from there. There doesn't necessarily have to be life there. It is another way that you reciprocate emotion. Those who've had a baby know that there is a communication. There is a knowing, which is also very similar to what I am saying. If there is something wrong, women will often say, "I felt that something was wrong. I knew that something was wrong." It is a sensory for self-preservation. This is why women feel a lot of their emotions in the lower part of their body and men feel them in the upper chest area in a more cerebral manner.

How big of a role do chakras play in telepathy?

Chakras deserve some credit, but chakra points are really fueling stations. They are exactly what you have learned in my book *Meditation within Eternity*. They are designed to give you energy for a spectrum of different results. Your lower chakra, again, is more structural energy. Your heart chakra is more emotional so it is going to affect the lower and upper chakras. The more that you meditate on your heart chakra, the more likely you will develop a higher empathic level of consciousness. When you combine it with your mind chakra, you get that willful telepathic combination. You are going to have both of the resources in combination for better results. But remember, it is the fuel behind the sensory.

A lot of people associate telepathy with the throat chakra. Is there any truth to that?

Well, I disagree. I associate the throat chakra with your health. I don't think it is really necessary to fully meditate on that. The best position is heart, mind, and your lower chakra and they will affect all the other ones. If you work on the other chakra points, you just increase the amount of time it takes for you to develop your consciousness.

Could two people have a conversation without talking?

Well, the two people would have to be very open and trusting of one another. It goes back to being in a test situation. When you are taking a test, your subconscious creates barriers. When people have used a hallucinogenic, like acid or LSD, they often reported a telepathic communication. It is as if they can read each other's minds. It is not that they really hear each other's words, but they know the other person's intentions. For instance, they both get up to go outdoors or they both think about playing Ping-Pong at the same time. Maybe one of them thinks of something really funny and the other person knows exactly what they are laughing about.

That is telepathy. The LSD removed the anxiety, the *Governor* of observation. The barriers have been removed so the mind no longer has to conform to social structure.

The Doe is always subconsciously governing your decisions. It's different because you can say, "Well, what about people who drink alcohol?" Alcohol affects a different center of the brain. LSD is a different story. I am not suggesting that anyone should go out and use LSD because it tears these doorways open. There are other ways to achieve things like this that are safer.

If you wanted to work with someone to do this, you would have to feel very comfortable with them. You would have to be able to trust them. When you are trying to get information from other people, there is a certain amount of sneakiness involved. You know your intentions and do not have any fear because you are getting information about someone else in a very stealth-like manner. As soon as the person knows or suspects this, there is a big shutdown.

When two people are practicing telepathy, they can get the information to flow if they feel absolutely comfortable and they can relax and clear their minds. I would suggest utilizing the meditation system that I teach. When you finish with that, have the intention to begin practicing together. Get pictures of a rabbit, a building, and a couch. Instead of invoking the images of those objects, feel them. Feel those objects and broadcast that feeling to the other person and then see what that person ends up describing. Even if your answers are only within the ballpark in the beginning, you will get better and better as you perfect your skills.

Do people unconsciously have telepathic experiences?

Yes, and it happens because the Governor is thrown off balance. There is a spike in some of the information that your unconscious mind feels. There's a need to know something. Again, it is a part of that primitive instinct. It's very similar to a mother waking up in the middle of the night knowing something is wrong, or when you sense that something bad is going to happen in the near future. You are already picking up on a network of vibrations telepathically. Haven't you ever been in another room and known that the people around the corner are talking about you in a negative way? That's telepathy. I don't care how scientific you want to get, that's clearly and boldly telepathy. They are invoking your consciousness and you are within range.

Yet, sometimes you can be far away and still have a knowing that you are being talked about. You know if the conversation is negative or positive. Generally, we pick up on the negative because we feel intruded upon or concerned about it, but you are really getting information. However, you don't know the specifics of the information because you think with your rational brain instead of just clearing it and trying to internalize it inside of you. If you did that, you could interpret those emotions.

Here is an example. I received a phone call from a very close friend of mine from the other side of the country. She said that she was very concerned that her husband was cheating. I asked her what made her feel that way and did she have any proof? She said she didn't know exactly why she felt that way because she didn't have any evidence. I asked if her husband was acting any different. She said no, so I asked how and why she felt that way. She said she felt it deep within, like a gut feeling. She just knew in her gut. I told her to trust her instincts. Her instincts were communicating something to her and because she was so close to her husband, she was able to feel it. That is telepathy. Sure enough, her husband was promiscuous and eventually they ended up separating. Her instinctual feelings were a form of telepathy.

Telepathy is really very emotionally based and you need to trust your feelings. You have to be able to discern what is artificially created within your mind and what you are actually receiving. That is the most difficult thing about developing telepathically. If you can learn to be clear when approaching something with the intent of knowing, you will get a good reception. You have to be very careful to keep the brain very calm. If the brain is excited, it is going to start throwing rubbish at you.

Imagery is also a form of telepathy. It is often used with psychometry to see the future. You can get images from a person. That is how mediums talk to deceased members of their client's family. The client is often amazed at how the psychic knows this information. So the medium is not really talking to the deceased person. They are actually picking up fragmented memories or emotional thoughts from the client. The medium thinks or believes he is picking up on a being, whereas the information is actually coming from the family.

If you observe the other person, you can begin to get information in the form of images; this takes skill and practice. For example, your intent would be to know what his wife looks like. At first, you will get very faint images. Those may not be very clear because you are skeptical; you have doubt. You have to find a way of relaxing your doubt or just saying to yourself, "Well, it doesn't matter if I'm right or wrong. Let's just see what I get."

You will progress and your accuracy gets better and better when you learn to trust yourself with the information. If it is someone you know, you are more apt to be fearful of being wrong because you are envisioning and inserting information that you already know about that person. It's ideal to practice on someone that you don't know at all and you don't feel like they're testing you. You're not in a position to be nervous. A stranger is less likely to question your skills or your abilities. You have to take a friendly approach and tell that person you are practicing on them but your skill level may not be very good yet. As you build more trust with yourself, your accuracy will increase dramatically and the information you access will get better and better. Like anything else, it takes practice.

What is the relationship between the pineal gland and telepathy?

The pineal gland definitely is a significant contributor to the sensory field. There are three stages of the human brain: the mammalian, neo-cortex, and reptilian. You are after the reptilian portion of the brain, the primitive part, which I believe holds a higher sensory. You are taking the more advanced part of the brain and trying to make use of the primitive, less complicated, parts of the brain. You are now enhancing your sixth sense ability by uniting these two parts of the brain.

The pineal gland is often referred to as the *third eye* or your *mind's eye*. If you close your eyes, you can see images. They appear to be in front of you, but slightly upward. This comes from the pineal gland, or the center of the third eye. There is believed to be a connection between the two.

Is it harder to practice telepathy as you get older?

There are certain advantages in aging; sometimes older people are better at telepathy. If you go back to my firemen story, you will notice the key element to telepathy is experience. There is no substitute for wisdom and experience. Therefore, as you grow older, provided your mental faculties are still intact, you will have a much larger database of human emotions and understanding. You have the experience and knowledge to get an understanding of what you feel or pick up that can be converted into an image in your mind. In some ways, older people have a definite advantage over younger people.

What about children?

There is a level of naiveté in children. They cannot react to their emotions as well as an adult can. As a child, you might know if somebody has bad intentions for you but you do not fight them. You are suckered along, but you know. There is a heightened sense of knowing, but there is also a limited reaction of how you can process that. However, I do think children are highly sensitive. In many ways, they are more psychic and more sensitive than adults. I think they lose it as they begin to conform to society. Everybody in their youth can attest to the fact that they are able to feel the adults' intentions, as well as the intentions of their environment a lot better. They just cannot articulate or formulate that sense in themselves very well.

How do you know when you have gone beyond just reading facial features?

You really have to internalize or share the information by following up on what you are getting. I encourage you to read facial features. Also ask yourself if you are judging the person based on your own sociological beliefs of what you believe is a good person or a bad person. In some countries, gambling is considered acceptable. If you have a very strong sense that gambling is wrong because of your religious beliefs, you might judge them as being a bad person. Judgment is defined by your perceptions.

You can gain some information from facial expressions. You can tell when somebody is lying or telling the truth. Some people are better at recognizing deception than others. There have been studies using lie detectors. Ironically, a Buddhist monk was the most accurate, and scored the highest, when reading people's faces and determining whether they were telling the truth or lying. There is information from facial expression, but it is broken down into what are called microseconds. You have to pick up the facial expression in a microsecond. By observing facial expressions, you can pick up on a vast amount of information. We pick it up all the time on an unconscious level. Having said that, I also believe that is only one level of telepathy, and that information can then transcend to more complex levels. It is like getting a sense or knowing what a woman is like and what kind of person she is. You are not going to get that from someone's facial structure. You have now moved beyond reading facial features, to reading something about that person from an unconscious level of their experience.

Also, information from facial expressions is only available if you are physically able to see that person's facial structures. That's not including people who might be a distance away that you cannot see very well, and yet you are getting feelings and vibrations of that person's presence. Or in a group, you could walk past somebody who just bumped into you and you get a very strong sensation about this person. Obviously, it goes well beyond the telepathic level in the means of physical-biological information that is shared.

Is it harder to pick up thoughts in a crowded room?

I'll give you an example. I remember when I was younger, in school, and there was a study hall. Sometimes, I would lay my head down because I was a little tired from being at school all day. There might be a lot of talking going on, but when I was in the zone, I could slip into a daydream and the daydream was very vivid and very clear. Then, something loud would happen that snapped me out of the daydream. I would then hear the noise around me, which I wasn't even aware of before.

So you can be in a crowd and if you are absorbed in deep concentration, it is almost as if sound slows down. You are aware of it, but you are focusing on whatever has your attention. It is a matter of how well you can prevent yourself from being distracted. It's unconscious thought, but requires a consciousness behind it.

What about somebody who you've only seen in a picture?

This gets into something besides telepathy now. You are entering what I call the Grid, or the Matrix. When you get an image of someone and get information from that image, that is called Psychometry. Many of the cases I've worked in the past have involved only photographs. I just connected with this higher grid of consciousness, the Gaia Mind, and retrieved data about the person in the photo.

Sometimes a person will only think about random numbers and that is all you have to work with. You just get information from those random numbers. It depends on how well you can tune into the grid. Your skill really depends on how much effort you put into practicing.

When do people generally develop telepathic abilities?

Most people use telepathy based on fear. Psychic ability comes from primitive times; it is a survival instinct. You used telepathy and scanning to feel the environment for survival, but it was all fear-based. People often think of telepathy in a negative way because you feel it when someone is talking badly about you, or you sense something negative in the environment, usually because you are fearful. It is very hard to see this in a positive way unless you absolutely understand it.

When fear kicks in, your level of telepathy increases. An entity communicates with you using emotion and you feel that emotion as if it was something threatening you. Then, as in primitive times it would be the same as if a lion, wolf, or other predatory animal want to eat you. You would feel their intention. Sensing entities is really no different. They broadcast a vibration, a feeling and you internalize it. Your body begins to react with fear.

Where do telepathic abilities come from?

For the most part, they come from your emotional center, but it is very much an organic process. Your sixth sense does not come from your soul. It is not in your dimensional body. The sixth sense is the most finite level of your organic senses. You have five senses and this would be a very unique sensory that isn't really utilized. It is an unfamiliar one. It is an organic sensory within the brain. The sixth sense is designed to help build our dimensional bodies to prepare us for what is beyond this physical life. It is the tool that you develop in order to experience and reflect on your dimensional bodies.

The more information you can collect through your senses, the more efficiently you can gather energy for the dimensional body. Perception isn't just what you see. Perception can be touch, smell, or hearing. It is the sixth sense that puts it all together. It's like building a car and adding everything you need except for the battery. You are not going anywhere without it. You can have all the parts of the car without the battery, but it isn't complete. You have five senses but you are missing a critical element if you do not understand that.

You may say, "How is this going to help me spiritually?" Well, how did you get to where you are now? How did you even begin to reflect spiritually? You did it because of your five senses, with myriads of different possibilities and experiences collectively contributing to your evolution. Acknowledging the sixth sense will give you that final push so that you can become whole.

How does telepathy contribute towards spiritual awakening?

It's a learning process. If you feel enough people telepathically, and I use the word "feel" because that's what it is, then you learn to experience human nature in another way. What is human nature but the human spirit? You have now learned another way to receive love. The mind begins to ponder the scope of these experiences and begins to look at them in different ways after you have experienced enough of this.

You internalize it just like you internalize all your other experiences; whether it is touching the face of someone you love, their smell, and the sight of them, or the sound of their voice. Now you have another interpretation of a divine experience. You internalize this, and when it comes to the point of understanding the Universe or God or something beyond yourself, you have a whole different way of approaching it. That approach is what opens the final doorways for you.

You have matured to a higher frequency because you have internalized this knowledge by going out and experiencing all the little things that build up to a higher understanding.

Where did emotion come from?

Emotion comes from your survival instinct. You developed emotion before you could talk; it is more familiar to you than words. As a caveman, you had to emotionally feel what was going on with others because you didn't have a form of verbal communication, only grunts and hand gestures. You really had to be very perceptive in communicating information. This evolved to complex emotions with the frustrations of wanting to communicate well. At one point, you became very sensitive to this information and your brain began to evolve.

Your brain eventually began to recognize the hand gestures instead of emotional broadcasts. You became very receptive to the hand motions and the grunting. It was more convenient for this dimension to communicate in that manner. So as you evolved, you developed a larynx and the voice moved up to your esophagus. The reason that children cannot talk as quickly as adults is because their larynx has not moved up into the right position. Once a child gets older, it moves up and then they are physically able to make the sounds necessary to form words.

In primitive times, you did not have the larynx in that location, so you had a much higher level of sensory and emotional broadcasting due to the lack of direct communication. If you read about the Aborigines, there are stories about them walking hundreds of miles through the outback and then meeting up at a precise location with other tribe members. Asked how they knew how to do that, the Aborigines would say they spoke to each other through their minds. It was really because they got a feeling of the place they needed to go. It wasn't exactly having a conversation. It was actually telepathy.

As a human being, your sense of communication was further developed. The guttural sounds turned into words and you became more dependent on that form of communication because it was easier after the human brain began to evolve. In turn, a lot of that telepathic ability was lost. As a species, if you had developed both physical and emotional sensory, then you would be much more advanced now and in greater harmony.

Does the Earth communicate with nature through emotion?

I believe so, but I think that it's unique and alien to our perspective. When spiritual people say they feel the embrace of nature, I think they mean that quite literally. The pagans or Druids called this the Mother Goddess. They have found a method of conveying this experience; they commune or convey with that emotional sense. I feel that same communion with the Earth. There is a total union that I experience as I am part of this greater organism. I also am able to feel that for our galaxy and then, of course, our universe. Some people say, "Well, how can you feel the Universe? It's so vast." I say, "How can you feel the Earth? It's so big." It's just a matter of perspective. Like the planet, I can feel the entire Universe because I'm in it.

Could you telepathically communicate with the Earth, and would that be considered the Akashic Records or is that something else?

Yes, it would be considered the Akashic Records. When I go into the Akashic Records, there are two different things going on. I am conveying down here, in this dimension, but my mind is in this higher place with the intent to find information that's coming from our conversation. Then I convey it from my mind back into the organic brain. I try to organize it in a method that I can communicate. I am inundated with feelings that I need to express. It is absolutely a form of telepathy, but it is a different variation of it.

Do you have to meditate in order to build your telepathic skills?

Yes, you need energy to communicate. It's like anything else in this universe, there is always an exchange of energy. Through meditation and understanding Prana, you gather the energy needed for telepathic communication. Your endurance level determines the depth of your communication and how long it will last. When you learn the Foundation Series, you're really learning to harness energy by keeping your mind clear. That's the reason why it is such a unique approach to meditation. You are learning a variety of things. When you apply yourself to these things, there is a level of success with your experiences. You do not have to give it a second's thought, as it is natural.

When you learn these things independently, it is more challenging because it isn't how you were first introduced. If you are going to learn something, learn the most complex thing you can because after you learn it, you internalize it. If you are constantly told to change or adapt to something, you will find a lot more resistance in the learning process. It is just how you absorb information. My approach utilizes all of these different things, and when you apply yourselves to them, it's going to be very natural for you to achieve these things. That's one of the factors for people's success and why they have such great breakthroughs.

Are people actively using energy while practicing telepathy?

Always.

If you practice this for a couple of hours, would you feel drained or tired?

Even if you can reach great levels spiritually, your footing or foundation is still in this physical dimension. Your physical body has requirements. It has needs and it is going to feel exhausted. You can only push yourself so much while you are in a physical body before it is going to react.

Can you project thoughts or emotions?

Yes, but it is always easier to receive than to broadcast. You are so used to interacting with reality on a physical level that it does not really make sense to interact on an emotional level. It's almost like you're not wired for it. If you want to react with another person physically, you talk. Or you touch, smell, see, taste, or listen for something; you internalize your external reality. You are constantly receiving. When you want to communicate, you have to communicate by broadcasting it out.

To send something out or broadcast seems to be a more complex task. You can do it, but the other person has to be receptive. If they are not receptive, that's where you have to say, "Hey, I'm sending something to you!" But you've got to do it with emotion, not words. The real question is, "How is this done?" You just have to overwhelm them.

Now you get into this whole area that we went into with *High Guard*. You have all these natural defense systems up. This brings up a myriad of problems. Sending is always more difficult than receiving. It is easier most of the time to receive at night. *So if you are going to broadcast, do it at night.* Make sure the person is sleeping because you can usually communicate with someone on a dream level. They are more receptive than if you try to communicate with them while their mind is busy with their daily life.

Use yourself as an example. There are times when you are thinking about something and you are on track and focused. Then you just stop; you're overwhelmed with someone's presence. All of a sudden, you are thinking very strongly of another person or you know this person is thinking of you. Well, how do you know that? Why do you feel that way? Do you think it's just random?

Ten to one, if you call that person, they will say, "I was just thinking of you," or "We were just talking about you." How many times has that happened in your life? Think about it. Now, you could say, it's just random coincidence. Well, get a pen and paper out and every time that happens, write it down and see just how random you think it is. How often do you find yourself reacting to it or noticing it? You feel it. You internalize it. Then what do you do? You carry on with your day. It is almost like you dismiss it and move on. Basically, you forget about even asking the person. That is the problem. You are not conscious; you are automated. You need to be mindful in order to react to these things or catch them when they happen so that the *Doe* doesn't drive you back into your normal process.

The idea is to sit down, clear your mind, and clear your thoughts. Your intention now is telepathy. It's not healing; it's not leaving your body; it's not enhancing your energy field. Your intent is to communicate with another person. The first thing you have to do is stop organizing your thoughts with words. Start feeling what you want to do; emotionalize your communication. Feel that person; invoke their feeling, their presence, their touch, their texture, and their smell. Do whatever you can but think heavily of this person. Do it in a very loving way. Remember what I said about *High Guard*. You need to have a very clear intention, a very friendly intention. You need to broadcast to that person.

Once you have developed this feeling towards this person, slowly release your intentions or your feelings. Communicate in emotion what you want to say to them. You might want to send them love. There is a difference between love and lust; you can feel the difference. Send love and hopefully they will be more receptive to that and reciprocate that feeling back to you. If you send lust, that person may not want your lust and that will immediately shove you out of their energy field. Or they may receive it well. But if they don't, it becomes a darker, more cynical energy, trying to control or dominate someone. Interpretation is very interesting.

You may want to convey to them a fear of going somewhere. You may know that there is trouble somewhere and you cannot find that person but you know they are heading into that trouble. You might want to broadcast that in a loving way. You would want to send information rather than broadcasting the trauma because if they receive just the trauma, they will block you out. You have to be very creative in how you broadcast information because most of it will be filtered out or rejected.

In a sense, it is very ritualistic. You have to sit down and apply yourself to a process: clarity, surrender, true intention. Remember: do not try to mix in too much information. The more complex the message, the more difficult it is to be received. If that person is really evolved, they can receive a lot of information.

How can you differentiate ownership of thoughts?

That internal sense that I explained earlier tells you what is yours and what isn't, if you choose to listen to it. You just stop and say, "Okay, where is this coming from?" You internalize it, and then you go back into the Doe, back into your process of doing things. Women do a better job internalizing emotion than men. If I discuss this with women, I see all their heads nodding, "Right!" And the guys are saying, "What do you mean?" Women are more aware of their emotions because their emotional centers are more developed. They possess a higher understanding of that communication. Right away, they know something funny is going on, whereas men are not as adept. They need to practice a bit at it.

What about projecting thoughts to someone to make them fall in love with you?

When two people are really in love, one of two things happens. They either project an intense emotion towards the other person who gives in and reciprocates, or they feel resentment. They feel that energy and they take it as an undesirable emotion. It's so dominating with such a powerful force behind it, they begin to reject it.

If you happen to go to a third party, such as a witchdoctor or voodooist, they will have a better chance of success than you would if the other person has mixed feelings about you. That's because the person you are sending to is looking for your energy; they are familiar with your energy. When it comes from someone that has no connection with you, it is unfamiliar. It doesn't necessarily mean it's coming with bad intention or good intention. They may start to get images and think it is their own thoughts. They may start to integrate this as their own thought process. Then the biological brain begins to imprint, creating the right chemicals to create this attraction. Yes, there's a truth to it; there's feasibility.

A person has to be at the right place at the right time for these things to happen. There is a greater chance it is not going to be successful because this person already is imprinted with somebody naturally or has other interests. But if they do not have anybody in particular in their life and they're not invoking somebody, there's a very good chance you can connect with this person, unless it goes against their nature. For example, if a man is trying to seduce another man but this is not their sexual interest, they might feel a friendship towards you but they are not going to want to cross that border. It is the same with a woman. If there is a chance that they could be interested, you can enhance the probability of success.

Are there rules you should follow when developing telepathic abilities?

Absolutely. There's one rule: do unto others as you would do unto you. Would you like to be manipulated? Would you like to be controlled? Would you like to be violated? What do you consider personal or impersonal? I think everybody has the right to privacy. If somebody comes to me and wants certain information, that's an open invitation for me to probe them. It's different than going out and purposely getting information to use against somebody. If I am going out to practice, I am going to work on random people; people whose lives I wouldn't even affect. They wouldn't even know who I am, or anything like that. I just have to be respectful and not harmful to other people. I certainly would want people to respect my vulnerabilities the same way that I would respect theirs. I think you can look at it any way you want. It's self-explanatory.

We all know right from wrong.

What is the best way to practice in the beginning?

Find people that you feel comfortable talking with. Just let them know you are practicing telepathy and that you need someone to be really honest with you. Now you've asked for permission. You might want to sit there and just pick random subjects. It could be about love or what kind of mate they have. You say something like, "I am going to tell you what kind of person I feel is in your life or not in your life," and you just listen to your feelings. When you create that intention inside of you, you will get a good response.

Do not try to analyze it. Just go with the flow and communicate it. Your first instinct will be to say less so that there is more room for interpretation. That's fine. Work with less so that you can get a more positive reaction. Build yourself up to more detailed answers as you build your confidence level.

You then might want to talk to them about their home and work situation. Talk about anything that's practical, such as work, love life, personal time, hobbies, friendships, family members, any crises, or what their house looks like. Or just start describing things that you feel from them. If you get an image of a house, describe the house. If there are trees out front, or out back, describe the trees. If you get images of people, describe them; just start randomly describing what you are seeing. This, hopefully, will be received with a positive reaction that will help you to become more confident with your descriptions and to develop a good sense of what is correct information and what is not. Then you can start using telepathy on a broader scale, meaning you can go out and scan people or environments in different ways.

Work with someone who is about to sleep. Sit down, clear your mind and intensely evoke that person. Then, hold an object, such as a shoe, and broadcast the feeling and textures of the object to the other person with the intention of projecting into their dream. Check in the next day to see if the object made an impression in their dreams

Another thing you can do is to work with someone. Of course, this is a more advanced level, so do it when you have passed the beginning level. Work with someone who is dreaming at night. After asking permission, sit down, clear your mind and intensely evoke that person. Then, for example, take a shoe and hold the shoe and broadcast the feeling and textures of the shoe. Then see if they come back and say, "Oh my God, all night I was dreaming about walking," or, "There were all these shoes," or, "I don't know why but I am fascinated with shoes." Even if it isn't a shoe, it's a sandal or even a foot, there is a connection there and you keep trying to develop that connection.

You could get a big white feather and stroke it and feel it as you are in that zone invoking them and sending that information in a very comfortable, positive way. Then see what they tell you the next day. Also, ask them what they dreamed about that whole week, even after you did this session. Maybe there is something more critical going on in their life so your broadcasts could not get through. It isn't the dominant purpose of their dreams. As soon as their life is not as dramatic and they are able to digest that information, it will be there. It was lingering in the ether where it is waiting to be downloaded.

Those are practical examples that you can work with. Make sure you get permission first, and that the person feels comfortable with it so they don't feel your presence. Ask, "What is it? What does this person want from me?" People are always fearful of the things they do not understand, so it is very important to seek out a very good communication with someone.

THE TECHNIQUE

Find a place where you will not be disturbed.

You will need to work with another person. One of you will be the 'projector' and the other will be the 'receiver.' Working with someone you do not know very well is preferred. The less you know about the person, the better.

Write the following emotions on separate pieces of paper. Then fold and place them inside a bowl.

- Joy
- Distress
- Happy
- Gloating
- Resentment
- Jealously
- Envy
- Sorry
- Hope
- Fear
- Satisfaction
- Relief
- Fear
- Pride
- Admiration
- Shame
- Reproach
- Liking
- Disliking
- Gratitude
- Anger
- Gratification
- Remorse
- Disappointment
- Hate
- Love

Have a pad of paper ready. You will be numbering each of these emotions as each is selected.

The projector must sit across from you (the receiver) or vice versa, about 5 feet away. The projector's job is to pull a paper from the bowl and form a list by numbering each emotion on the pad of paper in the sequence they were selected. (This will track the accuracy of the receiver.) The projector will then project the selected emotion. After the receiver guesses the emotion, the projector will silently note whether it was a hit or miss and draw the next piece of paper from the bowl.

1. At the first level of practice, the projector should project emotions with facial expressions and regular body language, similar to a charade. (*The projector can also try very subtle facial expressions to increase the challenge*)

The receiver should try to get above 50% accuracy before moving on. When they get to 60% or 70%, they should move to the next level of difficulty.

2. At the next level of difficulty, the person projecting should minimize any facial or body expressions while projecting the emotion (written on the paper) with the same intensity or focus. If 50% accuracy is surpassed, move to the next level of difficulty.

3. Now the projector should evoke a memory associated with a specific emotion, combine emotions, or put a spin on it for more complexity. (Example: the fear of heights)

The receiver should always try to write down any impressions they are receiving. Impressions received at level one will be quite obvious and will be received from any of the five senses. As accuracy increases, this exercise will begin to draw from the sixth sense in order to sense the specific emotion. Telepathy is about interpreting emotions. Emotions are universal. Everything has a frequency or feeling associated with it. So instead of being purely a visual or auditory experience like most parapsychologists imply, telepathy is more about sensing and understanding complex feelings or frequencies.

The trick is to figure out which impressions are legitimate and which are not. The brain will try to fill blank spaces, build onto impressions, try to match ideas by associations and, of course, babble. Keeping a clear or meditative mental state will allow impressions to enter with much less confusion or complication. This is why the meditation technique from my book, *Meditation within Eternity*, is a vital tool and must be used. It is designed to develop mental clarity while stimulating the sixth sense. This allows you to discover subtleties and experiences beyond what is apparent. This is necessary for telepathy to fully develop.

Telepathic ability is available to anyone who is willing to practice and learn how to increase this talent that is given to everyone at birth. When you follow all of the suggestions that I have given, you will become very proficient. So practice it, hone your skills and have fun with it!

CONTINUE YOUR JOURNEY

THANK YOU FOR joining me on this journey. My hope is that you take what you have learned, apply it, and watch your life transform as your spirituality flourishes. The light of knowledge is vital on your journey, but you must apply it. That is why I am giving you additional tools, you can download for free, to assist you in putting the methods you have discovered here into practice.

Before you do that, there is one thing I would ask of you: leave a short, honest review at Amazon.com.

Higher Balance is a dedicated, grass-roots organization. We rely on the power of people to help spread this knowledge. Assist others out there searching, like you, find this book.

GET YOUR READERS ONLY BONUS MATERIAL

As a reader you receive special reader-only bonus material you can download for free. You will get new tools and knowledge to enhance all the practices found in the book.

Receive:
- **Video training with Eric Pepin:** Watch as Eric leads you through applying the techniques from Silent Awakening, in practical and powerful ways.
- **Dreamscape Fantasy:** A guided, visual meditation that creates a lucid dream-canvas, exploring a fantasy-filled world. This tool will assist in pulling deeper emotional issues to the surface, with positive experiences, to reinforce healing and empowerment.
- **Guided Surrender Technique:** Listen to Eric Pepin as he guides you through a powerful Surrender session introduced in chapter one.
- **Deep Sleep:** A special album created with binaural technology designed to relieve stress, anxiety and attain a good night's sleep.

Go to
www.silent-awakening.com/readers-only

OTHER BOOKS BY ERIC PEPIN

What are you waiting for? There's no reason to stop now. Have you read these other books by Eric Pepin?

Intro. ***The Handbook of the Navigator***
www.navigatorhandbook.com

1. ***Meditation within Eternity***: The Modern Mystics Guide to Gaining Unlimited Spiritual Energy, Accessing Higher Consciousness and Meditation Techniques for Spiritual Growth
www.meditationwithineternity.com

2. ***Igniting the Sixth Sense***: The Lost Human Sensory that Holds the Key to Spiritual Awakening and Unlocking the Power of the Universe
www.ignitingthesixthsense.com

3. ***Silent Awakening:*** True Telepathy, Effective Energy Healing and the Journey to Infinite Awareness
www.silent-awakening.com

4. Book 4 – Coming Soon in Spring 2014

5. Book 5 – Coming Soon in Summer 2014

6. Book 6 – Coming Soon in Fall 2014

7. Book 7 – Coming Soon in Winter 2014

Books by other authors:

Bending God: A Memoir by Eric Robison
www.bendinggod.com

GET FIRST HAND EXPERIENCE

Discover techniques and knowledge to experience awakening yourself, beyond what has been discussed in this book. Attend meditation retreats, personal workshops, live video training online, or practice with at-home audio courses.

Visit www.higherbalance.com/experience to learn more.

Higher Balance Institute's programs were created with the purpose of stimulating and activating the dormant sixth sense, the missing link to spiritual awakening.

Our programs focus on methods and techniques that allow you to have incredible breakthroughs and real spiritual experiences – with your eyes wide open. A direct personal experience, not something you only hear or read about, will change and contribute to your life more than anything else can.

Higher Balance is the most unique and powerful program of its kind in the world. Join us and the thousands of others worldwide who have been transformed through the Higher Balance experience.

Higher Balance Institute
515 NW Saltzman Road #726
Portland, Oregon 97229

www.higherbalance.com/experience

Sit vis vobiscum.

CPSIA information can be obtained at www.ICGtesting.com
Printed in the USA
LVOW06s0559201213

365976LV00002B/4/P